AF248656

Comments

Bill Cabaniss has a great story to tell about winning and losing; being up and down. But mostly it's a story of patriotism, service, and character. Barbara and I are proud to call Bill and Catherine friends, and I gladly recommend that you read this story of an American life well lived.
George Herbert Walker Bush, 41st President of the United States

* * * * * * * *

An insightful read that looks at success through commitment to one's family, community and country. These pages tell the story of a full and successful life whose foundation is based on love of family, community and country.
Margaret Tutwiler, Former United States Ambassador to Morocco

* * * * * * * *

Bill Cabaniss remains the personification of dignity, diplomacy and service to state and nation. His life provides a profound example of true success, in business, politics, diplomacy and life. A superb illustration of one man's commitment to faith, family, and service to others.
Bob Riley, Former Governor of Alabama

* * * * * * * *

Uncertainty of purpose, shifting values at home and frustrations abroad trouble our country. It is both reassuring and comforting to read the story of Bill Cabaniss; the story of a life well lived. I hope that all who worry about our future will read this story; a story of family, business, public service and honor. After reading this account you will feel better about our society and the future of our country.

Bill Harris, Former Chairman of the Alabama Republican Party

* * * * * * * *

In times where political polarization paralyzes and endangers America, where people at the opposite ends of the political spectrum attend different churches, live in different neighborhoods, frequent different wine and coffee shops, and hardly speak civil words to one another, it is restorative and hopeful to read the biography of a leader who crossed lines and blurred stereotypes. Bill Cabaniss helped build Alabama Republicans into the majority party for the first time since Reconstruction. He served with distinction in both houses of the legislature and ran as a progressive, environmentally-friendly candidate for the U.S. Senate. He served with distinction as U.S. Ambassador to the Czech Republic. In retirement, he remained active in the American Friends of the Czech Republic and helped raise funds for the Václav Havel Library Foundation. The library, to be located in Prague, will become the first presidential library located in a nation other than the U.S. and will honor a notable worldwide leader of the democracy movement who was also one of the world's leading writers/intellectuals and president of his country. For all who despair of dysfunctional democracy at home, this biography will point to a path of hope.

Wayne Flynt, Distinguished University Professor Emeritus, Auburn University

FOR

Patricia
Michael, Curtis, Cynthia
Sarah, Margaret, Kevin
Abby, Jackson
Karina, Cade
Bramley, Hayes

+

Cynthia and Jenny

WILLIAM JELKS CABANISS, JR.
CROSSING LINES
In His Business, Political, and Diplomatic Life

A Biography
by
Worth Earlwood Norman, Jr.

William Jelks Cabaniss, Jr.
United States Ambassador to the Czech Republic
2004 – 2006

Cabaniss Family
Front L-R: Twins Maria Ballard and Frances Ballard; Kenny Johnson III
Back L-R: Dave Ballard, Mary Cabaniss Ballard, Bill Cabaniss, Catherine Cabaniss
Bill Johnson, Kenny Johnson, Mary Steele Johnson, Frances Cabaniss Johnson

Archdeacon Books/Archdeacon Press
an imprint of
Woody Norman LLC
Hoover, Alabama

Published in the United States of America

.

ARCHDEACON BOOKS

ISBN 978-0692240656

Revised

Cover
Fourth of July Celebration, 2005
United States Embassy Residence, Prague
United States Department of State Photo

State of Alabama Flag
Alabama Department of Archives and History

Crossed Flags of the United States of America and Czech Republic
http://www.crossed-flag-pins.com

In Memory of
William Jelks Cabaniss III
1968 - 1979

Whoever finds and speaks the right word
Is involved in creation out of chaos, and
Whoever keeps his word creates value in the world.

Georges Gusdorf

Speaking
(*La Parole*)
(Evanston: Northwestern University Press, 1965), 119-120

Contents

Foreword

I am honored to be the one to welcome you to this biography and hopefully provide a meaningful perspective. As you open this book and begin reading its pages, I believe that you will discover an outstanding work. The hero of this story, Bill Cabaniss, is a wonderful subject for study and examination, and the author has done a masterful job setting forth his story.

The major thrust of this biography is the focus of Bill Cabaniss's life of public service through elective and appointed offices. Although that time period spans the years 1978 to 2006, the author has done an extraordinary job developing the historical background leading up to and including these years of service. Whereas Bill Cabaniss is the product of his own family heritage, his local community, the State of Alabama, the United States of America, and the wider global community, it was imperative for the author to examine all of those components. In fact, the author provides a proper and thorough examination of all of these aspects. You will find that the author seamlessly blends local, state, national and international history and developments together in a way that is necessary to tell the story.

As you read about Bill's Huguenot and Virginia ancestors, and those who migrated over the years to the lower South, and as you learn of their public service and professional achievements, you will gain a better understanding of him: his motivations, drive, and passions. Similarly, as you read in this volume about the ante-bellum and post-bellum periods in Alabama, intermingled with older periods of American history and the history of the Czech Republic, you may find yourself wondering how all of the pieces fit together. But be patient and you will be rewarded; the author adeptly pulls all of these parts together in order to provide you with the best possible portrayal of this Alabama gentleman and American diplomat.

One major theme developed in this biography is Bill Cabaniss's desire to offer himself for public service in an effort to make the State of Alabama a better place. That is, Bill Cabaniss jumped into politics because he wanted to make Alabama a better place to live, to work, to be educated, and to enjoy a better standard of living. The author properly develops and presents this dominant theme. But it is more than a theme; this has been a driving force his entire life. Where all of us may want to make our state, our nation and our world better places, the truth of the matter is that very few of us are willing to take the risks and make the sacrifices necessary to serve in public office. Bill Cabaniss is the archetypal man in the arena that Teddy Roosevelt idealized in his 1910 speech entitled "Citizenship in a Republic." In keeping with the message of that speech, during his career in public service, Bill Cabaniss has come up short, but he has also experienced the triumph of his accomplishments. And you will have the pleasure of learning about that.

Bill Cabaniss has been a friend of mine for well over thirty years. If the reader hasn't already figured this out, Bill has been a hero and a role model for me for as long as I have known him. I served as a volunteer for Bill's early campaigns for the state legislature. Like so many others, I have taken great pride in his many accomplishments over the years. One aspect of Bill's life that I feel especially qualified to comment on is his spiritual life. In a different time, and a different church, Bill could have been described as a great churchman. That is an apt description, but it does not come close to properly describing the level of Bill's faith. I have had the pleasure of worshipping with Bill and Catherine Cabaniss for many years, and this spiritual component is essential to this biography. My personal knowledge is that Bill is a committed, evangelical Christian. He is not only a follower of the gospel of our Lord Jesus Christ, but he is an ardent disciple.

Finally, I might also point out that the author of this work, Woody Norman, is a close friend. He serves as a Deacon at Saint Peter's Anglican Church, Birmingham, where we have had the privilege to worship together for many years. Woody is a first rate researcher and writer. You will note as you read this biography, that very little, if anything, escapes his scrutiny. He has a marvelous talent as a writer, and he well deserves his given name, "Worth."

Now please sit back now and enjoy the following pages.

Stephen W. Still
Mountain Brook, Alabama

Preface

Writing a biography is a delicate craft, or an art as some would plea. The reader of this biography might want to know the author's method in producing this particular biography and the conditions which caused this project to begin. My first biography, published in 2012, was about a man who died in 1935. This biography is about a living person.

I knew little about Ambassador William Jelks Cabaniss, Jr. When he and Mrs. Cabaniss returned from the Czech Republic to Alabama in 2006 they began attending the same church as my wife and I attend. The initial characteristic one notices about Mr. Cabaniss is his physical stature and his confident, but never arrogant, demeanor. I knew that "he had to be somebody" simply because of the way he carried himself. When in conversation with him, no one is a stranger – you have his undivided attention. For my purposes I conducted a bit of research on Mr. Cabaniss, his family, his business, and his political career. Since I was at that time on the downside of completing my first biography I was looking for a new project.

One Sunday morning I approached him and asked him if he had planned to write his memoirs. "No," was his simple answer. "Would you consider a ghost writer, like me?" I asked. Showing what looked like some level of interest on his part, he asked me to send him a proposal. Of course, that is what good business leaders do. So I did. We met almost two months later to discuss my proposal. The end result was a biography where I would be an outsider. Herein rests my method with my subject, a living person.

The project began with several interviews with the Ambassador, interviews that I knew would not contain multiple perspectives. Therefore, I began a two-year trek traveling around most of Alabama and Washington, D.C. to interview former political colleagues, political party leaders, a former governor, a former Alabama chief justice, and former business partners. The output of these interviews (as well as time spent in libraries, archives, e-mail exchanges with genealogists across the nation) was distance. To write a biography of a living person requires distance between the subject and the biographer. For example, the Ambassador and I never ate dinner together. Once, when we spent the day at the office complex where his personal office is located, Mr. Cabaniss bought me a sandwich and a soft drink. I never paid him back, come to think of it. Otherwise, we both agreed to pay our own expenses on this project. There were no opportunities, certainly no intentions of my becoming emotionally involved in his life. We never attended social events together, and except for the closing weeks of this project, I had never been to his home, nor he mine. Distance!

Biography is history, but a person's life is always contextually historical, not his or her single thread from birth to death. Ambassador Cabaniss's family history is part of him. So, too, is the history of the State of Alabama and the American South, both politically and culturally. And when a person's life extends beyond the boundaries of state and nation to off-shore engagements, then all of a person's histories remain in the present. More importantly, personal integrity acts out and manages its historical core in all human relationships.

It is important to document Alabama's political development within the framework of a developing free enterprise trying to expand in Alabama. Historically, Birmingham was a boomtown beginning in the 1880s. Birmingham was not too dissimilar to the stories we read about the "wild, wild west." But business and labor problems then set the stage for future anti-business, politically-based attitudes. Bill Cabaniss's political career was activated by the unnecessary conflict between the lines of government and business that he experienced in the 1970s. Elements of turn of the century anti-business progressive ideology were alive and well within Alabama's political and social lifestyle. Something had to be done to correct this self-inflicted wound on his home state.

But foremost, this book is a biography of a man, who because of his then-current public service efforts and his subsequent first step into the political arena, set in motion an expansion of public service record of the highest quality. His public service contributions are local, statewide, national, and international.

Because William Jelks Cabaniss, Jr. was an international diplomat, this book attempts to present the reader with elements of the history of the modern-day Czech Republic. The early history of the City of Prague; Bohemia and Moravia; their struggle for their own identity; the Hussite religious struggle; the beginning of the State of Czechoslovakia that emerged out of World War I; their short-lived democracy that ended in 1938; their subjection to Communism in 1948; and finally the Velvet Revolution and division of Czechoslovakia into two free states – Slovakia and the Czech Republic.

A fair amount of space in this book chronicles Ambassador Cabaniss's family history beginning in Colonial Virginia. His roots on the Cabaniss side originate with French Huguenots. The Jelks family had its American beginning as indentured servants. The reader is encouraged to refer to the Appendices for details of the Cabaniss family history.

This project has been more than an almost four-year project for both of us – a business arrangement begun at my initiative and at Mr. Cabaniss's acceptance. I am grateful to Mr. Cabaniss and Mrs. Cabaniss for their time spent in interviews. I also thank them for their patience.

Worth Earlwood Norman Jr
Hoover, Alabama
All Saints' Day, 2014

Part One – Developing Lines

Serving his country and serving his local community were and remain high priorities in Bill Cabaniss's life. He never planned to enter the elective political arena. From his college days he wanted to marry, have a family, and make a career of the United States Army. His role model was his father who was not only a successful businessman but a patriot serving in the United States Navy in World War II in two Pacific theatre battles. But as life goes sometimes, Bill Cabaniss had to change his career military plans when things just did not go as he had hoped.

Chapter 1 Introduction

HIS AMBASSADORIAL APPOINTMENT TO THE CZECH REPUBLIC by U.S. President George W. Bush became the pinnacle of a stellar business and political career. He arrived in the central European capital city of Prague on a bitterly cold evening on January 9, 2004 and was officially received within days. Heads of state, history has revealed, like to make new ambassadors wait before official acceptance. And with a palace-like American embassy residence – second only to the one in Paris – as his new home away from home, this appointment looked cushy. But having to yield to diplomatic tradition, the 65-year old workaholic businessman-diplomat endured the obligatory diplomatic delay by climbing twenty-five feet up a tree – bum knee and all – with his younger deputy chief of mission, and a local guide, to shoot wild boar. After four days President Václav Klaus officially received William Jelks Cabaniss, Jr. as America's newest ambassador to the Czech Republic. Forty-eight hours later Ambassador Cabaniss and the Czech Foreign Minister flew into Baghdad under the cover of darkness.[1] Once in Baghdad the two men donned flak jackets and rode in an armored vehicle to a U.S. military compound. A little more than one month earlier things were quite different.

December 7, 2003 was a wintry-like Sunday evening on the Potomac at the Kennedy Center for the Performing Arts. The temperature that day rose no higher than 31 degrees Fahrenheit,[2] but it was to be an exciting evening. The lights shining on the dome of the Capitol always set the stage for a wonderful evening in Washington, D.C. regardless of the night of the week. And this evening Bill and Catherine Cabaniss and their friends would attend the annual Kennedy Center Honors awards. All were filled with excitement for the evening's events. Bill walked with a slight limp that night – his knee was acting up again. It was an old football injury from his college days at Vanderbilt University in Nashville. But for this particular weekend Bill and Catherine and their Alabama entourage were set for a gala three-day weekend in America's capital city.

At an earlier time that same day at the State Department, Secretary of State Colin Powell hosted[3] a dinner for that year's Kennedy Center Honors. Mike Nichols, Itzhak Perlman, James Brown, Carol Burnett, and Loretta Lynn were honored dinner guests in the Benjamin Franklin Dining Room. The largest of the diplomatic reception rooms is the Benjamin Franklin. Named for the "Father of the American Foreign Service" the spacious indoor expanse is the primary room used to entertain "both foreign and American guests." Even the room's carpet type is an inheritor of international diplomacy. The Savonnerie carpet has its origin in the French savon[4] and for many years was an exclusive product of and a diplomatic gift from the French Crown. In imitation of Turkish and Persian designs the Savonnerie took on the national character of France using medallions, pictorial settings, and flowery designs. The quality of the manufactured carpet included ninety Ghordes knots per square inch made mostly of wool wound with some silk. With intricate and beautiful designs the Savonnerie carpet in the Benjamin Franklin room includes the Great Seal of the United States, the four seasons of the early Republic and the fifty stars representing the states.

The Benjamin Franklin Room at the State Department is a space for individual honors and diplomatic receptions. Though beautiful and elegant, and breathtaking to the eye, the room approaches but does not match the eighteenth century elegance of France but could be considered by some as extravagant for a democratic republic. Secretary Powell used this room to honor Mike Nichols for his well-produced and popular films; Itzhak Perlman for his musical gift to the world; and to designate James Brown as the "Godfather of Soul and Foreign Minister of Funk." To Loretta Lynn he thanked her for her contributions as the "First Lady of Country Music" and Carol Burnett he honored as "America's Most Beloved Comedic Actress." Secretary Powell recalled that Miss Burnett's first big break in show business came when she sang a song on *The Jack Paar Tonight* show: "I Made a Fool of Myself Over John Foster Dulles." Dulles was United States Secretary of State from 1953 to 1959 in President Dwight D. Eisenhower's administration.[5] Powell lamented that he had to date received no such musical accolade. The Secretary also explained the reason for using this particular room.

Benjamin Franklin Room
United States Department of State Photo

The Benjamin Franklin Room is one of forty-two reception rooms at the State Department. The artwork is either original Americana or gifts from other nations. It is also a place where Secretaries of State swear in diplomatic officers of the nation. Powell made a point of telling the honorees and other guests that on the following Monday at twelve noon he would "swear in the new American Ambassador to the Czech Republic." Elaborating further, Secretary Powell noted that "It's not just a matter of sending them off in grand style; these surroundings show President [George W.] Bush's newest envoys that they continue a long tradition of selfless service." Bill Cabaniss would become America's newest envoy on the following Monday.

Catherine Cabaniss was at her husband's side during the swearing-in ceremony on Monday, December, 8, 2003. Other family members attending were Florence Parnegg of New Mexico; Frances and Kenny Johnson of Mobile; David and Nikki Etheridge and their daughters Jessica and Danielle of Wisconsin; Billy and Ann Harrison of Birmingham; Charles and Mary Ruth Caldwell of Birmingham; Lisa and Jared Flake of Birmingham; Jean Caldwell of Atlanta; and Frances Caldwell-Bennett and her husband Dr. Claude Bennett, former president of the University of Alabama at Birmingham. Other guests included Alabama Governor Bob Riley.

WILLIAM JELKS CABANISS, JR.

Swearing in ceremony as U.S. Ambassador to the Czech Republic
Bill Cabaniss, Catherine Cabaniss, Secretary of State Colin Powell
U.S. Department of State Photo

At the Swearing In Ceremony
Pavla Palousova, Secretary of State Colin Powell, Catherine Cabaniss,
Bill Cabaniss, and Czech Ambassador to the U.S. Martin Palous
U.S. Department of State Photo

Secretary of State Colin Powell administered the oath at noon. During the ceremony many people noticed a slight limp as Cabaniss walked to his position next to the Secretary. The press reported that the limp was due to an arthritic knee. Cabaniss, smiling broadly but with a seriousness appropriate to the office he was about to assume, took the oath and dedicated himself to his new assignment. Afterwards, aware that some concern about his limp circulated throughout the room, Cabaniss, a former Army lieutenant, joked that he was injured recently when General Powell ordered him back to Fort Benning for another round of Army airborne training.

The seating area at the Kennedy Center on the previous evening was tight and cramped and Cabaniss had to hold his knees together – there was little-to-no room to stretch his legs. By the time the concert ended his knee was the size of a pumpkin and possibly infected. He spent a miserable night trying to sleep. The pain continued Monday morning. He could hardly put any weight on that knee. He called his friend Sam Holt who lives in Washington, and told him about his knee and his current circumstance. Holt would contact his own orthopedic surgeon immediately. Cabaniss had a pre-scheduled breakfast with his very good friend Dr. James A. Smith who was in D.C. for the swearing in. Cabaniss called Smith early in the morning and asked him to take him to Sam Holt's doctor. Just two hours before the swearing in ceremony Holt's doctor drained Cabaniss's left knee and provided him with antibiotics. Like a good trooper, Cabaniss moved on to the State Department and took his oath of office.

L-R: Jean Caldwell, Frances Bennett, Florence Parnegg, Charles Caldwell
Kenny Johnson, Bill Cabaniss, Mary Ruth Caldwell, Catherine Cabaniss
Frances Johnson, Governor Bob Riley, Secretary of State Colin Powell

WILLIAM JELKS CABANISS, JR.

Swearing In Ceremonial Family Picture 2003
L-R: Kenny Johnson, Frances Johnson, Alabama Governor Bob Riley,
Catherine Cabaniss, Ambassador William J. Cabaniss, Jr.,
Secretary of State Colin Powell, Florence Parnegg, Charles Caldwell,
Mary Ruth Caldwell, Jean Caldwell, Frances Bennett
U.S. Department of State Photo

On the Saturday evening before the swearing-in, Mignon Smith hosted a dinner party for the entire Alabama entourage in honor of Cabaniss's new ambassadorial charge. Smith was the first Republican National Committeewoman from Alabama in the 1960s. She played a significant role in the re-emergence of the Republican Party in Alabama. On Monday Bill and Catherine returned to Birmingham to prepare for travel to their new work in Prague.[6]

Tsars Fell on Alabama

Cabaniss never had any intention of entering the political arena. He had expected to have a career in the Army. His father was honored for distinguished service in the U.S. Navy in World War II: he was awarded the Bronze Star; one uncle was a Navy admiral, and another uncle was one of the very first U.S. Navy aviators. Cabaniss had no exposure to local, statewide, or national politics – at least no exposure to nor interest in elective politics during his formative years. But as a business-owner in Birmingham he sensed an anti-business environment among legislators.

One particular incident in Alabama's "government versus business" skirmishes occurred in 1977. The incident was viewed by many as stereotypical of the business climate of that day. It was the first week of January in Montgomery, Alabama and the seats in the Garrett Coliseum were filled with the press, special interest groups, and citizen observers. The coliseum seats normally held sports fans who would watch their favorite teams play basketball, volleyball, or an indoor western rodeo. Less than two weeks beyond Christmas, this Tuesday gathering seemed a little too early in the morning and inappropriate to watch a sporting event, unless it was the beginning of a series of playoff games, which it was not. January 4, 1977 saw a crowd estimated widely from 2,000 to 8,000 attendees gathering at the coliseum for a show. News media had set up cameras to record the event for the evening news on local Alabama television stations. Out-of-state media were present also. What was happening?

Garrett Coliseum
City of Montgomery, Alabama Photo

A senior vice president of Citibank from New York was present, as well as an executive from a leasing subsidiary of the Prudential Life Insurance Company who was seated and busy sorting through his papers.

Joe Farley, the chief executive of Alabama Power Company entered the building accompanied by other power company executives and their security squad. The event was not a corporate-sponsored sporting event but a public hearing – very public in fact – on a rate increase requested by Alabama Power Company the previous November. For a decade the company had been attempting to educate the public on its need for rate increases, increases to parallel the rapid growth which the state of Alabama was experiencing, a growth rate that state officials had been steadily encouraging. The Alabama Public Service Commission normally conducted its hearings on rate hike requests in the commission's offices, but this time the hearings were to be heard in the large coliseum where more public participation could be anticipated. Though not a sporting event, food vendors in the coliseum were selling popcorn and soft drinks as people took their seats while the song "Bridge Over Troubled Water" played on the public address system. It was a carnival-like atmosphere and orchestrated to intimidate Alabama Power Company officials for their rate hike request. The event was an expressed reinforcement of the spirit or the ideology of the State of Alabama that big business gouged its customers.

Newspapers statewide had already tried and convicted Alabama Power of applying excessive rates to its customers. It did not matter, apparently, that utility rates were government sanctioned. Governor George Wallace had been verbally hammering away at the alleged abuses of Alabama Power for some time. Some citizens, many business owners in fact, thought that Wallace's diatribes against Alabama Power would discourage people and businesses from locating in Alabama. Others thought that Wallace did not do enough to keep rate increases in check. But there was no doubt that having the hearings in a large coliseum would bring attention not only to the rate increase request by a "greedy corporation" but to Alabama itself. News spread across the country ahead of this scheduled hearing. For many outsiders this "rate hearing extravaganza" confirmed their suspicions that Alabama was an anti-business state. But as the proceedings unfolded, some surprising (and unexpected) pieces of information emerged for the ears of all to hear.

An executive from Citibank testifying before the commission explained that Alabama Power Company had lost its "A" bond rating because they did not meet the financial expectations of the investment community on Wall Street. The message delivered was that a lower bond rating is economically hurtful, not only to the bondholders, but to the general public that benefits from the company's service. And since Citibank was the lead bank in the syndicate of lenders to Alabama Power, it decided that the utility was no longer creditworthy, therefore it would cut off any future loans. If that were not bad enough, the Prudential Insurance executive told the commission that his company would no longer extend credit for operation of the utility's vehicles and fuel. This was not only bad news for APC, but bad news for Alabama. An embarrassing situation made doubly embarrassing simply by the Public Service Commission's move to conduct the hearings in the Garrett Coliseum instead of its regular offices. Or was the coliseum venue the Commission's doing?

A peculiar mindset hovered over Alabama. George Wallace was elected governor in 1962 and early on his target enemy was racially based. He always had a political enemy or scapegoat. At the beginning of his gubernatorial career his underlying political tactic was race-baiting. Once race-baiting was no longer politically useful Wallace shifted to an anti-business strategy using tactics of class differentiation. For Wallace, there always had to be an enemy of the people somewhere. Though seemingly conservative to outsiders, Alabama has a history of economic and political liberalism. Back in the 1890s strong populist tendencies focused on the state's control of railroads and banks, the easing of credit, and the regulation of dominant industries including steel and utilities.[7] Alabama Power Company thus became Wallace's whipping boy, a tactic that proved successful for Wallace and for Alabama Democratic politics. Even though APC wised-up and became by necessity a better political combatant, the Alabama mindset of opposition to big business – any business – continued in its inexorable crusade. The media and special interest groups made sure that they kept companies like APC on guard all the time, particularly the utilities that had to approach the state for rate increases. Even at later times journalist and opposition lawyers would mischaracterize corporate executives to the public by saying things like "There is no way you can get a straight answer from this man [APC's Farley]. He has more tricks up his sleeve than all the Rockefellers and

Fords combined." The relentless hammering away at business by government leaders and progressive social action groups kept the anti-business mindset alive and well in Alabama for years, with no ending in sight. Alabama, a former solid-South Democratic state, had been a one-party state since the end of Reconstruction. In the year 2010 the one-party (Democratic) strangle-hold was broken. Alabama is now a one-party Republican state. Up until around 1986 the Alabama electorate knew virtually nothing about competitive politics.[8] The Alabama Power Company incident summed up the ongoing government/business environment of Alabama. It was symbolic. On the other side of the world other nations and their regions experienced their own problems.

A Challenge in Central Europe

On January 7, 1977, a document known as *Charter 77* was published in Czechoslovakia – a document representing a human rights movement within a satellite nation of the Union of Soviet Socialist Republics. The document was actually prepared in 1976 by some notable writers, workers, and intellectuals, and was motivated partially by the arrest of members of a musical group known as *Plastic People of the Universe*.[9] The *Charter,* through its authors, intended "to create a nonviolent opposition to the totalitarian regime."[10] The *Charter* simply noted that two international covenants, one a covenant on "civil and political rights," the other a covenant on "economic, social, and cultural rights," had been accepted by the government and placed in its Register of Laws No. 120 on October 13, 1976. The mere publication of the acceptance and registering of these covenants by the government of Czechoslovakia served to expose the fact that those rights – human, economic, and social – existed on paper only. The *Charter* was challenging their government to live up to their own laws. It was not a political movement to take over power. The signatories identified the spokespersons for the Charter as professors Jan Patočka and Jiří Hájek, and poet-playwright Václav Havel."[11] Havel would later tell an audience at a Council of Europe meeting in Strasbourg (France) in 1990 that he and his *Charter* cohorts thought and dreamed of freedom, justice, human rights, democracy, political pluralism, a market economy and much more. They dreamed of a Europe without high walls and with no artificially separated nations.[12]

Twenty-seven years would pass before the Czech playwright and the Alabama gentleman would meet.

A Call to the Political

Cabaniss intended to make a career of Army service, but while stationed in Germany two Army physicians certified that his knee was too unstable to join Special Forces. Not wanting to become an Army desk jockey, Cabaniss resigned his commission in 1964. That was his first turning point. After returning to Birmingham Cabaniss went searching for work. Cabaniss's family heritage could be said to be a typical southern success story. Bill Cabaniss stood on the shoulders of parents and grandparents who were family oriented to a high degree and they and other ancestors were people who for the most part made good and fortuitous family business decisions.[13]

By 1977 Williams Jelks Cabaniss, Jr. had become a successful businessman in Alabama. It had not been an easy task. As he built his company along with business partner Walter McCullers, Cabaniss learned first-hand the regional problems experienced by Alabama businesses. Being the external man of his small company, he traveled weekly throughout the Southeast to sell his company's services and wares. With a heavy travel schedule five days per week for seven years Cabaniss learned a lot, especially about the business environments of his region of the United States. That region was growing at a rate faster than that of Alabama. Rustbelt[14] companies shut down their northern facilities and began establishing branches or relocating plants to North Carolina, Tennessee, Georgia, Mississippi, and Louisiana, but not to Alabama. Discovering these state-by-state disparities, Cabaniss asked rustbelt executives why they avoided Alabama. The answer was simple and straightforward. Alabama operated in an anti-business environment. Not only was the state's rhetoric discouraging companies wanting to relocate, Alabama business law presented a more negative reality – Alabama's tort law. A quirk in the state's co-employee liability laws allowed employees to sue for cause not only their employer but any employee up to and including the executive level. At this point in his life Cabaniss had no interest in becoming political. He said that when in grade school he must have been absent the day his class made a field trip to the state legislature in Montgomery. His purpose in life was to attend college, make a career in the army, marry, and raise a family. That he did, except for an army career. But in 1977 at the age of 39, he believed that he had to make some kind of commitment to change the way his beloved Alabama "conducts business." This recognition of Alabama's anti-business environment triggered the second turning point in Bill Cabaniss's life.

BIG JIM FOLSOM WAS A TOUGH ACT TO FOLLOW. Gordon Persons was elected governor of Alabama in 1950 and took office in 1951. Hardly the flamboyant personality of his predecessor, Persons, in his business-like manner, refused to have an inaugural parade or the customary black tie gala and ball. Dedicated to the job to which he was elected, Persons made not one speaking engagement while serving in office.[1] To the public eye he was as lackluster as Folsom was the center of attention.

Worldwide, the big news in the early 1950s was the accession of Queen Elizabeth II to the throne of England on February 6, 1952 upon the death of her father King George VI. The coronation ceremony was filmed and hurriedly transported to America for all to see. On October 26, 1952 the American television series known as *Victory at Sea* aired. A spectacular collection of movie reels from World War II were put together, making for exciting viewing of America's involvement in the South Pacific. It was a hit program on Sunday afternoons long before the National Football League came into its own as obligatory viewing for fathers, their sons, and other young men. Bill, Sr. and Bill, Jr. watched *Victory at Sea* together.

The series of filmed episodes of World War II battles were engaging and to some degree entertaining. The series was produced by the National Broadcasting Company and aired its first episode on Sunday afternoon October 26, 1952. The television series ran until May 3, 1953 and was a big hit. Those who remember *Victory at Sea* were struck by the introduction of the show with a dark, rolling ocean in the background, and a large letter "V" projected onto the screen, all accompanied by the music of Richard Rodgers. The music mimicked in sound the undulating sea behind the letter "V." One song represented a victory accomplished: "The Guadalcanal March;" and the calm that settled in after a stormy battle was musically depicted in the beguine "Beneath the Southern Cross." The tune was used later in a Broadway play and re-titled as "No Other Love [Than I]."[2] Those television episodes conveyed to viewers the heroic struggles the United States Navy and other military personnel contributed in defense of their country. To Bill Cabaniss, Sr., the shows recalled an ever-present and distinct memory. To Bill, Jr. it meant a form of hero worship.

Bill, Sr. had moved up the corporate ladder quite rapidly since being hired in 1935 by Southern Cement Company. Within months he was promoted from an assistant sales manager to the company treasurer's position and made a director. In 1940 he was elected secretary and his salary improved. But in August, 1942 he resigned as director of the company because he was commissioned as a Lieutenant in the United States Naval Reserve. During the years Bill, Sr. served on active duty in the Navy – 1943, 1944, and part of 1945 – Southern Cement paid him part of his salary but he received no compensation from any profits the company may have made.[3] The successful businessman turned sailor would serve on the *U.S.S. Birmingham*, a light cruiser, during the war and saw action mostly in the Pacific theatre.

During the Battle of Leyte Gulf the *U.S.S. Birmingham* was heavily damaged in an explosion of the aircraft carrier *U.S.S. Princeton*. The *Birmingham* was called to aid the *Princeton* after it received repeated air attacks from Japanese fighter aircraft. The *Birmingham* made two attempts at approaching the burning *Princeton*, both ships in the ocean's trough at 30 degrees. On the third attempt the starboard side of the *Birmingham* made a spring line to the *Princeton's* port side. Many officers and men of the *U.S.S. Birmingham* were topside manning hoses and tow lines when at approximately 1523 or 3:23pm in the afternoon the *U.S.S. Princeton* exploded, sending shrapnel and large objects in every direction. The *Birmingham* was swamped with debris from the explosion. The fuel reserves on the carrier eventually exploded, causing massive casualties, few on the *Princeton* but many on the *Birmingham*. Two hundred and twenty-nine sailors were killed instantly with more than four hundred wounded, half of them with serious injuries.[4] Just prior to the explosion Bill (Sr.) had moved from the *Birmingham's* starboard to port side of the light cruiser's conning tower which saved his life.

Shades Valley High School, New Merkle, and Slabtown

Bill Cabaniss began his freshman year at Shades Valley High School in Birmingham in the fall of 1952. Had it not been for his tactful negotiating skills at such a young age – a trait that could have been inherited from his dad or developed on his own – the younger Cabaniss might not have been watching *Victory at Sea* with his dad and he would have entered high school out of the state of Alabama. In Alabama a young boy could get a license to operate a motorcycle at age fourteen. Francis Crockard had a motorcycle, so did Cullom Walker. Young Cabaniss figured that since it was some distance from the neighborhood to Shades Valley High School, a motorcycle for him would actually relieve his parents of any responsibility of chauffeuring. Good thinking. It worked. The boys had many makes and models of motorocycles – Harley, BSA, service cycles, TWN, and others. It meant freedom for them.[5]

Not far from the Mountain Brook area was a community named New Merkle, now Cahaba Heights. It was a mining community in those days. It was also a place for moonshine and a gathering place for high school boys set free by the motorcycles. It was a place for beer drinking too. Situated on the Cahaba River, New Merkle was nicknamed "Slabtown." The mining residue or coal dust was everywhere, not just in Slabtown. The coal dust provided a dark and dirty look to anything it touched. The roads were black from the coal dust – those were the unpaved roads on the back side of Mountain Brook. The boys would actually swim in the murky Cahaba for recreation and just to be boys.

Bill Cabaniss on bike with Francis Crockard, circa 1952

An organized sports program was not known in the school system, at least no intramural sports to the extent evident in the twenty-first century. So the young men formed fraternities which seemed to them to be the only way to play some level of competitive, organized sports. Cabaniss and Crockard were *Alpha Sigma Delta* brothers. Crockard says he still is. Walker was a *Chi Sigma Chi.* "The boys at New Merkle loved to see us come out there to play. We were smirked at, and called 'Brookies.' We were considered sissies and rich kids."[6] This was – how it was.

The young boys of Mountain Brook went about their ways as young boys should in their high school days. They cared little about government or politics, even though Cabaniss's dad had served on the first town council of Mountain Brook and Cullom Walker's dad held an appointive office in Jefferson County. Crockard had a first cousin – Mignon Smith was her name – who would become a major player in Alabama Republican politics. Statewide, Alabama continued to be governed by the Democratic Party as it had been since 1874. Whoever won the Democratic primary election, or whoever was selected by the state Democratic Executive Committee in the summer of an election year, would always win in the fall's general election. Republicans had never been taken seriously since the end of Reconstruction, nor had the Alabama Republican party been highly organized. Internationally the Korean War was not to end for another year and 1952 was a national election year for the presidency. Both the Democratic and Republican national conventions were televised that year. The nation was beginning to experience a post war economic boom and the nation's population was growing at an accelerating rate. With an economy in a postwar upswing, and now television, some of the environment outside their high school and their self-made fraternities were making an impact on them, affecting their formation.

Young Bill Cabaniss already knew how to negotiate a successful deal. The deal with his father was not a small victory. It earned him one full year at Shades Valley High School after which he knew that he would spend the remaining three years of preparatory education in New Jersey. Bill Cabaniss, Sr. attended the Lawrenceville School and so would his son. That one year at Shades Valley was both a time for Bill Cabaniss, Jr. to enjoy the camaraderie of his Birmingham friends and a time to prepare for his three years of absence.

Eisenhower Republicans

Dwight David Eisenhower, the famous Army general of World War II and a Republican, defeated Democrat Adlai Stevenson in the general election of 1952. In Alabama during the campaign years – mostly 1951 and 1952 – businessman Winton Blount was appointed Alabama Chairman of "Citizens for Eisenhower." Not "Alabama Republicans for Eisenhower," just "Citizens." Given the Alabama state of mind, which has lingered since the end of Reconstruction, any mention of the word

Republican was invoked in the pejorative. Even though the "Solid [Democratic] South" fractured in 1948, Alabama went for Stevenson. In the South Eisenhower carried Virginia, Tennessee, Florida, and Texas. Republicans were traditionally strong in the northeast but there were signs of an emerging shift.

Political analysts and statisticians mused that Eisenhower Republicans were essentially professional and business persons, but mostly they were reform-minded, intending to make real a nationwide two-party system. Such a mindset present in the South was certainly felt as a challenge by entrenched Democratic leaders. Analysts also revealed that Republicans did well in urban areas and were attractive to more prosperous people. This attractiveness could be seen even in Alabama, if only in the tiny town of Mountain Brook. Eisenhower won there by almost 80% in 1952 and in 1956 by 77 percent.[7] There is no doubt that the economically successful leaders in the Birmingham area made their home in the upscale community to its south and east. There were other "over the mountain" affluent neighborhoods within the suburban cities of Vestavia Hills and Homewood. But it would be Mountain Brook that would receive negative scrutiny.

Eisenhower took office in January of 1953. On March 15, 1953, episode #19 of *Victory at Sea* aired on national network television. This was the *Battle of Leyte Gulf* and a few Sundays later on April 16, 1953 the battle for Okinawa was presented as *Suicide for Glory*, episode #25. Bill Cabaniss, Sr. served in both campaigns and the visual summary of those battles was viewed both by father and son. William Jelks Cabaniss, Jr. knew that his father was not only a patriot, he was a hero, and selflessly served his nation at its greatest time of need. These understandings and personal feelings stuck with young Bill as he prepared for his education and his own future. By this time Bill's dad was chief executive of a cement manufacturer, and had become quite successful. *The Pittsburgh Press* in March of 1954 headlined a story "Southern Cement Company Builds 1 Million Barrel Plant." The paper quoted Cabaniss, Sr. as saying "Post-war expansion of our company has been due primarily to the upsurge of business in our territory, which has multiplied demand for all our products." Birmingham itself was becoming the worldwide center for slag products or "aggregates" and had not yet reached its peak. Vulcan Materials of Birmingham would become the nation's largest aggregates producer.

The Korean War was about to end but not quite yet. Other parts of the world were in turmoil and under domination by the Soviet Union as part of the after-effects of settling World War II. There were some early challenges made to the communist system of government in 1953. The first was when the Allies broke Berlin into partitions. The Soviet Union controlled East Berlin in what was colloquially known as East Germany. The other challenge came from Plzeň in Czechoslovakia.

Due to poor economic conditions, citizens of both cities caused a level of public disturbances. But in Plzeň, as well as the rest of Czechoslovakia, the Soviets implemented a reform of the Czech currency, wiping out much of the population's savings. Spontaneously, strikes and demonstrations broke out against communist policies. There were riots in Plzeň which were put down by security police.[8] There was a new order in the world since the end of World War II with the United States becoming the strongest nation, both economically and militarily. But there developed a two-power construct in world affairs between a totalitarian model enforced on partitioned Eastern Europe, which threatened the rest of Europe, and a market-based/freedom-based economic model. The Korean War ended on July 27, 1953 after three years, one month, and two days of hostilities.

The Lawrenceville School

In the fall Bill Cabaniss entered the Lawrenceville School in New Jersey. Known primarily as a prep school for Princeton University, its graduates were also recruited by Yale. The all-boys school had a large contingent of southerners in the student body. Francis Crockard, a childhood friend of Cabaniss, attended Lawrenceville. The future chief justice of Alabama, Drayton Nabers, Jr., also of the Birmingham area, attended the prep academy but not in the same graduating class. A future bishop of the Episcopal Diocese of Alabama, Charles Colcock Jones Carpenter[9] attended the school in his youth, and his son Doug Carpenter did the same. By the end of Bill Cabaniss's first year at Lawrenceville the United States Supreme Court decided that the long-standing "separate but equal" schools in the South were not equal and struck down fifty-eight years of *Jim Crowism*. In 1896 the Supreme Court in the case *Plessy v. Ferguson* established the "separate but equal" standard.[10] In Alabama the Democratic nominee for state attorney general, Albert Patterson, was murdered in Phenix City on June 14, 1954. Phenix City was well known for its violence, corruption, and gangsterism. It was considered the "wickedest city in America."[11] 1954 was also an election year for the Alabama governor's office. James E. "Big Jim" Folsom was elected to begin his broken - but second - term at the beginning of 1955. Though governor from 1947 to 1951, while out of office between 1951 and 1954 he kept his face and name in the public eye by attending any event that would draw a crowd and the press. It was not difficult for a six foot, eight inch tall man to attract attention anyway.[12] A southern political liberal, a complexity difficult to nuance, Folsom's second term was marked by his "Farm-to-Market" road program.[13]

Lawrenceville School Football Team of 1956
Bill Cabaniss seated fourth from left.
Lawrenceville School Yearbook Photo

Bill Cabaniss returned to Lawrenceville in the fall of 1955 to begin his senior year. He became vice president of his class and as such was accorded the honor of sitting at the front of all school assemblies along with the class president and the headmaster of the school. Underclassman Drayton Nabers remembers those proud moments watching his fellow Alabamian in that leadership role.[14] At Lawrenceville Cabaniss was on the swimming team and played varsity football. He made friends with a classmate from Philadelphia, Dick Baruch. On the football team Baruch played quarterback and Cabaniss centered. Both planned to play football at nearby Princeton University after graduation.

Lawrenceville was unique in many ways. It was an all-boys school and they lived in houses, homes really, around a circle. There were no dormitories. Each house had a live-in house mother and house father. A Dr. and Mrs. Wright managed Bill Cabaniss's home away from home. And there were several southern boys studying at this New Jersey campus. Cabaniss figured that it must be a southern tradition for fathers to send their sons to Lawrenceville. Although Cabaniss had planned to join his friend at Princeton after graduating, it was not to be. Instead, he was accepted at Vanderbilt University in Nashville, Tennessee.

Montgomery Bus Boycott

In Montgomery, on October 31, 1954, a young Martin Luther King, Jr. of Atlanta would be installed as the minister of the Dexter Avenue Baptist Church and little more than one year later, on the first day of the Montgomery Bus Boycott, King was named president of the colored Montgomery Improvement Association, a position which would catapult him into national prominence as a civil rights leader.[15] The boycott began on December 1, 1955 when a black seamstress named Rosa Parks refused to give up her seat to a boarding white passenger. For this she was arrested by police. There existed at the time a Montgomery city ordinance requiring African Americans to give up their seats on a bus or any other public conveyance to a white person. That was the incident which prompted the successful Montgomery Bus Boycott. For her actions that day Mrs. Parks became known as "the mother of the modern civil rights movement." Alabama was becoming politically and socially restless even as it was transforming itself into a home for America's space-age development in Huntsville.

Martin Luther King, Jr.'s Montgomery home was bombed in January, 1956. Bombing was a tactic also used against African Americans in Birmingham following the end of World War II when there was a shortage of housing. Blacks began buying homes in previously all-white but transitional neighborhoods. Montgomery's bombing was intended to stop the leadership of the bus boycott. King declared that even if he were to meet his demise from the bombings or any other violence the movement "will not stop." And it didn't. In December of 1956 the Supreme Court banned segregated seating in public transit vehicles.[16] King and Parks were the first black people to ride in fully integrated buses in Montgomery.

Varieties of Change in Alabama

In North Alabama the Army Ballistic Missile Agency was established in 1956 at Huntsville's Redstone Arsenal, a move that would eventually make Huntsville and Alabama home to many of the world's best scientists. It was also a time when a young black woman named Autherine Lucy attempted to enter a summer school session at the University of Alabama in Tuscaloosa. Her first day in class went without incident, but on the second day rumblings began and rioting ensued. The university "excluded" Lucy from classes, citing the rioting but she later was "expelled" permanently from studying at the school. Her accompanying attorney was Arthur Shores, the first black man licensed to practice law in the State of Alabama. Shores's home in the western section of Birmingham was one of those homes bombed several times after the end of World War II.[17]

Bill Cabaniss was home in the summer of 1956 preparing to attend Vanderbilt University in Nashville, Tennessee. Cabaniss had also applied to Georgia Tech but decided on Vanderbilt where he played football for one season. A knee injury brought a sudden end to his football playing dreams, but he became captain of Vanderbilt's swimming team. Cabaniss majored in mathematics, was president of *Beta Theta Pi,* and a member of the Army Reserved Officer Training Corps.[18]

In Birmingham, Southern Cement was prospering and the Magic City, in addition to its steel production and steel fabrication, was riding high in the aggregates or gravel industry. In Montgomery Winton Blount, also known as "Red" and his brother, Houston, had developed a fairly large and prosperous contracting and construction company. Its heyday was yet to come when Houston accepted an offer from Charles Ireland, chairman of the Birmingham-based aggregates giant and recently renamed Vulcan Materials, to lead its new pipe division.[19]

Dwight D. Eisenhower won re-election in 1956 as president of the United States, receiving no electoral votes from Alabama. Adlai Stevenson, the Democratic candidate, received ten of Alabama's electoral votes. A lone elector decided to cast his vote for neither the Democratic nor Republican candidates. An Alabama woman, Mignon Smith, made history by becoming the state's first Young Republican Committeewoman. She served as a delegate to the 1956 and 1960 Republican National Conventions. She was actively attempting to re-start or resurrect the Republican Party in Alabama.[20]

By the time Bill Cabaniss graduated from Vanderbilt University the Soviet Union had launched "Sputnik" in 1957, followed by the launching of an American satellite in 1958 which was placed into orbit by Jupiter rockets designed and built in Huntsville, Alabama.[21] And John Patterson, a Democrat and the son of the slain Alabama attorney general candidate in 1954 from Phenix City, was elected governor in 1958. Patterson's term as governor was marked by his battles with African American civil rights groups in Alabama like the NAACP and the Tuskegee Civic Association, a group that organized a boycott against white merchants in Tuskegee.[22]

In June, 1960 Cabaniss graduated from Vanderbilt University and received a regular commission as a second lieutenant in the U.S. Army. Cabaniss intended to make the Army his career. He reported to Fort Benning, Georgia in the same month.[23] The 1960 census placed Alabama's population at 3.2 million; 980 thousand were African American. Alabama was now barely an urban state with 1.7 million urbanites and 1.6 million rural citizens.[24] While Cabaniss was serving in the Army at his first duty station in Germany, the political, demographic, and social landscape in Alabama was in the midst of rapid change — social turmoil.

A large number of Alabamians supported the Republican Party in the national elections of 1960. One of the factors swaying these Alabama voters was the religion of the Democratic presidential candidate, John F. Kennedy, a Roman Catholic. Another problem was the Democratic Platform. Republicans experienced victories in Alabama's largest cities but the Democrats won in all the other major elective offices, some with more than two-to-one margins. Alabama's Winton Blount was appointed as Richard Nixon's presidential campaign chairman for the Southeast.

Nixon visited Alabama and gave a speech at Birmingham's City Hall. Kennedy never visited Alabama but his vice-presidential running mate, Lyndon B. Johnson of Texas, did. Johnson's wife, affectionately known as "Lady Bird," was born in Texas of Alabama parents. Former president Harry S. Truman campaigned for Kennedy in Decatur, Alabama, and most of the Alabama congressional delegation campaigned around the state. Claude O. Vardaman was chairman of Alabama's Republican Party. In that election Democrats had to overcome the growing Republican opposition as well as a group named "Independents-for-Nixon." Alabama voters supported conservative Democrat Harry Byrd of Virginia. It was after the 1960 election that serious consideration was given to shoring up the Republican Party in Alabama by a new leadership.[25]

Alabama Young Republicans

It was Mignon Smith who brought a young attorney, John Grenier, into Alabama's Republican Party leadership. In 1960 Grenier became chairman of the Young Republicans and then chaired the state Republican Party in 1962. Up to this time Alabama Republicans were known as "Post Office Republicans." Though the state elected Democrats locally, Republicans held the presidency. Therefore, many local federal appointees were Republicans, but these Republicans had no political base in the state and therefore no chance of election victories at a local level or a statewide office. "There was no [highly organized] Republican Party [in Alabama] at all. The party could meet in a phone booth. [John] Grenier worked for [the Birmingham-based law firm of] Bradley Arant during the day and traveled around the state to set up county Republican organizations. ..." [26]John Grenier and his group of young Republicans replaced Vardaman and the old "Post Office Republican" system and transitioned the party into a formidable political opponent for Democrats. The effect was the transformation of state politics into a two-party system. But it would take five decades for Republicans to achieve political dominance.

Chapter 3 Alabama Republican Politics – 1961-1965

JOHN F. KENNEDY TOOK OFFICE AS PRESIDENT of the United States on January 20, 1961. He was not a popular president in Alabama where most of the votes went to United States Senator from Virginia Harry Byrd and Republicans experienced a strong showing, the strongest in decades. Kennedy did appoint an Alabamian, Dr. Luther Leonidas Terry, as Surgeon General of the United States. It was Terry who led the study which produced the famous report on the hazards of cigarette smoking. *Smoking and Health: Report of the Advisory committee to the Surgeon General of the United States* was released on January 1, 1964.[1]

1961 was also the year that Monroeville, Alabama native Harper Lee won the Pulitzer Prize for her novel *To Kill a Mockingbird*. The storyline of the book was set in the 1930s in Alabama and became not only a bestseller but was made into a movie starring actor Gregory Peck. America was becoming more involved in war-torn Vietnam and "Freedom Riders" were making bus trips through the South to put an end to segregation and racial discrimination. The Freedom Riders were testing the 1960 decision of the United State Supreme Court decision prohibiting segregation in bus and train terminals. Freedom Riders met with violent opposition upon reaching Alabama.

Bill Cabaniss was serving his nation in the United States Army as a second lieutenant. He was stationed in Germany.

Army Ranger Squad at Fort Benning, Georgia
Bill Cabaniss, top left, 1961

He and several of his Army buddies applied for service in the Army's elite Special Forces. Cabaniss was ordered to go through two medical exams due to his weak knee from a football injury in his freshman year at Vanderbilt University. The first medical opinion stated that Cabaniss had an unstable knee, the second opinion concurred. This information was difficult to receive for the young Army officer. Even though he was already committed to an Army career, Cabaniss was inspired at his college graduation ceremony in a speech delivered by Army Four-Star General William "Westy" Westmoreland.[2] The result of the two medical examinations was devastating to Cabaniss. He had dreamed of becoming a Special Forces Army Ranger. The dream quashed was an unplanned and unexpected turning point in his life. "I did not want to be a desk jockey. I wanted to be in an active unit." In July, 1962 he returned to the U.S. for training in firing missiles at White Sands Missile Range in New Mexico. While on leave Bill Cabaniss and Catherine Caldwell were married in Birmingham.

Wedding Picture July 20, 1962
Bill and Catherine Cabaniss

Afterwards, the couple departed for Zweibrucken, Germany for Bill to serve out his remaining assignment. When Cabaniss returned to the states in 1964 he resigned his Army commission while at Fort McClellan. Married, he and Catherine went home looking for a job.[3]

Republican Party or Conservative In-roads in Alabama

For many years the two United States Senators from Alabama, John Sparkman and Lister Hill, were popular but they were liberal in an increasingly conservative-minded state. In 1962 the Alabama Democratic Party received a big scare in the re-election campaign of Lister Hill. Hill's Republican challenger, Jim Martin from Gadsden, almost defeated him. Only 6,803 votes separated the two. John Grenier had taken over the Alabama Republican Party in 1962 and immediately began building a statewide organization. "… The Republican Senate candidate, a novice politician, had been nominated by the Republican state convention after an 'insurgent group largely representative of the newer and younger urban business-professional wing of the party' took control."[4]

Grenier began recruitment of candidates for a national House seat for the 1964 election. Between Martin and Grenier, the two made strong efforts to shore up Republican strength by strategically targeting offices. In Martin's race with Hill, Grenier knew that there would be low voter turnout in the general election because in the one-party state of Alabama the big election was the Democratic primary. Whoever wins the Democratic primary is the almost automatic winner of the general election. Since only a small percentage of the electorate was expected to show up at the general election, Martin and Grenier targeted only that small percentage for campaign purposes. There was no need to canvass the entire state – it would have been a waste of time, effort, and expense. It almost worked. The election was too close for comfort for Senator Hill. For all intents and purposes that 1962 election was the beginning of the end of Hill's political career. Former Alabama Republican Party chairman Bill Harris mused: "I think we actually won the 1962 race. A lot of ballots were thrown out."[5]

Another phenomenon that occurred in that 1962 general election – mostly obscured by Martin's strong showing – was the fact that eighteen Republican candidates contested seats in the Alabama state legislature – two of them were successful.[6] These two electoral successes were the beginnings of the upsurge of Republican visibility and vitality that transformed into a movement. "The money behind the [Republican] movement [in Alabama] came from Mignon [Smith], Herbert Stockham, Red Blount, and Tom Brigham."[7]

Nobody in Alabama Votes Republican

The difficulties facing Republican candidates could be seen at the voter level. In Greene County a voter showed up at the polls to vote. Asked what party, the voter said "Republican" and was not allowed to vote. John Grenier learned of the incident that day, reported it to the Federal Bureau of Investigation who saw to it that the voter could exercise his rights. The local registrar simply said that "nobody votes Republican."[8] Don Collins, originally from Etowah County, Alabama and later a Democratic representative to the Alabama House, had campaigned for Richard Nixon in 1960, not for Kennedy. When Collins went before the Jefferson County probate judge to register himself as a Democratic candidate for the House from Birmingham, the judge required him to sign a loyalty oath to the state Democratic Party. Collins then felt compelled to advise the judge that he had voted for Republican Richard Nixon in 1960. The probate judge said "Never mind that, go ahead and sign it." Collins never forgot that moment of hypocrisy.[9] Alabama was actually a "no-party" state but no serious candidate for public office ever considered running as a Republican.

Carpetbaggin', Scalawaggin', Race-mixin' Liar

Breaking with his former mentor Jim Folsom, George C. Wallace was elected governor in 1962 and assumed office in January, 1963. Wallace's populist style of campaigning and speech-making made him a political spectacle not only in Alabama but throughout the entire nation. That did not bother Wallace. He sought the limelight constantly just as did Folsom. A prime example of Wallace's public style – which permeates a national perception of most southern politicians – is the way Wallace sparred with federal judge, and former law school classmate, Frank Johnson. Refusing to give the United States Civil Rights Commission grand jury records, Wallace was cited with contempt. With the possibility of real jail time, Wallace clandestinely returned the records so that the Commission would receive them. But publically Wallace excoriated the encroachment of federal agencies into Alabama as a violation of the constitution. His ready-reference was Judge Johnson whom Wallace labeled as "a low-down, carpetbaggin', scalawaggin', race-mixin' liar."[10] Such phraseology coupled with a physical swagger of the hips left to right and back and forth, and a sassy, vocal delivery, was apparently pleasant to the ears of the electorate, and prevailed as a caricature of loud-mouth, southern politicians to the rest of the nation.

Wallace's election – he lost in the primary four years earlier to John Patterson who appeared more racist than Wallace himself – began a new phase of racial strife of social division in Alabama. The bombings continued, this time to the home of the brother of Martin Luther King, Jr., the office of the Southern Christian Leadership Conference, and the Sixteenth Street Baptist Church in Birmingham. Four young African American girls were killed in the church bombing. All of this in 1963.

Civil Rights demonstrations continued and many blacks were jailed, including King. It was from a Birmingham jail that King wrote his famous letter responding to local clergy inaction. It was also a year when two young African American students entered the University of Alabama and the newly elected governor, George Wallace, stood in the school's doorway in a standoff with the federal government. Wallace capitulated but with bravado he stood for "States' Rights" against an intrusive "Central Government."[11]

In Mobile, Alabama the new University of South Alabama opened its doors. 1963 was a year with an unusual mix of social and political strife. On the national scene the United States Senator from Arizona, Barry Goldwater, a Republican, was preparing for his 1964 race against incumbent president John F. Kennedy. Although John Grenier would play a significant role in Goldwater's national campaign, the Republican Party in Alabama was struggling. It was only in 1963 that a permanent staff was established at its headquarters. Under Grenier's leadership this group of young professionals traveled around the state organizing previously unorganized or non-existent county political groups and committees. In Jefferson County, the home of Birmingham, precinct organizations were developed.[12]

In late November when President John F. Kennedy was assassinated, it was said that Goldwater lost his motivation for running for president in

1964. Goldwater respected Kennedy for his capabilities and had looked forward to the race. He had no regard for Lyndon Johnson who became president immediately following the assassination. By this time Goldwater had been deep in his campaign effort, but he wanted to quit. Young Republican devotees met with Goldwater to encourage him to continue the race. But Goldwater understood public opinion, especially when it involved the assassination of the nation's president. He knew he had no chance of defeating Johnson under those circumstances. It was John Grenier and several other young advisors who convinced Goldwater to stay in the race because the conservative movement was undergoing a shift in support from the old Republicans of the northeast to new Republicans in the south and southwest.[13]

Bill Cabaniss Returns Home from Army Duty

Bill Cabaniss returned to Birmingham from his Army assignment in Germany in time to see the politics of 1964. His first priority, however, was finding a job. So he began pounding the pavement seeking employment, but he avoided Southern Cement Company. Cabaniss's father had been chief executive officer of Southern Cement for many years, and the young Cabaniss wanted to make it on his own. At first Cabaniss thought he had an offer from Birmingham's Woodward Iron Works. Joe Shaw was CEO at the time and he got Bill excited about the company and a particular job he had in mind for him. But that offer was one year into the future and Cabaniss couldn't wait. "Mr. Shaw, I need work now." He was married and it was also time to think about beginning a family. Then one day Cabaniss received a call from "Slick" Ellison, the chief executive of Southern Cement. "I hear you need a job." Cabaniss replied simply, "Yes, sir." "Then why haven't you called me. Don't answer that. I know why. If you want a job, then come and see me." Cabaniss did call on Ellison and accepted a position as safety engineer at Southern Cement's Shelby County plant.

Cabaniss worked from 1964 to 1970 and gained experience at the Martin-Marietta subsidiary. He worked at the plant level for three years and then moved to the Birmingham office where the marketing development group worked. That was where he gained experience with the sales force. Marketing and sales worked together to assess how

Southern Cement's products measured up to their competition. They developed new products when the need was discovered. He traveled to Louisiana to field test the company's newly developed masonry cement with Larry Kirchoff. Kirchoff was the salesman in charge of Louisiana.

A few days after Cabaniss returned to Birmingham he received a call from Dave Shearer, Southern Cement's CEO, who told him that Kirchoff had had a heart attack and asked Cabaniss to hold together the sales territory while Kirchoff recovered. For the next eight weeks Cabaniss flew to New Orleans on Sunday evenings, met with Kirchoff in the Ochsner Clinic, to work through his itinerary and then on Mondays began meeting with Kirchoff's customers. Kirchoff was punctual. His customers knew by the minute when he would arrive. Taking on this work Cabaniss got to know Louisiana very well and Kirchoff's customers even better.

The Alabama political climate in 1964 experienced a significant impact and the national scene would see some judicial earthquakes. Strom Thurmond, the former Dixiecrat candidate for president in 1948 and a Democratic United States Senator from South Carolina switched parties. In 1964 Thurmond became a Republican, the first Republican Senator from the Deep South in the twentieth century. In the same year the United States Supreme Court made a decision in the "one man, one vote" case of *Reynolds v. Sims*, which had the effect of favoring Republican strongholds in urban and suburban areas. This decision and another decision, *Baker v. Carr*, advanced the development of two-party political systems in the United States. The 1964 General Election results made Alabama a political focal point for the future of the Republican Party.

The Goldwater Sweep in Alabama 1964

It was labeled "The Goldwater Sweep" in Alabama. Barry Goldwater lost his presidential bid by a landslide in the general election but in Alabama he garnered 69.5% of the popular vote. Clearly a southern state with a presidential candidate from the southwest, the Republican party both nationally and in Alabama made its significant re-birth, giving notice to the nation that the once "Solid South" is really dead and politics are changing forever. Several GOP candidates in Alabama won elections that year including Guy Hunt as probate judge from Cullman County. For the longest time the "Republican Party was without credibility in Alabama. It was a patronage party in those days. Rural post masters were appointed. But in the sweep of 1964 five Republicans were elected to the United States Congress."[14] Bill Dickinson of Montgomery and Jack Edwards of Mobile won congressional seats longtime held by Democrats. Following the general election Alabama Republican leader John Grenier became executive director of the National Republican Party.

Less than a month after Lyndon Johnson assumed the presidency on January 20, 1965 through his own outright election, Alabama native and crooner Nat King Cole died in Santa Monica, California on February 15th. He sold over 50 million records and was the first African-American male to host his own weekly television program.[15] Three weeks later in Selma, Alabama approximately six hundred demonstrators made an attempt to march to Montgomery to oppose voting restrictions on black Americans. The marchers were violently rebuffed by state and local law enforcement and not allowed to proceed. The confrontation was captured by the print and television news media and was viewed across the nation. A second attempt made no forward progress and the marchers knelt in prayer. On March 21 a successful third attempt consisted of more than a five-fold increase in the number of marchers and on the capitol steps in Montgomery 25,000 demonstrators heard Martin Luther King, Jr. say that "we are on the move now … and no wave of racism will stop us." In August President Johnson signed the Voting Rights Bill into law.[16]

Growth of the Alabama Republican Party emerged in small steps. Bill Armistead, then a student at Howard College (now Samford University in Birmingham), in 1964 started the student Republican Club at Howard. This was after Armistead had called the Republican Party office asking them if he could help with the election of presidential candidate Barry Goldwater. The unexpected call was received favorably and Armistead was asked to come downtown to the office at 21st Street and Magnolia. Once there he met John Grenier and was given a stack of materials. Armistead campaigned not only for Goldwater but in-state he supported congressional candidates. In the future he would run an unsuccessful campaign for Alabama Lieutenant Governor. Today he is chairman of the Alabama Republican Party.[17]

Bill Cabaniss, still employed by Southern Cement and traveling throughout the southeast, was assisting old customers and prospecting for new ones. On November 22, 1965 Catherine Cabaniss gave birth to the couple's first child, Mary Caldwell Cabaniss.[18]

LELAND CHILDS OF MOUNTAIN BROOK WAS, IN 1966, THE FIRST Republican elected to the Alabama Senate since Reconstruction.[1] Jim Martin gave up his seat in Congress that he won in 1964, and ran for governor of Alabama, opposing Democrat Lurleen Wallace. He lost. However, even though the election experienced a low-voter turnout, the total amount of votes cast for Martin, 262,000, were to be more than those garnered by Richard Nixon in Alabama in the high-voter turnout in 1968. Nixon received 147,000 votes

Alabama Republican Party Internal Problems

But the Alabama Republican Party began to suffer an internal split. Two wings had developed within the party, one being a modern wing led by John Grenier and the other a more ideological group who followed the John Birch Society and former Democratic "Dixiecrats." There was a Grenier/Martin squabble which did not help things. Due to the struggle, Grenier lost his leadership position to a conservative group led by Albert Lee Smith. The far right of the party did not like the more moderate Grenier.[2]

"In 1966 probably as many blacks voted for James Martin as voted for Mrs. Wallace. While there are instances on record, Negro support for Republican nominees is not an important aspect of Alabama politics."[3] Alabama Republicans had a difficult time growing their party as long as George Wallace was around. Other southern states were growing their Republican parties and they started winning elections. But Alabama had Wallace who in the 1960s was extremely popular among the electorate which made it very difficult for Republicans. "In the long range perspective, the most significant result in 1966 was Ronald Reagan's victory in California. ... Some of Reagan's supporters began thinking of a presidential race in 1968 as the dimension of his landslide over [California governor Pat] Brown emerged. The big winner [nationally] in 1966, however, was Richard Nixon, who now saw his path to the nomination in 1968 open up."[4]

WILLIAM JELKS CABANISS, JR.

Lurleen Wallace

In early 1967 Lurleen Wallace was inaugurated as Alabama's first woman governor. She ran for governor in the 1966 campaign to facilitate husband George Wallace's presidential run in 1968. She died in office in 1968 and Albert Brewer completed her term.[5] Brewer served until 1971. Brewer's legislative achievement during those years was successfully moving through an educational reform package, the best Alabama had ever seen. Brewer was progressive in his ideas on education as well as in legislative reapportionment, and updating rules for the legal profession. George Wallace promised Brewer that he would not run when election time came. However, Wallace reneged on his promise to Brewer and entered the race shortly before the filing deadline. Wallace entered the race and won.[6]

Local Events, World Events

Catherine Cabaniss gave birth to their second child, a son, William Jelks Cabaniss III who was born on February 4, 1968. With high anti-war sentiment against America's involvement in Vietnam, President Lyndon Johnson spoke to the nation on a Sunday evening, March 31, 1968, and announced that he would not seek re-election. That news opened the doors for other Democratic candidates to enter the presidential campaign which included Eugene McCarthy and Robert Kennedy. On June 5, 1968 Kennedy was shot in an assassination attempt in Los Angeles at the Ambassador Hotel after accepting the nomination from the California Democratic Convention. He died at Good Samaritan Hospital on June 6. All was not well with the rest of the world either.

The Prague Spring of 1968

In the spring of 1968 Alexander Dubček attempted to put a human face on socialism inside Czechoslovakia. It was a brief period of political liberation. "The Prague Spring had three basic aims: political liberation, economic liberalization, and the federalization of the national economic system. ... At the heart of each of these reforms lay political liberalization, or the wish for greater freedom and pluralism to emerge within the restrictions of the Communist political system. Prompted by pressures from students, writers, and the economic elite, 'socialism with a human face'" resulted in a political model closer to pre-World War II Czechoslovak democracy than the post-World War II Stalinist bureaucracy. On August 21, 1968, five Warsaw Pact member countries invaded Czechoslovakia and Soviet troops continued to occupy the country until 1989. During the "Spring" Miloslav Vlk was ordained a priest at the ripe old age of thirty-six on June 23, 1968. But the state did not allow him to exercise his priestly ministry and Vlk was forced to live underground. Eventually he became the cardinal archbishop of Prague.[7] The "Spring" was crushed.[8]

George Wallace for President

In the United States George Wallace ran for president under the banner of the American Independent Party in 1968. In Alabama Republican Perry Hooper, Sr. lost the open U.S. Senate seat vacated by the retiring Lister Hill. Hooper lost big to former Lieutenant Governor James B. Allen whose conservative political views were similar to if not identical with those of Hooper. But Allen was a Democrat and still a safe bet in Alabama even if times were changing. Hooper also received more popular votes than Richard Nixon did in Alabama. By the end of 1968 Richard Nixon had won the presidency and Alabama businessman Winton Blount had been elected president of the United States Chamber of Commerce. Shortly after assuming the Office of the President in 1969 Nixon appointed Blount United States Postmaster General, which was at that time a cabinet position.

UAH, UAB, and the Talladega Speedway

Both the University of Alabama at Huntsville (UAH) and the University of Alabama at Birmingham (UAB) were established in 1969. The university system's medical and dental schools were already in place since the 1940s. In September the Talladega Speedway opened with the first running of the *Talladega 500*, won by Richard Brickhouse and attracting a crowd of 65,000 race fans.[9] By the year 1970 the population of Alabama was sitting at 3.444 million with 2.533 million whites and 0.903 million blacks. The urban population had grown to 2.0 million to 1.4 million rural.[10]

It was the year that Bill Cabaniss would become an independent businessman. It was rough-going at first. As Cabaniss traveled around Alabama and the southeast building his business – he was the only company salesman – he began to notice some reluctance by many out-of-state companies to do business with Alabama enterprises. The negative image of Alabama held by outsiders was that it was a one-party state, the brunt of the Civil Rights Movement, and the fact that labor unions and plaintiff lawyers controlled the state.[11]

GEORGE WALLACE WAS ELECTED GOVERNOR OF ALABAMA again in 1970 and began his newest term in January of 1971. But in Maryland in 1972 while campaigning for the presidency, an assassination attempt on him left him crippled for life. Jere Beasley became acting governor in June, 1972 filling in for Wallace as he underwent a series of surgeries and rehabilitation programs.[1] Winton Blount, the Alabama construction company magnate who was picked by President Richard Nixon to be United States Postmaster General, was now overseeing the transition of the Post Office as an executive agency of the federal government. No longer would the Postmaster General be a member of the President's cabinet.[2] Blount decided that it was time to seek elective office.

Blount's business enterprises were fundamentally construction requiring subcontractors in the electrical, steel, aggregates, and concrete industries. In the mid-1950s he and his brother Houston split when Houston moved to Birmingham to run a newly created division of Vulcan Materials. Winton, or "Red" as he was known to many, decided to enter the political arena as a candidate for the United States Senate from Alabama in the early 1970s. Blount called on the young Bill Cabaniss to manage his campaign in the Birmingham-Jefferson County area of the state. Blount's selection of Cabaniss gave evidence to Cabaniss's operational and management skills, not to mention his trustworthiness.

But the thirty-three year-old Cabaniss declined Blount's request and in a letter dated December 27, 1971 he cited his unavailability to provide the sufficient amount of time to effect a successful campaign outcome. Cabaniss had just started his new company and his first priorities were his family and his new business.[3] The principled and purposeful Bill Cabaniss dedicated himself to the success of his new company. As it turned out, a young George W. Bush came to Birmingham to work as Red Blount's political director from May to November. Bush stayed at the home of Houston and Frances Blount. In the first ever Republican primary in Alabama, Red Blount defeated Gadsden businessman and former United States Congressman James Martin[4] but lost to incumbent

Alabama Senator John Sparkman in the general election. Ironically, or within the turbulent winds of politics, Blount received virtually no help from his old boss President Nixon. Nixon knew he could depend on Sparkman's votes for legislation he wanted to push through the Senate and provided little visible support for fellow Republican Blount.[5] Blount would remain a strong leader in the emerging Republican Party in Alabama.

Precision Grinding and Machinery

Bill Cabaniss acquired the assets of Birmingham-based Precision Grinding and Machinery Company and was busy growing his new company which required a lot of his time on the road and away from home. His new business partner, Walter McCullers, managed the plant operations. The working arrangement between the two men went quite well. Cabaniss was the outgoing sales personality type and McCullers the operational and engineering specialist. Cabaniss had already made a name for himself while working for Southern Cement. He was a capable and reliable person, a person who could be trusted. He always kept his word.

McCullers had been a manufacturer's representative for J.T. Sudduth & Co. in Birmingham. Joe Sudduth owned several small businesses, one of which was Mechanical Components, Inc. McCullers was a salesman for Mechanical Components (MC) and when Sudduth started up Precision Grinding he used his MC salesmen to sell for Precision also. Executives at United States Steel Corporation (U.S.S.) suggested to Sudduth that there was a large market for critical, precision, steel and metals grinding. There was a company in town already in that business but it was not doing well – Gulf States Grinding. When the owner decided to shut the company down Sudduth bought it and hired the sons of the owner of Gulf States to run the renamed Precision Grinding and Machinery, Inc. The working relationship between Sudduth and the previous owner was not going well so Sudduth decided it was time to get out. McCullers believed that it was about that time that Sudduth and Bill Cabaniss met, but he did not know how and under what circumstances. Once Cabaniss bought the company he wanted someone to manage the company's operations while he "got his feet wet." Initially leasing a company's building from Joe Sudduth, Cabaniss then decided to build his own building on Wenonah Oxmoor Road in southwest Birmingham. The machinery was still mortgaged but once that relocation occurred "that's when we really got into the business."[6]

Aerial View of Precision Grinding Plant
in the Oxmoor Valley of Birmingham, Alabama
Precision Grinding, Inc. Photo

The first principle that Bill Cabaniss decided on with McCullers was the company's business consistency. They needed to always know their costs because they were a service company, not a manufacturer. At that time there was a lot of "reciprocity" business going on. Purchasing department heads of large companies tended to look favorably on vendor companies who provided "perks" and other benefits. Apparently this kind of activity went on at the middle management or supervisory level of an organization and not at the C-level[7].

Purchasing managers, as one example, wielded a fair amount of reciprocity leverage on companies eager to do business with the giants. Bill Cabaniss and Walter McCullers did not want to get into that game. McCullers said that "I always felt that Bill was a straight shooter. We tried to do business without buying the business. Bill always said that we will earn the business with good service." Sharpening industrial knives had to be according to customer specification. The old Precision Grinding was not producing at a high quality level, but over time the new Precision Grinding met and exceeded customer specifications.

Management and Staff of Precision Grinding, Inc., 1975.
Bill Cabaniss top row, second from right.
Courtesy Precision Grinding, Inc. Photo

It was a business that was going to be earned or there would be no business. There was no other method, no reciprocity perks. "We dealt with them fair, and they dealt with us fair. There were times when the output of Precision Grinding was returned for rework. Financial losses were incurred, but the company always lived up to its promises for precision work. Bill said 'Our word is our word. If any of our work is bad we will refund the customer's money or re-work it at our cost.'"[8] At one point in their business startup, McCullers told Cabaniss that Precision Grinding could not afford him and McCullers offered to resign. The company had not been profitable early on. Cabaniss, however, told McCullers that "the company cannot afford either of us." But neither could the company move forward without both of them.[9]

Alabama Politics in the 1970s

Bill Harris got involved with the Alabama Republican Party in 1972. Eventually he would become the party's executive director through 1976 and then he was elected party chairman in 1977. It was Harris that Bill Cabaniss met with in 1977 to discuss running for the Alabama State House.[10] Traditional Republican counties in Alabama are those in which Republican presidential candidates received thirty-five percent of the vote in three-fourths of the presidential elections from 1900 to 1948, excluding 1912. Chilton, Cullman, De Kalb, Fayette, Franklin, St. Clair, and Winston counties match those criteria. With the exception of Chilton County, all are in the northern section of the state. During Civil War times much of the northern Alabama counties were Unionists who had little to no affinity with what became Confederates. Lingering in the minds of most Alabamians is a negative connotation attached to the word "Republican." Republican candidates have fared well in those counties with large cities. The urban parts of the state up to this time were more willing to support Republicans than rural areas.[11] By 1970 the rural population of Alabama had fallen to forty-one percent and would drop to just below forty percent in 1980.[12]

World oil prices quadrupled in the early 1970s, effecting a large transfer of wealth from the world at large to the Middle East. Those oil producing nations in the Middle East invested their new wealth in upgrading of their petrochemical plants but also their infrastructures, including hospitals, universities, and military bases. The broad scope of the infrastructure projects could not be handled internally and many international, mostly American, companies were hired to do the work. Alabama's *Blount Industries* was one of the major construction firms with projects in Saudi Arabia. Blount is responsible for the construction of the University of Riyadh, now King Saud University.[13]

Catherine Cabaniss had their third child, Frances Caldwell Cabaniss, on December 30, 1970.

The Judicial Article

In Alabama the voters went to the polls on December 18, 1973 to make a change to one of the articles in the 1901 Constitution, a constitution that when ratified, disfranchised most African Americans and many indigent whites. But this particular referendum sought to change a judicial article of the constitution. With only seven percent of eligible voters participating, the *Judicial Article* was passed by a heavy margin. Several significant alterations were made. One made the appointment of state judges a thing of the past. Judges would now be elected, thus politicizing the judicial branch of government. The amendment also provided lifetime pensions for judges in every county of the state and without any regard for cost. The architect and champion of the Judicial Amendment was Alabama's Chief Justice Howell Heflin.[14]

Perhaps Heflin was planning for his own political future. But Heflin lobbied legislators long and hard to get the measure through both House and Senate. Doubtless he worked all of the county Democratic organizations and probate judges, promising the latter pensions. The upside of the amendment change was a more healthy structure for the courts in Alabama. Indeed the change was heralded throughout the United States as one of the best reorganizations of a state judicial structure. Governor George Wallace signed it into law on October 10, 1975.[15] Heflin had put together a formidable team to develop the judicial article's legislative package. One of those team members, new to politics, was Ann Bedsole of Mobile. According to Bedsole "that got me into politics."[16]

The Watergate Scandal forced President Richard Nixon out of office and Gerald Ford became president in August, 1974. Less than one month later, on a Sunday afternoon, Ford issued a full and complete pardon for Nixon.[17] Ford would certainly be remembered for the infamous pardon, and his many presidential vetoes of Democratic spending bills. What goes virtually unknown is his posthumous pardoning of Confederate General Robert E. Lee. In a ceremony on August 5, 1975 at Arlington House – the renamed Custis-Lee Mansion, Lee's home, President Ford signed Public Law 94-67 – the result of Congressional Joint Resolution 23, restoring Robert E. Lee to full citizenship as of June 13, 1975.[18]

Single-Member Districts

In Alabama there was an ordered re-apportionment and single-member districts were implemented.[19] Douglas Hale, a Republican from Huntsville, was elected to the Alabama House of Representatives as was

Bert Nettles of Mobile in 1970. In 1974 both Republicans lost their elections. *The Anniston Star* headlined an article with "Alabama only state with no GOPers." By contrast Nebraska had no Democrats. Although both men said they would be back, they posed for a picture coupled in a Huntsville telephone booth demonstrating the "strength" of Republicans in the Alabama House of Representatives.[20]

George Wallace had been elected governor again in 1975 and assumed his new term in January, 1976. The Republican National Convention was held in Kansas City. Missouri. Many of the Alabama delegates favored Ronald Reagan, but Gerald Ford received the party's nomination. John Grenier, as an advisor, was involved in the effort to nominate Ford.[21] Hall Thompson, a Birmingham businessman, asked Bill Cabaniss to become involved with the Ford nomination effort. Cabaniss chaired a fund-raising dinner for a ten-state television hook-up.[22] Alabama in the general election went for fellow southerner, and Democrat, Jimmy Carter of Georgia.

Dinner Party Politics

Adrian Bewley and Bill Cabaniss were friends in their youth growing up in Mountain Brook. Adrian and his wife Judy, Pat Brock and his wife Nina, and Bill and Catherine, enjoyed time together at dinner one evening in late December, 1976. After dinner Pat Brock, the brother of former United States Senator Bill Brock of Tennessee, moved Bill and Adrian to a corner of the room and said "OK, one of you guys has to run for office." Brock was talking of an office in Alabama state government. Republican Party representation in the House and Senate of Alabama was all but non-existent. Cabaniss looked over at Judy Bewley and told her that if he ever did run for office he would call on her to manage his campaign.[23]

Bill Harris was elected chairman of the Alabama Republican Party after many years as its executive director. Harris and his team assessed what was going on in Alabama politically and decided to concentrate on the Alabama State Legislature rather than national offices. Republicans could claim no political muscle whatsoever so the party organization had to build from the bottom up, again. First of all they needed to establish credibility because they had clout neither with the business nor the donor communities. Alabama was neither a one-party nor a two-party state. The Democratic Party was simply a vehicle of convenience for people to get themselves elected to office. So the Democratic primaries would be little more than personality contests since issues were of less importance in a no-party state. It was in the primaries where the business community participated in order to elect their man. Whoever won the primary would win the general election later in the year. Therefore, the business and donor communities had no need to pump in funds for the general election. Even when there was a Republican candidate in the general election, the Democrat would always win because the electorate never took Republicans seriously. It was so bad that even Republicans didn't take themselves seriously. The upsurge of the Republican Party in the 1960s fizzled when intra-party squabbling tore it apart.

Alabama Republican Party Chairman and Bill Cabaniss Meet

Bill Harris's tasks in 1977 were recruitment of qualified candidates and creation of a party operation to support those candidates. He targeted specific districts and he worked to get business people and other people of means to contribute to a fund for campaigning. This was an uphill task.[24] Interested in running for office from his district, Bill Cabaniss showed up one day to talk with Bill Harris. Harris had called a meeting of a group of people to help finance campaigns. Cabaniss attended. Most of the people there were ideologically oriented, but not Cabaniss. After the meeting Cabaniss and Harris continued to talk and Cabaniss said that he would like to run for office. That news set well with Harris because he knew that a Cabaniss candidacy would be extraordinarily helpful to the Alabama Republican Party. It would be good for the party to have such a well-respected leader to run and serve. Harris believed that Cabaniss's presence in the election elevated the status of the other people who ran for office.[25]

Cabaniss met with Harris and Margaret Tutwiler who worked with Harris in the Alabama Republican Party. Later Cabaniss and Tutwiler met and talked about campaign tactics. While they talked Tutwiler broke out a legal size yellow pad and began writing. She gave Cabaniss three hand-written sheets of notes on how to run a grass roots political campaign. Cabaniss would follow her directives word for word.[26]

Margaret Tutwiler was one of three key people working directly for James A. Baker III when he was Secretary of State (1989-1992) under President George H.W. Bush. She was Baker's Assistant Secretary for Public Affairs and spokesperson. She was involved in the Republican political campaigns of Gerald Ford in 1976 and Ronald Reagan's re-election campaign in 1984. According to Baker, Richard Nixon said that Tutwiler "has a nice, soft southern accent. At the same time, she's tough, mean, and devious. Perfect!" Baker recognized her ability to cut through the clutter of argument and policy doublespeak to determine the bottom line.[27] For Bill Cabaniss and his inaugural campaign for the Alabama House, he could not have had a better tutor. Cabaniss also had excellent legal advice on many campaign issues from his good friend Hobart McWhorter, a Birmingham attorney then with the firm of Bradley Arant.

1977 – "Charter 77" and a Turning Point in Central Europe

On the other side of the world the Soviet Bloc nations continued to be in some level of turmoil. On Epiphany, January 6, 1977, a document known as *Charter 77* was published in Czechoslovakia. The *Charter* represented a human rights movement. Prepared in 1976 by some notable writers and philosophers, the development of the document was motivated in part by the arrest of members of a psychedelic musical group known as "Plastic People of the Universe." One of the proponents of the document was Jan Patočka, a Czech philosopher. Many Czech and Slovak intellectuals were officially banned by the government, forcing them to operate in an underground university. Patočka, like many other undesirables, underwent intense interrogations by the secret police. Two months later Patočka died. He had just endured an eleven-hour interrogation session.[28]

BILL CABANISS AND HIS FAMILY WENT INTO FULL CAMPAIGN mode in 1978. As promised, Judy Bewley became Cabaniss's campaign manager and Peggy Balliet coordinated the work of all the campaign volunteers. Alice Williams, an important campaign volunteer, focused on organizing key campaign objectives. Balliet had recently assumed the position of executive director of the Alabama Kidney Foundation, an unpaid position.[1] The entire team began working Cabaniss's Alabama House district, mostly the town of Mountain Brook. Following Margaret Tutwiler's handwritten yellow pad directions, Cabaniss and his children began knocking on doors and passing out leaflets in parking lots.

Campaigning in 1978

In January there was a special election in Etowah County. Cabaniss went to Gadsden to assist in electing a Republican. He worked as a recruiter around the state even while he was campaigning for office.[2] Bill Cabaniss had his first forum in the Avondale section of Birmingham. It was in the heat of July. Cabaniss, a studious person, had prepared himself, researched the budget issues, and the over-spending problems in Montgomery. As an astute businessman he knew that he had to be on top of all the issues that affected the economic well-being of Alabama's citizens. Though somewhat uneasy about his first meeting with the general public, Cabaniss took his first question. An elderly woman stood and asked "Mr. Cabaniss, what is your position on abortion?" Dumbfounded, he had no position and said so. "Young man I think you should find your position if you want to represent us," the woman said. Dejected and once at home in bed and re-living the night's event at the political forum, he said to Catherine "You'll never guess what the first question to me was. A lady asked me about my position on abortion." After a few moments of silence passed, Catherine said, "Well, what is your position?" "I don't have one," he answered. "Then you'd better get one," she said.[3]

WILLIAM JELKS CABANISS, JR.

Four Republicans Elected to Alabama House

Bill Cabaniss and three other Republicans were elected as Representatives to the Alabama House on November 7, 1978. That might not seem important or significant, but it was. Although they were not the first Republicans elected since Reconstruction, they were the first to continue in public office long enough to establish the voice and credibility of Republican leadership in the State of Alabama. And it would be Cabaniss who would emerge as the natural leader among not only his fellow Republicans but allied Democrats. Four Republicans elected into the Alabama House, and in the same election year, was a major break-through in itself. A poetic prelude, perhaps, to the election of the Republican foursome, was a performance on the previous Saturday evening at the Birmingham Civic Center by Luciano Pavarotti.[4]

Former Alabama Governor Bob Riley, a Republican, recalled his grandfather who ran a dry goods store in rural Clay County. "I remember he had one thing on his mind – a little statue of FDR [Franklin Delano Roosevelt] driving the ship of state. [FDR] was close to deity to my grandpa." Riley's grandfather would say that "[Herbert] Hoover got us into this mess and FDR got us out." This attitude was reflective of most Alabamians. It was almost impossible to get elected to a local office without being a Democrat. Years later when Riley told his father that he was going to run for a seat in the United States Congress as a Republican, his father replied "Son I don't see how you can win as a Republican."[5] Gerald Dial, a former Democrat who also grew up in Clay County, said that when he was a little boy "a Republican came to town and they closed the school so that we could all go out and see him."[6]

As reported by Al Fox in *The Birmingham News* on November 8, 1978, there were two Republicans who had served in the previous session of the Alabama legislature who would not be returning to office. One was beaten in the general election and the other decided not to run for reelection. Bert Nettles, a native of Monroeville, was the winner of a special election in 1969. Nettles was the only Republican serving in the Alabama House of Representatives in 1969. A few years earlier Nettles became active in the Alabama Republican Party and in 1968 served as chairman of the state Republican Convention. Nettles was elected to a full term in the election of 1970.[7] The second Republican since Reconstruction in the Alabama House of Representatives was Doug Hale of Huntsville. With nothing to lose, Hale introduced an ethics bill near the end of the 1973 legislative session. If Hale had wanted to make a career of politics in Alabama he said he would have run as a Democrat. But since his goal was to help make Alabama a two-party political system, he had nothing to lose personally. Hale's ethics bill was placed in committee by Speaker Sage Lyons, thinking that the bill would be killed in committee. Lyons, knowing the House rules, invoked the Discharge Rule that allowed voting on a bill even though it was in committee and destined to be a dead-end. The bill passed 61-1. The Senate had already approved it. The passage of that bill was Hale's signature accomplishment as one of only two Republicans in the Alabama House.[8]

Before the official returns had been released it appeared that the Alabama Senate would remain solidly Democratic with thirty-five, three of whom were African American. The House retained 13 African Americans (all Democrats) of the 105 seats, but now there were four Republicans. There was a geographical significance to the winning Republicans; they were elected from Jefferson (Birmingham) and Mobile counties. V.M. Parker of Chickasaw in Mobile County succeeded fellow Republican Dal Younce of Saraland who did not seek reelection. Ann Bedsole of Mobile was elected to her first term and became the first Republican woman elected to office in Alabama. Long term mayor of Birmingham, George Seibels defeated two-term incumbent Francis Falkenburg. Had Bill Townes of Oneonta not lost his bid to Bob Harvey, Republicans would have had five seats in the House.

Bill Cabaniss defeated Wally Retan. The newspaper report cited both Retan and Cabaniss as residents of Birmingham, but Cabaniss was a resident of Mountain Brook who would be attacked politically in the future as a wealthy elitist not interested in the common Alabama citizen. Cabaniss did not receive much media coverage in this first election. In fact, his name was not mentioned in the article narrative by reporter Al Fox. The only mention of Cabaniss came in the detailed listing of the winners and losers in the subheading of HOUSE BY DISTRICTS where in District 31 the line read "Bill Cabaniss (R) defeated Wally Retan (D), both of Birmingham."[9]

Prior to his 1978 election Cabaniss clearly explained his political, social, and economic positions in his campaign advertisements. Addressing his remarks to the House District 31 electorate the advertisement's headline states that "He knows how you feel. You know where he stands." Cabaniss polled his district by both questionnaire and in person months prior to this first election and pledged to be a strong voice in Montgomery if elected. The outline of his position in 1978 remained steady during his twelve years in the State Legislature (eight years as a Senator).

His first program item was "Honesty in Government" or ethics in which he said he wanted to eliminate opportunities for self-interest of legislators and remove any possibility of conflicts of interest. Education was his second political priority where he said that a "quality education for our children is one of the most important responsibilities of state government." This particular priority would bring him into a virtual working relationship with one of Alabama's leading liberals, Wayne Flynt. At least, Cabaniss and Flynt were proponents of better education in Alabama. Flynt, the prominent Alabama historian and Auburn University professor, shared the same interest in education with Cabaniss. "Home Rule" occupied Cabaniss's third platform position. He wanted to see a constitution that provided for a better operating state government that would also provide "home rule." The 1901 Alabama Constitution, which is still in effect today, limits the amount of decision making (home rule) Alabama counties and cities can make thus giving the state legislature broad control over local governments. For example, the legislators from Jefferson County, as a group as well as the entire legislature, have ultimate control over many of the decisions made by city councils or county commissions.

Officials elected to local offices find themselves limited in what they can effect in their own counties and cities. Cabaniss wanted this aspect of the 1901 Constitution changed to a "degree." Fourthly, he wanted a "Fiscally Responsible [state] Government" in order to get state operations more orderly and to control spending. At the time Cabaniss entered elective politics there were virtually no business people serving in the legislature. Educators, trial lawyers, and union people dominated the legislature. The fifth element in Cabaniss's campaign promises was the work for "A Healthy Business Climate."

He not only wanted to keep Alabama a right-to-work state, he wanted a legal climate that attracted rather than repelled businesses from coming into Alabama, and to encourage Alabama businesses to expand within the state rather than leave for more attractive opportunities elsewhere. Those five items or causes as advertised and promoted by Bill Cabaniss in his first run for elective office remained the core of his entire legislative career. It is the fifth item, the healthy business climate, that burned as the "fire in his belly" causing him to seek election.[10]

Alabama was for years a one-party state of Democratic governors and legislators. Here and there a Republican would succeed in an election, but would not serve in office for a substantially long period of time. Alabama Republican Party chairman Edgar Welden (1975 to 1983) believes there are three significant dates in the modern day Alabama Republican Party history – 1964, 1986, and 2010.[11] The "Goldwater Landslide/Sweep of 1964" in Alabama placed five Republicans in U.S. Congressional seats. In 1986 Republican Guy Hunt was elected governor, the first Republican elected since Reconstruction days. And the election of 2010, perhaps the sweetest of all, gave Republicans majorities in both the House and the Senate. It was a long haul from the end of Reconstruction to the year 2010 for Alabama Republicans and it took a certain kind of sustained effort and leadership to pull off that remarkable election.

The election of 1978, however, should not be forgotten or dismissed as trivial, given that only four Republicans were elected. Indeed, an argument can be made that, in retrospect, the 1978 election of Bill Cabaniss of Mountain Brook, Ann Bedsole and V.M. Parker of Mobile, and George Seibels (former mayor) of Birmingham, was pivotal and foundational toward future Republican successes in Alabama. It marked the potential emergence of Alabama as a two-party state where Alabama citizens could experience competitive political engagement, an engagement that would benefit Alabama with competing ideas on policy and governance. It is important to recognize that four legislators from the years 1978 through 1982 constituted the largest number of Republicans in the Alabama legislature since Reconstruction. Could four people make any difference?

A foreshadowing of future Republican victories occurred in the 1978 election. Democrat Forrest Hood "Fob" James defeated Republican Guy Hunt for Governor, and Alabama Supreme Court Chief Justice Howell Heflin was elected to the United States Senate. Hunt's political fortunes would change in 1986.

Jim Martin made another attempt at elective office in 1978. He ran for the United States Senate seat held by Jim Allen who died unexpectedly. But he lost to State Senator Donald Stewart. Martin won majorities only in Winston, Jefferson, Shelby, Montgomery, Houston, Mobile, and Baldwin counties. Martin had originally planned to run against State Supreme Court Justice Howell Heflin who was running for an open seat. But when Allen died in office Martin switched races thinking he had a better chance against Stewart to fill Allen's remaining term.[12] James defeated Bill Baxley, Jere Beasley, and Albert Brewer in the state's Democratic primary and went on to win the general election, as was the Alabama political norm.[13]

Howell Heflin's entry into the 1978 race for the U.S. Senate seat turned out to be quite easy. In the beginning Heflin campaigned in the state Democratic primary against George Wallace. But Wallace withdrew, leaving the nomination to Heflin. Heflin was a popular candidate in Alabama as was George Wallace. In this race Heflin was riding high on his success with the *Judicial Article* and getting it passed through the Legislature. The net of the Article's passage was that every judge and lawyer in every county in Alabama owed a great deal to Heflin for their personal employment and security. Therefore they became the core of Heflin's future political support. Heflin said "they were my foundation in campaigning and elections and were very helpful. Since we got the probate judges [in every county] a retirement system, some were active in the campaign, and the circuit clerks and registrars were all happy because the Judicial Article had improved their financial condition."[14]

This political base for Heflin would be secure for the next twelve years. In fact the base grew because of Heflin's support for some select Alabama businesses, particularly Alabama's insurance companies.

Cabaniss, too, had already established himself as pro-business around the state. He had served on the board of Protective Life Insurance Company of Birmingham, a company founded by his great uncle and former governor, William Dorsey Jelks.

"Fob" James, a businessman, became Alabama's governor, the first time around, in January, 1978. When Bill Cabaniss stepped foot on the floor of the Alabama Legislature for the very first time – a friendly person and always eager to make new friends – a legislator from the town of Phil Campbell approached him. With no time to send or receive an introduction or greeting the Democratic legislator said "What are you Republicans going to do to us today?" The unexpected and illogical question prompted Cabaniss to ask in return "My friend, what can four Republicans do in a House of 105 legislators?"[15] Ann Besole, from the Mobile area, also experienced the difficulties of being a Republican legislator.

Early in that first legislative year, Bedsole went to the microphone to make a point on a piece of legislation. But the House floor was too noisy, Bedsole thought, so she asked Democratic Speaker Joe McCorquodale for order. It was possible, and probable, that some of the legislators ignored her because she was a woman; it was possible that they thought Mrs. Bedsole had nothing important to say, or both. "The Lady wants you to pay attention to her." No change. More noise. Gavel. "The Lady wants you to pay attention." Quietness was difficult to come by. The Speaker had known the representative from Mobile since she was a young girl. The Speaker then turned to Bedsole and said "If you have something to say, they will listen to you."[16]

Bill Cabaniss made a surprising discovery about the Speaker. It was a common routine, if not a ritual, for freshman representatives to meet with the Speaker before the first session of the House. For Bill Cabaniss that felt rather odd since most of the legislators for more than one hundred years were Democrats. He asked for a meeting. When Cabaniss met with McCorquodale they ended up having a lengthy chat. The Speaker displayed strong conservative inclinations and appeared to be pro-business. From that one conversation Cabaniss discerned that the Speaker was not a diehard Democrat. The relationship between the Democratic

Speaker and the freshman Republican from Mountain Brook began on a positive and hopeful note, and blossomed.

McCorquodale owned a considerable amount of land in Clarke County in South Alabama. There were many times from the point of their first meeting that at the invitation of the Speaker, Cabaniss and the Speaker's leadership team went hunting together – always several Democrats and the lone Republican.[17] This relationship fell easily into the manner in which Cabaniss conducts business. The side of the aisle matters little. The important element was the ability to work together to get work accomplished. This was a good start for Cabaniss, and it was a good change for the House Democrats even if they were initially unaware. To the dismay of most of the House Democrats, Speaker McCorquodale later appointed Cabaniss chairman of the Insurance Committee. Infuriated Democrats blasted their Speaker who reminded them that they were all here to do the work of the State.[18]

After a few weeks in the House Cabaniss observed how the power structure operated, and recognized who were the crucial links in that structure. Cabaniss was pleased and surprised when he discovered the conservative-leaning political disposition of the Speaker. He also saw that the teachers' union and its leader Paul Hubbert were not only gaining strength in the House, but that Hubbert challenged Speaker McCorquodale on many if not most issues.[19] It was a time when interest groups thrived in Alabama and legislators were surrounded by special interest lobbyists.[20]

From Cabaniss's point of view there were many bad bills presented and passed in the House and the only alternative for him and his three Republican colleagues was to find ways to stop bad legislation. To Cabaniss a bad piece of legislation was one not thoroughly researched with no consideration of future costs to Alabama taxpayers. A bad bill also inhibited business, thus stifling any economic growth potential in the state. He was already aware of out-of-state perceptions of Alabama's anti-business climate and its civil rights problems. That is why he ran for office in the first place, to try to do something about those issues. But the Republicans could not stop bad legislation alone, they needed help from across the aisle.

Cullom Walker, a Birmingham businessman and life-long friend of Cabaniss, said that "Bill was always straight as an arrow." Walker was surprised that his childhood buddy went into politics. He could not see Cabaniss compromising on anything in which he believed. He never waivered on his opinions.[21] Ann Bedsole noticed that early on, too. "When he made a decision about some piece of legislation, he could not be swayed. But he didn't make up his mind too easily. He worked through it before he made up his mind." But the Republicans still needed political help which could only come from the Democrats. To some extent Cabaniss knew he could make a good argument to the Speaker. Once Cabaniss's reputation for conservative principles became known, and they became known quickly, he found two Democratic allies, Larry Dixon and Gerald Dial. Dixon, from Montgomery, said that he was a Democrat only because that is how you get elected in Montgomery. But he was not a Democrat in spirit, but in a pragmatic sense. Dixon and Cabaniss not only became conservative allies, they became fast friends.[22] Because of a sharing of conservative values, Gerald Dial of Clay County and Cabaniss bonded almost immediately. Dial, once a U.S. Army private who rose to become a brigadier general in the National Guard, also shared common military aspirations. "He was a Ranger, I was a Ranger. We both knew what we went through. He was a Republican and I was a Democrat, a weird Democrat because I was a Conservative."[23]

Bill Cabaniss was not like most Alabama politicians at that time. He was smooth, he was educated, and he knew how to ask a question. More importantly, he knew, doggedly, how to ask the same question five times or more before finally getting the right answer.[24] "The way Bill Cabaniss discussed a topic was the way I understand. He and I had a common way of looking at things," according to Dixon. As far as House seating arrangements were concerned, Cabaniss and Dixon were seated on opposite sides of the chamber. Dixon sat near Bedsole, so the two of them became friends and political allies on many issues. Alabama Republican Party chairman Edgar Welden noted that Bill Cabaniss came along at a time when it was difficult to grow the Republican Party. Although Cabaniss had been active in supporting Republican candidates, it was not until he entered politics and presented himself as a legislative participant that things began to change.

David Bronner, long time chief executive officer of the Retirement Systems of Alabama (RSA), considered Cabaniss a most interesting person. The first thing he and most people notice is how Cabaniss carries himself. You knew he was somebody of importance and someone with a purpose. For Bronner it was an adventure to work with Bill Cabaniss, a person who wanted to pursue something for the state. For a bill pending in the Legislature, most of the time no one would study the bill to determine the cost and not just the initial but long term costs. But Cabaniss did. Most politicians who came to Bronner's office simply asked questions and left. "Cabaniss would delve into the details with me."[25]

The first year in the Legislature for Bill Cabaniss was exciting and to a certain extent enjoyable. There would be moments in future sessions when getting anything through or stopped would be all but impossible. But the first year was an eye-opener on how things get done in Alabama politically. But not everything in 1979 was good.

Family Tragedy

In August 1979 Catherine Cabaniss, with her oldest daughter Mary and her sister Frances Caldwell, decided to visit the coast of Maine. Frances had friends in Kennebunkport, Adam and Linda Lewis. Frances was a colleague of Adam Lewis at Doyle, Dane and Bernback in New York where she was working on her successful Volkswagon television advertisements in the 1970s. After visiting in Kennebunkport, Catherine and Mary went to Bay Head, New Jersey to visit friends Dodie and Corbin Day. Bill and their son Bill flew up to be with everyone for the weekend. During the weekend young Bill developed a severe headache, a headache so bad that he had to be taken to a New York hospital. The eleven year old boy had a brain aneurism and immediate surgery was required. So the doctors operated on him and found that it was too late. Within hours, on August 26, 1979 William Jelks Cabaniss III died. Bill and Catherine were devastated. Sisters Mary and Frances no longer had their brother. The Cabanisses had the presence of mind to donate some of Bill's organs but the medical laws of New York made organ donation a tedious bureaucratic exercise that Bill and Catherine had no time with which to deal. Bill called his friend Richard "Dick" Hill, a physician and the President of the University of Alabama at Birmingham. Dick told Bill to "bring him home. We can handle the donation of his kidneys." That part settled, they went home.[26] Judy Bewley got a call about Billy's death from a friend. All she could see in her mind was the handsome, young blonde-headed boy. It was a shock to everyone and knowing that the Cabanisses were a very private couple, she wondered how they would get through this family tragedy.[27] Bill Cabaniss knew how he was to cope. As a businessman and a new state legislator he had work to occupy his mind. Catherine's ability to cope worried him.

Cabaniss Family in Happier Times
L-R: Mary, Bill III, Frances, Catherine, Bill

Cabaniss Family Christmas, 1975

Front Row L-R: Bill Cabaniss III, Frances Cabaniss, William Jelks Cabaniss, Sr., Ceci Harrison, Will Etheridge, Florence Cabaniss, David Etheridge **Back Row** L-R: Mary Cabaniss, Catherine Cabaniss, Bill Cabaniss, Jr., Joan Harrison, Dr. Randy Harrison, Catherine Harrison, Billy Harrison, Florence Parnegg, Hannes Parnegg, Sandy Etheridge

Grief, Mourning, Coping, Reaching Out

In 1980, less than a year after her son's death Catherine Cabaniss, and her good friend Carolyn Wade, enrolled in the art program at the University of Alabama at Birmingham (UAB). There was no bachelor of fine arts degree at the time she entered UAB, but in 1985 Catherine graduated with her B.F.A. degree and her art exhibit was held in the Visual Arts Gallery at UAB. Bill delved deeper into his own business and the business of the state. One of his friends, noticing that he was not really coping well with the loss of his son, gave him a short paperback book and suggested that he read it. *Tracks of a Fellow Struggler* affected Cabaniss so profoundly that he wrote a handwritten letter to the book's author, John Claypool. The senior pastor at Northminster Baptist Church in Jackson, Mississippi, had a difficult time accepting the death of his eight-year old daughter when he was senior pastor of College Hills Baptist Church in Louisville, Kentucky, so he wrote *Tracks*.

Less than ninety days after losing his young son, Cabaniss wrote in his letter to Claypool "After reading your book 'Tracks of a Fellow Struggler' more than once recently, I do not feel that we are strangers.

Catherine and I lost our 11 year old son, Bill, on Aug. 26. A spirited & very athletic boy Bill had without any warning or prior knowledge a sudden & massive brain hemorrhage caused by a malformation of the arteries. Apparently something very rare & which had existed from birth. He was in a coma for 1 week before passing away. ... Catherine & I are hurting over Bill's loss in different ways. He was as much a spirit for her as he was to me but in different ways. They were both good tennis players and loved playing with each other. ... I have been tormented by the complete absence of any rational reason or explanation. ... I'm bending under the pressure of what I can maybe interpret as a 'no confidence vote' in God in my life. ... My faith is probably being put to the ultimate test and during my frantic search for an answer of some type, someone sent us your book & we read it. I have reread parts of it many times. Your story, your grief, your search, your ultimate faith has helped us. ..."[28] Although not dated, Claypool's reply to Cabaniss was prompt.

"... Please do not think some fault in you is the cause of this event. The whole realm of 'why' things happen is so complex. ... Gratitude was the only way I found to make it through the night. We have been blessed by having these gifts of these gift[s]/children at all. ..." Claypool included a copy of one of his sermons in the hope that it too would give comfort to Bill and Catherine. Since Cabaniss had mentioned in his letter that he was self-employed and a member of the Alabama Legislature, Claypool ended his letter by saying the Alabama Congressman John Buchanan was his first cousin.[29] The exchange of letters meant a lot to Cabaniss.

A memorial to their son is in the Birmingham Museum of Art, a sculpture by Jacques Lipchitz entitled "Mother and Child." The benefactors to the Art Museum are the Meyer Foundation and Mr. & Mrs. William J. Cabaniss, Jr. in memory of William Jelks Cabaniss III.

* * * * *

Charter 77 Violated

In 1979 Václav Havel, the political dissident and playwright in Czechoslovakia, was sentenced to four and one half years in prison for his involvement in the Czech human rights movement.[30]

* * * * *

The Bush Family

The Cabaniss family spent many summer vacations in Florida. Catherine Cabaniss now wanted to change that venue to Maine in 1980. So Bill Cabaniss called his friend Tom Rast and asked him for the name of a realtor in Kennebunkport. The family rented a house there which became their summer retreat for the next twenty years. Bill drove Catherine and their daughters up to Maine at the beginning of the summer and he would fly there several times during the summer over those twenty years. Early on, Cabaniss flew on an upstart airline, *Peoples Express*, for a $95.00 ticket. That airline, with one-stop flights between Portland, Maine and Birmingham, allowed Cabaniss to visit on weekends.[31]

Bill Cabaniss loved to jog. On his weekends in Kennebunkport he would jog around the neighborhood. While jogging one summer Bill met a young George W. Bush. His father, George Herbert Walker Bush, had been in office as Vice-President of the United States for less than six months. This was a time when George was simply one of the sons of George H.W. and Barbara Bush.

Bill and Catherine Cabaniss with former U.S. President George H.W. Bush
Birmingham, Alabama April 1990

It was 1981. Cabaniss and the younger Bush ran together and talked about politics. Bush knew about Alabama politics because he had been in Birmingham ten years earlier working on the U.S. Senate campaign for Winton "Red" Blount, the job that Cabaniss declined.[32]

Detroit was the site of the Republican National Convention in 1980, between July 14 and July 17 in the Joe Louis Arena. This was the year that Ronald Reagan received his party's nomination for President of the United States. "The Republican platform reflected Reagan's beliefs and the thinking of GOP conservatives who were able at last to tailor the document to their liking. On economic policy the delegates called for lower tax rates and a balanced budget."[33] In Alabama Admiral Jeremiah Denton of Mobile was elected to the United States Senate. He was the first popularly elected Republican Senator in Alabama history. Denton was also the first Vietnam prisoner-of-war to step foot on American soil at war's end. There were only four other southern Republicans elected to the U.S. Senate in 1980.[34]

Internationally, 1980 was the year that Soviet Prime Minister Mikhail Gorbachev introduced *Perestroika*, a policy that unintentionally sparked the final years of the Soviet Union and freed nations such as Czechoslovakia.[35]

Part Two – Alabama Industry and Politics

The ending of the American Civil War brought on the beginning of southern industrial development. Alabama was no exception and the new post-war city of Birmingham would become both the center of the state's industrial might and the hub for a new kind of politics. A hybrid politics consisting of remnants of antebellum agricultural planter dominance and the newer industrial magnates changed Alabama's political landscape.

ON JANUARY 11, 1861 THE ALABAMA SECESSION CONVENTION passed an Ordinance of Secession declaring that Alabama was a sovereign and independent state. Alabama became the fourth state to secede from the Union by a vote of 61 to 39. Abraham Lincoln, a Republican, became the sixteenth President of the United States. From February to May, 1861 Montgomery, Alabama served as the capital of the Confederate States of America. The capital was moved to Richmond, Virginia.[1] The Third Alabama Regiment was being organized in April at Montgomery from among many locally-formed rifle companies.

On May 4, 1861 more than one-thousand men left Alabama for Lynchburg, Virginia where the so-named Third Alabama Regiment was the first Alabama unit mustered into Confederate military service. The unit was ordered to join a temporary brigade at Norfolk, Virginia composed of the First and Twelfth Virginia regiments under the command of Colonel J.M. Withers. Colonel Withers soon was succeeded by Virginia Colonel Mahone. The brigade would stay in Norfolk for almost one full year before seeing any action.[2]

In Alabama John Gill Shorter served as governor from 1861 to 1863. Born in Monticello, Georgia in 1818, Shorter moved to east Alabama in 1833 settling in Irwinton, later known as Eufaula. Shorter, somewhat a progressive when he was young, became a Jacksonian Democrat and became governor when Alabamians were beginning to feel the negative effects of the Civil War.[3] Alabama and the nation were at war.

Dixie Eagles Rifle Company

Joseph William Dorsey Jelks (see Appendix C) formed a rifle company from Union Springs, Alabama in early 1862. He was elected captain of the company by his troops and by prior arrangement he made his company part of the Third Alabama Regiment, already in service at Norfolk, Virginia. Also joining the regiment was the Southern Rifles Company from Union Springs, captained by R.H. Powell.[4] Jelks's company was nicknamed the "Dixie Eagles" and was identified as

Company L within the Regiment. His naming of the company as "Dixie" Eagle could have been based simply on the fact that the South is Dixie, or he could have named the company for his six-year old daughter Martha Frazier Jelks, who was nicknamed Dixie.[5]

The Dixie Eagles left Union Springs on April 12, 1862, staying in homes overnight in Tuskegee before going to Auburn the next day. After camping in Auburn for ten days the Dixie Eagles went to Columbus, Georgia where they received their military gear and from there they boarded a train for Norfolk, arriving on or about May 1, 1862.[6] Things then began to happen quickly.

Once in Norfolk, Jelks and his Dixie Eagles Company joined the Third Alabama Regiment which had been stationed there for one year, primarily as a non-combative security detail. But on May 5, 1862 Norfolk was evacuated. By May 10 Union troops would occupy the cities of Norfolk and Portsmouth, and Norfolk mayor William Lamb surrendered his city to Union General John E. Wool. The ship *C.S.S. Virginia*, also known as the *Merrimac* – one of the two ironclad ships that fought in the battle at Hampton Roads – was so un-seaworthy it could not power itself up the James River to remove itself from harm's way. So the *Virginia* was scuttled for scrap instead.[7] The Third Alabama Regiment along with its Virginia complement marched over land to Richmond from Norfolk in order to strengthen the Confederate forces gathering there under the command of General Joseph E. Johnston. Johnston's purpose was to defend Richmond from the city's outskirts. Union General George McClellan's Army of the Potomac had been threatening the Confederate capital city after his army's siege of Yorktown in early May. The siege forced Johnston's Confederate troops at Yorktown to withdraw up the peninsula toward Richmond.   As they made their withdrawal, Confederates deliberately slowed McClellan's advance to Richmond. After a brief battle on May 4 in Williamsburg between the Confederate rear guard and the advancing Union army, the movement to Richmond continued. The Alabama troops in Norfolk advancing inland, and Johnston's troops retreating in parallel on the peninsula, converged outside of Richmond and consolidated their forces. On the night of May 31, 1862 there was a large explosion in the area of Seven Pines outside Richmond. The ensuing skirmish was an inept, tactical battle and the two-day confrontation ended in a stalemate, but with heavy casualties. Joseph William Dorsey Jelks was either killed in battle or died shortly afterwards. Circumstance places him at the Battle of Seven Pines (May 31-June 1, 1862).[8] Joseph William Dorsey (J.W.D.) Jelks was the father of William J. Cabaniss, Jr.'s paternal grandmother.

Jelks left behind his wife Jane, three sons, and one daughter. He was forty-three years old at the time of his death. He is buried in Oak Hill Cemetery in Union Springs, Alabama. Marcellus Bolivar Jelks, J.W.D.'s brother, served as a sergeant in the 39th Alabama Infantry, Company E. Marcellus was born in Halifax, North Carolina in 1825 and is buried in Oak Grove Baptist Church Cemetery in Calhoun County, Alabama. His date of death is unknown. J.W.D.'s half-brother Charles Napoleon Jelks[9] was a sergeant in the 51st Alabama Cavalry Partisan Rangers. He died in 1904 and is buried at Oak Grove Baptist Church Cemetery in Calhoun County, Alabama.[10] J.W.D. Jelks was a great-grandfather of William J. Cabaniss, Jr. Another great-grandfather, George Augustus Berrien Cabaniss of Georgia, also fought in the Civil War at Cheat Mountain in 1861. A great-uncle, Thomas Banks Cabaniss also of Georgia and brother to George Augustus, served in the war from 1861 to 1865 and was assigned to General Robert E. Lee's Army of Northern Virginia when it surrendered at Appomattox Court House in 1865.[11]

Alabama in the Remaining War Year

On January 1, 1863 Abraham Lincoln signed and placed into effect the Emancipation Proclamation. Thomas H. Watts, the attorney general of the Confederate States of America, was serving in Richmond, Virginia when he was overwhelmingly elected governor of Alabama, defeating incumbent John Gill Shorter. Watts never campaigned for office because he was in Richmond but he let it be known that if elected governor he would serve. Watts governed Alabama from 1863 to May, 1865.[12] In 1862 a British shipbuilding company launched the *C.S.S. Alabama* for the Confederate Navy. The ship's captain was Raphael Semmes of Mobile. The ship never anchored at a port in the Confederate South but ran successful raiding missions on the high seas of Union merchant and naval vessels. On June 10, 1864 the *Alabama* was destroyed and sunk by the *U.S.S. Kearsarge* in the *Battle of Cherbourge* off the coast of France.

Later, on August 5, 1864, Admiral David Farragut and a large flotilla of Union ships – wooden and ironclad – and 2,700 men assaulted the Confederate defenses guarding the approach to Mobile Bay. This *Battle of Mobile Bay* effectively removed Mobile as the center of blockade-running and freed Union troops already stationed nearby for service in the Virginia theatre.[13] Five years earlier, before the hostilities of the Civil War had begun, the last cargo of slaves arrived in the United States at Mobile. From 110 to 160 Africans were transported on the schooner *Clotilde* by Captain William Foster. Foster worked for Mobile shipbuilder Timothy Meaher, but the illegal trafficking scheme was intercepted by Federal authorities. At the time fifty percent of Alabama's free black population lived in Mobile County, approximately 1,350. Pre-Civil War slave population was more than 435,000 in 1860.[14] Lincoln was re-elected and began his second term on March 4, 1865. On April 9, 1865 at Appomattox Courthouse in Virginia, Confederate General Robert E. Lee surrendered to Union forces. Six days later Lincoln was assassinated on April 15, 1865 and Andrew Johnson became the seventeenth president of the United States. Johnson stayed in office until March 4, 1869. He was a member of the Democratic National Union Party, and eventually the *No Party* party.

President Johnson appointed Lewis E. Parsons as provisional governor of Alabama, and he served from June to December, 1865. Parsons was a pre-war Whig and then a Know-Nothing.[15] He served as an Alabama elector for Whig presidential candidate Millard Fillmore in 1856. Not an Alabama native, Parsons was born in Lisle, New York in 1817 and represented Talladega County in the Alabama House of Representatives from 1859 to 1861.[16] Parsons's successor was Robert M. Patton who served from December 1865 to March, 1867. Another non-native, Patton was born in Virginia and was elected to the Alabama Legislature in 1832 and served with distinction as a Whig in both houses. Patton had always opposed secession.[17]

Reconstruction and Politics in Alabama

In September, 1865 the Alabama State Constitutional Convention assembled. In November, 1865 at Mobile, the first Alabama statewide Colored Convention was held. Fifty-six delegates, mostly church ministers, were chosen from local areas around the state. None of their resolutions contained anything which white Alabama people might consider objectionable.[18] "… Unionists expected to direct the reorganization of postwar Alabama. They believed that the Confederacy's collapse vindicated their earlier opposition to secession. …"[19] A program of Reconstruction was begun by President Lincoln shortly after the war began. Congress later wrested control for Reconstruction from the executive branch. Many presidential aspects of Reconstruction were reversed or dropped by the congressional version of Reconstruction. Citizenship for Confederate soldiers, office holders, and plantation owners was withheld and subject to more rigorous scrutiny before citizenship would be restored. Radical Reconstruction was met with fierce opposition by southerners. Alabama was under military governance in 1867 when President Johnson appointed Wager Swayne, a native of Ohio, to be its military "governor." Swayne served from March to December of that year. Swayne was an assistant commissioner of the Freedmen's Bureau for Alabama during the years of Reconstruction when Parsons and Patton served as governor.[20]

With the Reconstruction Acts of 1867 came wholesale changes in the way the South was governed. No longer would political offices be held by white men only. Blacks became fair game politically.[21] "In May, 1867, the second statewide Colored Convention met in Mobile. The differences between it and the 1865 convention were indicative of the growing Republican radicalism of black political leaders. The convention was not entirely representative of the state's Negro population – one-half of the delegates were from Mobile and the remainder came from only twelve other counties. Most of the Black Belt counties, however, were represented, and many of the delegates were typical of a new breed of semi-professional black politicians."[22] "The Colored Convention may have gone by another name. Another meeting to arouse interest in the formation of the Republican Party in Alabama was the Freedmen's State Convention, held in Mobile on May 1, 1867, under the direction of General Swayne. Black citizens at the convention issued a series of resolutions and proclaimed themselves a part of the Republican Party because this was the only party to attempt to extend the Negroes privileges."[23]

Alabama Republican Party Chartered

"Over three hundred blacks and whites met in Montgomery on June 4-5, 1867, and formally chartered the state Republican Party. They endorsed congressional Reconstruction and the Fourteenth Amendment and condemned civil and political discrimination. Central to the indoctrination of black Republicans in Alabama and throughout the South was the Union League. Set up locally throughout the south, the Union League acted as a wing of the Republican Party."[24] "One of the chief instruments through which the Republican Party was established in Alabama was the Union League, an organization that had originated in the North during the war as a patriotic organization, but which rapidly after the war became a bulwark of the Republican Party in most Southern states. It was the Union League that first enlisted most blacks behind the Republican Party. Its period of effective political influence in Alabama lasted only about a year. By late 1868, because of attacks by the Ku Klux Klan and because its purposes were served just as well by the Republican Party, it had practically ceased to exist."[25]

"On June 4, 1867, the Union Republican Convention met in Montgomery with the Union League Convention. About fifty whites and one hundred blacks attended ..."[26] By the end of the year 1867 Alabama was a two-party state. The state government had been reorganized and blacks had been given the franchise.[27] In 1868 the newly ratified Alabama Constitution became the first of the Reconstruction constitutions completed and submitted to the people.[28] William Hugh Smith assumed the office of Alabama governor in July, 1868 and was the first Republican in history to do so. The Republican Party was composed mostly of freedmen. Smith refused to take office initially because, opposing his own party, he did not want to enforce ratification. The U.S. Congress placed him in office anyway.[29]

Andrew Applegate became Alabama's lieutenant governor under the 1867 constitution. A carpetbagger from Ohio, Applegate was known to Alabamians as "Jack Appletoddy." Those elected to office under the 1867 Constitution included 100 members of the Alabama House of which ninety-seven were Republicans (26 African Americans) and three

Democrats. House terms were only two years. The thirty-three member Senate had 32 Republicans, one of whom was African American, Benjamin Royal; and one Democrat.[30]

Ratification of the Alabama Constitution of 1868

The ratification election of the new Alabama Constitution was held on February 4, 1868. Even though the vast majority of the votes (70,812 to 1,005) cast favored the new constitution, the law actually required a majority of the 170,631 registered voters for passage. Even though General Meade suggested that the constitutional convention reassemble itself, the Republicans favored immediate admission. Congress passed the Fourth Reconstruction Act of March 11, 1868 which provided for a majority of those voting to win passage of the constitution.[31] On June 25, 1868 Alabama was readmitted to the Union.[32] "By summer 1868 the Ku Klux Klan and the Knights of the White Camellia were active in Alabama, especially in the counties of the Tennessee Valley and western Alabama Black Belt.[33]

Two famous Alabama Democrats, David P. Lewis of Madison County and Alexander McKinstry of Mobile, switched to the Republican Party in 1869. By 1870 Alabama's population had grown to just short of one million citizens. The first census with no slave count, the African American population numbered 475,510 to 521,384 whites. "Perhaps it was too much to expect a party based on the tenuous alliance of such diverse groups as blacks, carpetbaggers, and scalawags (who themselves consisted of the unlikely combination of Black Belt planters seeking to maintain control over their ex-slaves and northern Alabama farmers resentful of the large planters) to remain in power for long. Blacks, who formed the vast majority of Republican voters, were by the early 1870s demanding the increased share of offices to which they thought their numbers entitled them. These demands, however, met the formidable opposition of most scalawags. Scalawags chafed at the prominent position of carpetbaggers within the party."[34]

Robert Burns Lindsay, a native of Lochmaben, Scotland and a Democrat, was elected and served as Alabama governor from 1870 to 1872. He defeated incumbent governor William Hugh Smith by 1,439 votes. Democrats also retook the House, winning 57 seats to thirty-eight

Republican. Nineteen of those 38 Republican seats were held by African Americans. There was no Senate race in Alabama in 1870.[35]

THE CITY OF BIRMINGHAM, ALABAMA WAS FOUNDED BY THE Elyton Land Company in 1871. As a political entity, Birmingham did not exist during the years of the Civil War. The new industrial city would become a magnet not only to fortune-seeking industrialists but workers and laborers. Birmingham would become a city that attracted the northern investor and would become Alabama's first city of competing ethnic and racial groups. Former slaves eager to leave the plantations and farms of their previous masters would leave the Black Belt counties for labor jobs in the new city. Indeed, Birmingham would be called the "Magic City" in almost no time at all. Birmingham grew geographically by annexing neighboring towns.

In 1872 Republican David P. Lewis, a native of Virginia, was elected as Alabama's second Republican governor. During his two-year term there was an election-results dispute that produced two legislatures. When the issue was settled the Republicans held a two-seat majority in the House and the Democrats a one-seat majority in the Senate. The 1872 legislature included 19 House Republican African Americans and five African Americans in the Senate. "Having lost the governorship in 1870, Republicans realized that their party's success in 1872 required the support of the state's Unionists of 1860. Republican leaders agreed to compose a state electoral ticket entirely of native Unionists, especially those from north Alabama, an area that had been rife with opposition to secession."[1] An epidemic of cholera and a nation-wide business depression in 1873 left Birmingham very nearly dead … and stock in the Elyton Land Company fell.[2] The so-called Panic of 1873 was merciless on Alabama, which was already reeling from bad railroad deals between 1868 and 1872. The state's credit was virtually destroyed by Alabama governors.[3] Also in the 1868 and 1872 national presidential elections, Alabama voted for Republican Ulysses S. Grant. Between 1876 and 1948 Alabama voted for Democratic presidential candidates.

WILLIAM JELKS CABANISS, JR.

W.D. Jelks and E.H. Cabaniss attend Mercer University

In 1873 young William Dorsey Jelks, of Union Springs, Alabama, entered Mercer University, a Baptist college in Macon, Georgia. Jelks was born in 1855 and became fatherless in 1862. J.W.D. Jelks, his father, died in Richmond while serving in the Third Alabama Infantry Regiment. His mother Jane remarried in 1865 to Robert Green Wright. Given the national and state financial situation that year, it seemed that 1873 was a difficult time to begin (and pay for) college. Jelks was a hardworking young boy and knew that he wanted to attend college. He saved his earnings and with additional funds loaned to him by family friends, Jelks left Union Springs for Georgia with the blessings and goodwill of his community to begin his college studies. His time spent at Mercer, the classes that he would study, and the friends he would make, would set the stage for his future.

At the same time that W.D. Jelks began his education at Mercer in 1873, a sixteen year-old named Edward Harman Cabaniss, of Forsyth, Georgia, entered his sophomore year. Cabaniss entered college in 1872 (seven years after the end of the Civil War), the same year that his grandfather Judge Elbridge Gerry Cabaniss died. It is probable that the two young Mercer men met and knew each other during some of their college years. They might have had several encounters in classes or in extra-curricular activities, like the debate club. Cabaniss's forebears were lawyers. His father George Augustus Cabaniss trained in law but after serving in the Civil War in a Georgia regiment he decided to become a merchant. Edward Cabaniss's grandfather, Elbridge Gerry Cabaniss, was not only a judge but an active partisan politician.

Edward H. Cabaniss

William Dorsey Jelks

Alabama Department of Archives and History Photos

Both young men, W.D. Jelks and E.H. Cabaniss, studied at Mercer to prepare for their futures. Both men are ancestors of William Jelks Cabaniss, Jr. W.D. Jelks was Cabaniss's great uncle, and E.H. Cabaniss was his paternal grandfather. Character, work ethic, perseverance, and strong family ties mark the lineage of both families. E.H. Cabaniss probably had no intention of leaving Georgia or at least he probably gave little thought to leaving his state. After all, his was one of the leading families of Monroe County, Georgia. From the time of his great-grandfather George (third-generation Cabaniss) to his own time, Forsyth was the family home. His education was in public schools. Edward Cabaniss graduated from Mercer in 1875, one year before Jelks. He earned a bachelor's degree, finishing second in a large class. Later he earned a masters degree. Though he never earned a degree in law, E.H. Cabaniss read for law at local law firms, and one summer went to Charlottesville, Virginia to study law under the famed John B. Minor.

Minor was considered the best lawyer of his day. Five years before Cabaniss graduated from Mercer University, John B. Minor established a summer law course for practitioners who needed to supplement their legal skills. In 1870 Minor published his *Institutes of Common and Statute Law* cementing his reputation as the leading legal professor in the South and boosting the enrollment of the law school dramatically. Minor succeeded the also famous attorney and legal scholar Henry St. George

Tucker. Minor was the only law professor at the University of Virginia until 1851. He taught law for 50 years. That summer course in Virginia prepared Edward H. Cabaniss not only for his legal profession but for his life.[4]

While at Mercer W.D. Jelks developed an appreciation for writing and journalism which probably grew out of his love for Greek and Latin literary classics, an appreciation that would lead him into the profession of journalism. Jelks was the brother of Bill Cabaniss's maternal grandmother Martha Frazier Jelks Cabaniss. W.D. Jelks received his degree in 1876.[5] While he was attending college in Georgia his native Alabama would experience a change in its political orientation.

Alabama's Political Reorientation 1874

Alabama politics changed in 1874. For the next quarter century a coalition of planters and new industrialists would control state politics. They were the conservative Democrat Bourbon Redeemers. How did they win? The Democrats were more united than Republicans. "From 1870 to 1874 Republicans and Democrats struggled for control of the state, and in 1874, through a combination of Republican disunity, Democratic intimidation of black voters, and the appeal for all whites to band together behind the 'white man's party,' the Republicans were permanently driven from power. In Alabama, as in other Southern states, black participation in politics had been greatly reduced by the late 1870s and would later be almost entirely eliminated."[6] "... In Dallas County, Alabama [in the western Black Belt], in August 1874, robed Klansmen assassinated two Republican leaders, one black and one white. At Spring Hill near Eufuala [in the eastern Black Belt], in Barbour County, Democrats stormed a polling place at twilight, shot out the lantern, fired at the Republican official who had been counting the votes, fatally wounding his sixteen year old son, and stole the ballot box which contained more than 1,700 mostly Republican votes. In Russell County on the state line, Georgia Democrats crossed over and voted freely in the Alabama election."[7]

It would fall to George S. Houston, a Redeemer Democrat, to end Republican power in Alabama.[8] Now that the Republicans no longer controlled Alabama government, Democrats began the process of creating a new state constitution, a constitution to relieve Alabama of the rule of carpetbaggers and scalawags. They would replace the 1868 Constitution with a conservative document that would give the Democrats, in general, and the Black Belt planters, in particular, a stronghold on their re-acquired power. This new constitution would be Alabama's fourth in fifteen years. The constitutional convention delegates were dominated by eighty Democrats, 12 Republicans, four of whom were African American, and seven Independents.[9] What could twelve Republicans do? Nothing! The Constitution of 1875 was ratified and put into place.

In East Orange, New Jersey in 1876, a future Alabama mining executive, Harold R. Sanson, was born. Later, the Sanson and Pierson families of New Jersey would marry to begin the maternal side of Bill Cabaniss's legacy.[10] By 1876 the Republican Party, a new party beginning with the election of Abraham Lincoln, had held the presidency of the United States for four full terms.[11] Rutherford B. Hayes assumed the office of President in 1878 and Rufus W. Cobb became governor of Alabama. From Shelby County, a coal mining area south and southeast of Jefferson County and Birmingham, Cobb would be Alabama's second Bourbon governor.[12] Edward H. Cabaniss was admitted to the practice of law in Union Springs.[13] Within one year Cabaniss became one of the editors and co-owner of the *Union Springs Herald*, the local newspaper. His business partners were D.F McCall and William Dorsey Jelks.[14] It is possible that Cabaniss and Jelks might have talked about going into business with one another while attending Mercer. Whatever their motivations, the two men were in business together if only for a short time. Cabaniss had a preference for the practice of law; journalism was not his ambition, but perhaps it was a way to make money. Newspaper editors in Alabama and around the South became powerful influencers over time. In 1879 Jelks acquired a large interest in the *Eufaula Times*. He eventually became owner and editor of the *Times* in 1880 with the backing of Congressman William C. Oates, and then relocated to his new home.[15] Jelks himself became highly influential in Alabama politics with his large statewide newspaper distribution. He made friends easily and eventually established a broad political base for his point of view.

Though he possessed and articulated his strong political views, he was fair-minded and provided space in his newspaper for opposing positions.

The 1880 Alabama census placed the state's population at 1.262 million. Whites outnumbered blacks by only 62,082 and the state was considerably rural. The rural population stood at 1.193 million, urban at 68,518.[16] 1880 was the year that the black National Baptist Convention organized itself in Montgomery.

ON FEBRUARY 10, 1881 THE ALABAMA LEGISLATURE established the Tuskegee Institute in Macon County in the eastern Black Belt. Tuskegee would be a training school for colored teachers and the law stipulated that graduates must agree to teach for two years in Alabama schools. This action by the Legislature would produce an historic legacy in Alabama. A process began where Booker T. Washington would become the school's first superintendent.[1]

President Chester A. Arthur took office on September 19, 1881 upon the assassination of James A. Garfield. Both presidents were Republicans. Garfield had only been president since March 4, 1881. Arthur would serve until 1885. In 1882 Edward A. O'Neal would serve as Alabama's governor to 1886. O'Neal, a Democrat, continued in the line of "redeeming" Bourbon governors faithful to the old Confederate cause. Republicans made an attempt at the governor's seat by creating a coalition of independents and *Greenbackers* supporting James Lawrence Sheffield of Marshall County.[2] The control of state government, beginning in 1874, would be in the hands of those with pre-Civil War political and social sentiments. Marshall County and other northern Alabama counties were mostly Unionists and never favored secession. It would become more and more difficult for a Unionist, Republican, carpetbagger, or scalawag to win statewide elections for many years to come.

Jelks, Cabaniss Families Marry

Edward H. Cabaniss, the lawyer-publisher, fell in love with the sister of one of his newspaper business partners. Martha Frazier Jelks and Cabaniss married on December 13, 1882 in Union Springs. Martha's parents were Joseph William Dorsey Jelks, who died in Richmond during the Civil War, and Jane Goodrum Frazier Jelks. Martha had three brothers – the closest in age was William Dorsey. Edward and Martha would have five children, all sons. The following year Cabaniss would end his newspaper publishing career to devote himself to the practice of law.[3] Less than six months after E.H. Cabaniss married, William Dorsey

Jelks married Alice Keitt Shorter on June 7, 1883 in Eufaula, Alabama. Alice's uncle was former governor John Gill Shorter and her first cousin was the Populist Reuben Kolb, both historic figures in Alabama politics. Her father, Henry Shorter, was a well-to-do Eufaula attorney who was also president of Alabama's state railroad commission, a very powerful position.

Eufaula is situated high on a bluff on the west side of the Chattahoochee River, The area around the bluff was home to several Indian tribes. The Uchees, the Actahoochees, and the Eufaulas were the dominant tribes, each speaking their own dialect. The area was within the Creek Nation as defined by the United States Government. But the white man could not stay outside the defined borders and the Intruders War began in 1827. White settlers were eventually allowed to purchase claims from the Indian tribes. The first settler was Carson Winslett and the first store was established by a Mr. Allen and a partner, William Irwin. Eufaula was renamed Irwinton. The Irwinton Bridge Bank was chartered and named after the first bridge built across the Chattahoochee River that connected with Georgia. In 1842 the name of Irwinton was changed to Eufaula. A town in Georgia by a similar name apparently confused those who made postal and commercial deliveries. Called "The Bluff City," Eufaula was considered one of the most beautiful towns along the Chattahoochee.[4] It still is.

Another uncle of Alice Keitt Shorter was Eli S. Shorter who served in the United States Congress from Alabama before the Civil War. Another first cousin was Clement Clay Shorter who was Speaker of the Alabama House of Representatives at the age of twenty-six.[5] Neither Cabaniss nor Jelks had any political connections in Alabama until their marriages. Cabaniss was the son of a solid and successful Georgia family and Jelks was the son of a founder and captain of an Alabama military unit in the Civil War. Cabaniss's and Jelks's careers would soon take off.

Robert Wright Cabaniss

Robert Wright Cabaniss, the first of five sons of Edward H. and Martha J. Cabaniss, was born on January 3, 1884 in Union Springs. It is probable that this son was so named because Martha's step-father was Robert Green Wright. Martha hardly knew her Civil War-fallen father,

Joseph William Dorsey Jelks. In 1865 her mother Jane married Wright who was Martha's father figure for almost twenty years. R.W. Cabaniss would eventually attend the United States Naval Academy at Annapolis, Maryland.

Grover Cleveland, a Democrat from New York, became President of the United States in 1886, serving the first of his two separate terms. Cleveland was the only Democrat to break the Republican Party hold on the nation's presidency. His first term ended in 1889. In 1886 Thomas Seay became governor of Alabama. There was some discontent with Bourbon rule by 1886. Seay won the Democratic nomination on the thirtieth ballot. He defeated the Republican Arthur Bingham handily in the general election.[6]

Cabaniss Law Firm in Birmingham

Edward H. Cabaniss ran for and was elected to the Alabama State Senate from Bullock County, Alabama in 1886. Cabaniss was not only a Democrat, but a Baptist who belonged to no secret societies. The term of office was four years but Cabaniss resigned his seat in 1887 in order to relocate to Birmingham, a boomtown by this time.[7]

On April 27, 1887 the Union Springs *Herald and Times* published an announcement about Cabaniss's departure and relocation.

Senator E.H. Cabaniss has decided to locate in Birmingham, and will leave for that place next month. His family will remain here some time. Senator Cabaniss is one of the most highly esteemed citizens of Bullock. He has resided here twelve years, and has won for himself that high regard from the people which any man might envy. He is one of the ablest young lawyers in the State, and will win fame and fortune in the growing city which is to be his home. Last year he was nominated for Senator from this county which is the 26th senatorial district, by the Democratic convention and the fact that he was nominated by acclamation, without one dissenting voice, shows the appreciation in which he is held by the people of Bullock. He represented our district in the legislature in a manner acceptable to all, and reflected great credit upon his constituency. Every citizen in the county will regret to learn that he has decided to locate elsewhere, and will join in the wish that prosperity and success may attend him. He and his interesting family will prove a most valuable acquisition to Birmingham.[8]

Once in Birmingham Cabaniss entered into a one-year partnership with James J. Banks. Cabaniss and Banks were related by marriage. Their wives were first cousins. Banks would become an Alabama circuit court judge for a while and then move to Colorado and Hawaii. Banks became an Associate Justice of the Supreme Court of the Territory of Hawaii. Cabaniss would form a new partnership with Samuel Davies Weakley in 1889. That partnership would last for seven years.[9] While working with Cabaniss, Weakley was serving as Birmingham's city attorney and his major contribution in that position was a compilation of a code of city ordinances. Later, Weakley served as Chief Justice of the Supreme Court of Alabama, receiving his appointment from former Cabaniss in-law, Governor William Dorsey Jelks.[10] An Alabama historical magazine provides a description of E. H. Cabaniss as "a gentleman of marked dignity; he is a clear, logical speaker, calm and imperturbable in manner, and he impresses his listeners with confidence in the integrity of his argument."[11]

When E.H. Cabaniss died in 1936 the Birmingham Bar Association paid high tribute to the man and his service in a formal resolution dated December 18, 1936. It read in part

His career at the bar is one in which a place of singular honor and distinction was inevitable from its beginning. Intellectual integrity of the highest order made it impossible for Mr. Cabaniss to accept that which was merely expedient. In consequence he never found himself in blind alleys or forced to compromise or retreat. This quality, added to mental energy of the first order, and a deep and abiding respect for the jurisprudence of England and America and the principles of constitutional liberty which that system took for its own, rationalized and perpetuated, which together constitute the greatest contribution of the English speaking people to social order, assured from the outset that Mr. Cabaniss would take and maintain to the end a premier position at any bar in America before which he might practice. ... Edward H. Cabaniss stands today in our regard as by far the most distinguished member of the profession in the history of the bar of North Alabama. ... He would have graced the judiciary of any court; he would have made a brilliant diplomat.[12]

It appears that the Birmingham Bar Association's 1936 resolution envisioning a future "brilliant diplomat" to one of its own would be fulfilled by E.H.'s grandson who would be born eighteen months later.

Farmers' Alliance Politics in Alabama

In state politics the Farmers' Alliance grew from 1887 to 1896. It grew out of the earlier Grange and Agricultural Wheel organizations, 1870s for the former, 1880s, the latter. It evolved into the Populist movement which challenged conservative Democrats for control of Alabama state politics.[13] The Farmers' Alliance held a convention in Montgomery in 1889 and Governor Seay was asked to attend and speak. But he withdrew because in his opinion the group was becoming too political.[14] Thomas Goode Jones served as Alabama's governor from 1890 to 1894. Although a faithful Bourbon Democrat, Jones had liberal opinions about race relations and maintained good relations with many Republicans. But his campaign was tainted by its racism and the suspected manipulation of African American votes. The main purpose of that election was to block the nomination of Reuben Kolb.[15]

African American Alienation from Republican Party

Still a predominantly rural state in 1890, Alabama's population now stood at 1.513 million people. Only ten percent of the population was urban. The African American population was 678,489 strong and the white 833,718.[16] It became obvious by 1890 that Alabama Republicans could not successfully come together to elect anyone to statewide office, particularly that of governor. If that practical fact were not enough, a move by the national Republican Party may have become the tipping point which caused the alienation of African Americans from its own political roots. Three important bills in the United States Senate competed for attention in 1890. There was a federal elections bill pending that would provide suffrage nationwide, especially for blacks. Two other bills, a silver purchase act and a tariff act competed with the election bill and the United States Senate was in gridlock. The legislative gridlock was broken by dropping the federal election bill and passage of the two other bills. Known as the Compromise of 1890 or the Henry Cabot Lodge bill, this action by Senate Republicans signaled what is believed to be the beginning of the end of Republican Commitment to African American suffrage on a national level.[17] A slow shift or exchange in the policy of the Democratic and Republican parties was in the works. Change was afoot. Business, politics, race issues, and industrialization were picking up speed across the nation and particularly in the northern part of Alabama where the Magic City of Birmingham had become not only a place of employment and investment, but the center of a state government and business coalition – Bourbon Governors and Big Mule businessmen.

On October 15, 1889, the Alabama Penny Savings bank was organized in Birmingham by African Americans. As Birmingham grew and its new industrial base began to expand, opportunities for all people opened up.

In Europe in1890, the Czech National museum opened in Prague.[18] Victoria had been Queen of England since 1837. The southern part of Africa was being explored and dominated by European governments and Cecil Rhodes became an active industrialist in Africa's diamond mines.

FORMER DEMOCRATIC AGRICULTURE COMMISSIONER Reuben Kolb, a "Jeffersonian Democrat" challenged incumbent Thomas Goode Jones for governor, getting support from farmers, blacks, Populists, and Republicans. The period of years between 1892 and 1899 saw the development of "fusion" election tickets composed of Populists and Republicans, dominant mostly in the hill counties of St. Clair, Marshall, Shelby, and Chilton. The merger of Populists and Republicans for this particular election was known as the People's Party. What Kolb did was to challenge Bourbon control of the Black Belt by promising blacks protection of their political rights.[1]

The First Iron Bowl Football Game

On February 22, 1893, the first football game between Auburn University and the University of Alabama was played in Birmingham at Lakeview Park. Five thousand spectators attended. Auburn won 32-22. The series of games ended in 1907 and would not resume until 1948.[2] Later that year on September 30, Julia Tutwiler persuaded the University of Alabama Board of Trustees to experiment with a form of co-education. A faculty committee agreed to it, provided that the young women students were at least 18 years old and of good character. They would take examinations for entrance as second year students or higher. In 1893 only two women were admitted.[3]

William C. Oates, the former United States Congressman from Alabama and financial backer of William Dorsey Jelks's purchase of the *Eufaula Times*, became Governor of Alabama in 1894. Democratic Party insiders wanted Oates to run, figuring that Kolb would run for office again. Oates held the right positions, the party leaders thought, to fight off the Farmers' Alliance and the semi-populist wing of the party. Kolb did run again with Populist and Republican support, losing to Oates by more than 25,000 votes.[4] Controversy prevailed over that campaign. Joseph F. Johnston would serve as Alabama governor from 1896 to 1900. Challenges by Populists and Jeffersonian Democrats were not as vigorous in Johnston's campaign.[5]

At Tuskegee Institute in Macon County, Dr. George Washington Carver joined the faculty in 1896 to head the institute's agricultural school. Born a slave in Missouri during the Civil War, Carver was studying in Iowa when he was invited by Booker T. Washington to come to Tuskegee.[6] A Republican candidate was elected to the Alabama House from Marshall County. Truman H. Aldrich, a Republican, served Alabama in the 54th United States Congress from 1896 to 1897. William F. Aldrich, Truman's brother, also a Republican, served not only in the 54th Congress but the 55th and 56th. Even though all of William's elections were disputed, the U.S. Congress settled them and seated him. After William Aldrich left Congress in 1901, no Alabama Republican would serve in Congress until 1964.[7]

Alabama Senator W.D. Jelks

In 1897 William McKinley became the twenty-fifth President of the United States and in 1898 William Dorsey Jelks was elected to a four-year term to the Alabama Senate from Barbour County. In the senate Jelks chaired the all-important Committee on Constitution, Constitutional Revision and Amendment. Prior to this election Jelks's only election was as member of the Eufaula city school board. At the end of the 1900 session of the Alabama legislature Jelks was elected President of the Senate.[8]

In 1899 Harold Sanson, Bill Cabaniss's maternal grandfather, graduated from the Stevens Institute of Technology in Hoboken, New Jersey.[9] The year 1900 began the Progressive Era which would last forty years. The word "Bourbon" would be dropped from the political vocabulary of Alabama and the terms "conservative" and "progressive" became operative.[10] William J. Samford would serve as governor between December, 1900 and June, 1901. Samford's family moved to Chambers, Alabama from Greenville, Georgia where he was born. His father was a planter and edited several newspapers in Alabama. Samford studied at the Classical School in Oak Bowery in Chambers County and served in the 46th Alabama Regiment during the Civil War. A prisoner of war, he was held on Johnson Island in Lake Erie not far from the shore of Toledo, Ohio. He served one term as United States Representative from Alabama's Third District beginning in 1878.[11] Samford was unable to take office in December, 1900 due to a heart problem. He left the state for treatment and returned later in December. During his absence Senate leader William D. Jelks assumed the role of acting governor for twenty-six days. On December 11, 1900 Jelks signed into law a bill that authorized a constitutional convention in 1901. That was his last official act as acting governor before Samford returned.[12]

Alabama continued to be predominantly rural. Of its population of 1.828 million in 1900 the rural to urban ratio was seven to one. More than 5,600 manufacturing establishments were accounted for by this time.[13]

MANY FAMOUS ENTERTAINERS HAVE COME FROM Alabama. On January 31, 1902, Tallulah Bankhead was born in Huntsville, Alabama. Three weeks later her mother died of blood poisoning. An actress, Bankhead was well known in the 1930s, 40s, and 50s. What is probably not known to those persons living outside Alabama, is the fact that Tallulah came from one of the strongest political family powerhouses in northern Alabama, if not the entire state.

Alabama Democratic Political Families

The Bankhead and Brockman political and family alliance was one of the strongest in America. William Brockman Bankhead, Tallulah's father, was Democratic Speaker of the United States House of Representatives from 1936 to 1940. Her grandfather, Democrat John H. Bankhead, was a United States Senator from 1907 to 1920, and her uncle, Democrat John H. Bankhead II, was a United States Senator from 1931 to 1946. Both senators were elected for three terms and both died while in office. And both were conservative Democrats as were most southern Democrats at that time. John II was preceded in his senate seat by J. Thomas Heflin, the flamboyant uncle of future Alabama Chief Justice and United States Senator Howell Heflin. John II's senatorial contemporaries from Alabama were Hugo Black, former governor Bibb Graves, and Lister Hill.[1] Despite the appellation "conservative," a latent liberalism was resident in the Alabama Democratic Party, but it would take years to blossom. Northern Alabama, in the Tennessee River Valley region of the state, had more in common with Tennessee than the rest of Alabama. Before and during the Civil War this region was more sympathetic to the Union and not the Confederacy. Progressivism[2] was to take hold first in this region of Alabama.

On March 2, 1901, Governor William J. Samford and the Trustees of the planned Alabama Department of Archives and History [ADAH] met to organize what would become the nation's first state archival agency.[3] This would be Samford's major contribution to the state and his legacy in his shortened term as Alabama's governor. A year earlier William Dorsey

Jelks of Eufaula was elected president of the Alabama State Senate by his peers, a remarkable vote of confidence for a freshman senator. Samford had been elected governor in the same year and it was common knowledge that Samford suffered from a weak heart. It is probably for that reason that the Senate made Jelks their leader, knowing Samford's health might well fail. In any case, Jelks had proven his capabilities over the years as an editor and publisher of several newspapers and his statewide political influence was credible. Samford's health was so bad that he was unable to attend his own inauguration on December 1, 1900 and the existing state constitution had no provision for a lieutenant governor. Samford left the state for treatment and the office of temporary governor passed to Jelks. Jelks served until December 26, 1900 when Samford returned, and Jelks resumed his senate leadership role.

Alabama Governor William Dorsey Jelks

On June 11, 1901 Governor Samford died and William Dorsey Jelks assumed the office of governor for the remaining years of Samford's two-year term. A new state constitutional convention had been underway to create a constitution that would limit suffrage. Most African Americans and many poor whites would lose any voting rights enjoyed up to passage and ratification. By September 1, 1901 the Constitutional Convention had done its work and created a new set of laws. On September 14, 1901, Republican Theodore Roosevelt became the twenty-sixth President of the United States. Roosevelt would serve the remainder of William McKinley's term until his own election in 1904. Jelks, now Governor of Alabama,[4] set the date for ratification or rejection by the people for November 11, 1901. The constitution was ratified and Jelks set the effective date as November 28, 1901 – Thanksgiving Day.[5] The uniqueness of the bill's (the new 1901 State Constitution's) passage revolves around the serendipitous rise in Jelks's political career. He had chaired a senate committee which revised the existing constitution during the term of Samford's gubernatorial predecessor. Jelks later chaired a joint committee to perfect the bill, and days after being sworn into the office of governor, Jelks signed the bill and set the date for ratification. Jelks not only initiated the bill for creating the new constitution, he signed it into law.[6]

The 1901 Alabama State Constitution created provisions for the office of lieutenant governor and four-year terms for statewide elective offices (including both Senate and House terms). Jelks ran for governor on his own after serving the remaining eighteen months of Governor Samford's two-year term. He won after standing for nomination in the Democratic Party primary held on August 25, 1902. In the primary he defeated Joseph F. Johnston,[7] and in the general election on November 4, 1902 he defeated Republican J.W.A. Smith of Jefferson County.

As governor, Jelks made significant changes to the way state government operated. Even though the new constitution reduced the tax rate on income to the state, Jelks was able to find funds to increase pensions four-fold for old soldiers. A law requiring uniform statewide school book acquisitions saved the state hundreds of thousands of dollars; and a significant portion of the bonded debt of the state was refunded with the balance refinanced at better rates. Governor Jelks disapproved of the state practice of monthly leasing of state convicts. He moved to make sure that the state would protect the health of convicts, clothe, feed, and guard them. Though not a perfect program by any measurement, the governor wanted to ensure improvement in the health and moral condition of the state's convicts. The state made money from the leasing of convicts. It is recorded that the income to the state under Jelks's changes increased perhaps ten times over the previous state convict leasing program. The legislature authorized large sums to the common schools and directed funds to the universities in Tuscaloosa, Auburn, and Montevallo for the construction of "splendid halls."[8]

Probably the two largest items attached to Governor Jelks's legacy are the 1901 Alabama State Constitution and his operational efficiency in managing state government – primarily by leaving a surplus in the State Treasury. He had his own health issues while serving as governor and had to leave office for a period of time. Because the new constitution provided for a lieutenant governor, Russell M. Cunningham, a physician, became acting governor during Jelks's absence. Jelks's service as governor was five years and eight months, the longest term of service at that time. "Jelks seemed to enjoy positions of leadership. In Union Springs, at the age of twenty-two, he had served on the Common Council."[9]

Jelks's affable personality, his strong political inclinations, and his knack for efficiency led him to strengthen his statewide organization for governor. He appointed S.D. Weakley as his state campaign chairman and received support from many influential persons including United States Congressman Henry D. Clayton, Jr. Also, William C. Oates, a conservative Democrat, lent Jelks his support. His work as a newspaper owner and editor forged relationships with Clark Howell and Roby Robinson who were editor and business manager, respectively, of the *Atlanta Constitution* newspaper.[10] Jelks handily won election as governor outright in 1902.

Jelks an Effective, Principled, and Honest Governor

As governor, William Dorsey Jelks was a dedicated executive. Even though he engaged in patronage quite heavily, there is no evidence of corruption. On examination of his correspondence, both personal and professional, one can conclude that Jelks was a meticulous administrator. He was a resourceful person in running state government as evidenced by his payoff of state debt and the restructuring of the balance at lower interest rates, and by the fact that he left office with a $1.8 million surplus. He successfully crafted a state bond issue in 1905.[11]

Jelks was not only thrifty, he was honest. Jelks's chauffeur recalled one day when their vehicle ran over and killed a pig in Georgia. The governor wanted to stop and find the animal's owner and pay him for his loss. When found, the governor told the owner that he wanted to pay for the pig. The farmer, fully aware of his potential gain rather than loss, said "That pig was female, and she would have so many and so many [more piglets]." The farmer went on and on; therefore Jelks quickly gave him his business address so that they could confer later in Birmingham. Jelks's chauffeur said the governor wanted to do the right thing but he could see that he needed to be careful in this situation. He wanted to pay only for the one pig, not future generations. This is an example of his thriftiness.[12]

An example of principle is when "Jelks declined to officially accept [an honorary Doctor of Laws] degree from the University of Alabama because he was serving on that institution's Board of Trustees at the time."[13]

Although well known as an editor and proponent of the movement of the Alabama Democratic Party, William Dorsey Jelks made it clear when he was a newspaper owner-editor, his newspaper was not a Democratic "organ." He stressed that he would never put aside his personal conviction if it differed with or contradicted the policies adopted by the Democratic Party. In that way he was a free thinker of his day. Jelks took positions with clarity and rarely changed his mind. That is not to say that he didn't change his mind, but his readers knew pretty much Jelks's position on any issue facing Alabama.[14]

Jelks's biographer, David Alsobrook, wrote that "In summary, Jelks was a party man, and any factor that appeared to weaken the party was anathema in his eyes. Democratic Party unity was his editorial battle cry, and his tolerance for other political 'faiths' ended when this unity was challenged. The following editorial fragment expressed Jelks's complete devotion to the party: 'We don't care if a man favors the abolition of National banks, an income tax or the government ownership of railroads or any other plank in the Ocala document. For when he submits his claims to a beat meeting,[15] a county convention, a State, and finally to a national convention and in that last grafts his doctrines on the Party platform, it becomes democratic doctrine and the fellow that can't stand it must get out.'"[16]

Jelks's newspaper dispensed more than just political news and analysis. He editorialized for the benefit of young people with several articles on university education and agricultural training. As a graduate of Mercer University in the classics, in an editorial Jelks agreed with the *Gadsden News* that the "average college graduate is as well fitted for the government of an empire as he is the ordinary business of life ... He may be able to write a love story in Greek or an essay in Latin, but these accomplishments will not help him earn his daily bread ... Let the workshop precede the college. There is more to be admired in a boy who can plow a straight furrow or groove and can tongue pine boards than there is in the sickly youth who can parse a sentence in Latin or write a letter in Greek."[17]

Jelks was a big promoter of Eufaula itself and wrote about a town's capability for economic activity. He wrote that "every strictly mercantile community necessarily has its season of business depression, a condition which can be provided against only by the introduction of manufacturing enterprises, which are productive year round. To this end the Eufaula Investment and Security Company merits the unreserved encouragement and support of every citizen of Eufaula." By way of example he wrote a decade earlier that "the arrival of five different trains and nearly as many steamboats … gives some idea of the vast amount of goods and travel that reach Eufaula. On the Alabama side, wagons loaded with the products of the farm come from eighty miles around, sell out, and return loaded with the necessary supplies. The river traffic is wonderful."[18]

Jelks was a man who encouraged widespread and diverse economic activity. Always the promoter, he encouraged his town to grow out of the old cotton-oriented South. He believed there needed to be more diverse industry ranging from agriculture to manufacturing, from shipping to railroads. According to biographer Alsobrook, "Jelks stressed that the North would never respect the South as long as there existed 'the slightest semblance of dependence upon them.'"[19]

That statement, written only fifteen years after the end of the Civil War and three years following the collapse of Reconstruction, perhaps betrays a certain level of felt southern inferiority to the North. Or perhaps it was Jelks's way of representing a new reality for southern living marking the end of antebellum Romanticism and entrance into the cold, hard world of business enterprise and political engagement. In that sense William Dorsey Jelks was a pragmatist, not a short term manipulator. He took the long view.

Sanson-Pierson

According to the *Chi Psi* Fraternity journal for 6th Decennial Catalog of 1902, Harold Sanson – Bill Cabaniss's maternal grandfather – was listed as manager at Southern Cement Company in Birmingham, Alabama.[20] The catalog also recorded the marriage of Sanson to Miss Florence Pierson on October 29, 1902. They were married at the home of the bride in East Orange, New Jersey. The groom's brother, F.B. Sanson, was the best man. Both groom and best man were listed as graduate engineers of the Stevens Institute of Technology in Hoboken.[21] It was also the year that William Dorsey Jelks sought a full 4-year term as governor of Alabama. The 1901 Alabama constitution allowed for a term of four years instead of two.[22]

Daniel Pierson, Jr. and an investment group known as the Associates of New Jersey purchased the Southern Cahaba Mining Company for $270,000 in 1903. The company's new officers were listed as Daniel Pierson, Jr., President & Treasurer; Harold R. Sanson, Vice President and Manager; and W.T. Archer. The former owners were Truman H. Aldrich and P.B. Thomas of Birmingham.[23]

In the spring of 1904 Alabama Governor William Dorsey Jelks contracted tuberculosis and traveled to the New Mexico Territory for treatment. Lt. Gov. Russell Cunningham was left in charge for nearly one year[24] from April 1904 to March 1905. A physician, Cunningham attended Louisville Medical College from 1874 to 1875. He completed his medical studies in New York City at Bellevue Hospital Medical College in 1879.[25] On May 1, 1904 Czech composer Antonin Dvořák, who at one period of his life lived and worked in the United States, died. Colonel William Crawford Gorgas of Alabama began elimination of scourges of yellow fever and malaria in the Panama Canal Zone[26] and sculptor Guiseppe Moretti created an iron statue of Vulcan to represent Alabama Industry and Birmingham at the St. Louis World's Fair.[27]

Chilton County, Alabama elected in 1904 Republican Lewis W. Reynolds as Probate Judge. He was re-elected in 1916. Chilton County was heavily Republican between 1900-1912.[28]

The Cahaba Southern Coal Mining Company of Birmingham, founded by Harold Sanson, was dissolved on April 23, 1906. Other names mentioned on the dissolution record were Augustus Benners and J.L. Dillon. The company was classified as an Alabama Domestic Corporation.[29] *Directory of American Cement Industries* cites Southern Cement Company, Birmingham and Ensley, Alabama; Daniel Pierson, Jr., president and treasurer, and director. Harold R. Sanson was the company's secretary and general manager as well as a director. C.J. Curtin, of New York City, was a director. The authorized capitalization of the company was $500 thousand and $50 thousand was listed as paid up.[30] The Southern Cement Company would see its best days during the leadership of William Jelks Cabaniss, senior, in the 1950s and 60s.

Upon the death of Alabama Chief Justice McClellan in February, 1906, Governor William D. Jelks, E.H. Cabaniss's brother-in-law, appointed Samuel D. Weakley, Jr., E.H. Cabaniss's law firm partner, to fill the remainder of McClellan's term. Weakley served until November, 1906.[31]

The Tennessee Coal and Iron Company in Birmingham was purchased in 1908 by United States Steel Corporation of Pittsburgh, Pennsylvania,[32] which would have a national as well as local Alabama impact. 1907 was also the year Braxton Bragg Comer became governor. Scion of a well-to-do family, he was a successful industrialist and planter who spent four stormy years as Alabama's governor. Comer's brand of progressivism – which sought to serve the new industrial-urban interests while not disturbing the traditions of the old plantation system – brought numerous collisions with powerful interests.[33] "When William Dorsey Jelks left office in 1907 he had served longer than any other governor before him. He left a cash balance in the treasury of $1.8 million, which he recommended be spent on education."[34] George Augustus Cabaniss, Bill Cabaniss's paternal great-grandfather, died on December 14, 1907 in Fulton County, Georgia.[35]

After leaving office, William Dorsey Jelks founded Protective Life Insurance Company in Birmingham in a year of national financial "panic," 1907. Southern country banks were forced to limit the dollar amounts of their customer withdrawals and the people of Birmingham had to use clearing house certificates in lieu of currency. This was the time when President Theodore Roosevelt intervened and permitted Pittsburgh, Pennsylvania-based United States Steel Corporation to enter Alabama as purchaser of the Tennessee Coal and Iron Company – this action was intended to give impetus to processes leading to a gradual business recovery from a nation-wide depression.[36]

In 1909 Republican William Howard Taft became the twenty-seventh president of the United States. Taft previously served as Secretary of War. In the same year Wilbur and Orville Wright established a "flying school" near Montgomery, Alabama, today the home of Maxwell Air Force Base. This was six years after their historic flight. An interesting side note: Tallulah Bankhead, the actress, claimed that Orville and Wilbur attended her first public performance.

In Europe an explosion of Czech modern music began with Vítězslav Novák (1870 - 1949), who studied composition at the Prague Conservatory under Dvořák. As professor of the senior class in composing (1909 - 39), he taught a generation of Czech and foreign - largely Slavic - composers. Czech modernism matured in the course of the long musical career of the much older Leoš Janáček (1854-1928). When Queen Victoria, of the House of Hanover, died in 1901, her son, Edward VII, of the House of Saxe-Coburg, became king. In 1910, upon Edward's death, George V became king. Between 1910 and 1917 George V was a Saxe-Coburg, but became part of the House of Windsor until his death in 1936.

On December 14, 1910, Florence Pierson Sanson, Bill Cabaniss's mother, was born. The population of the State of Alabama stood at 2,138,093 at the 1910 census. White population accounted for 1,228,832 and the African-American population was 908,282. But Alabama was still a rural state even though industrial Birmingham was booming. The number of manufacturing establishments was listed as 3,398, but the urban population was only 17.3% of the state's total population.[37]

In elections around the state in 1910 Republicans made little, but some, headway. Franklin County elected Republican S.J. Petree as probate judge, Cullman County elected C.C Scheuing as its County Sheriff, and J.B. Sloan was elected to a state senate district made up of Blount, Cullman, and Winston Counties. J.J. Curtis of Winston County became first Republican Circuit Judge for Winston and Walker Counties – the first since Reconstruction.[38]

There had been ten different state chairmen of the Alabama Republican Party between 1867 and 1900. Julius W. Davidson served as state chairman between 1901 and 1904. Joseph Oswalt Thompson served between 1904 and 1911.[39] The party would remain small and ineffective for seventy-five years. It would become dominant in Alabama in 2010.

THE SECOND DECADE OF THE TWENTIETH CENTURY SET THE stage not only for the hope of freedom and independence for millions of people around the world, it also produced the beginning of totalitarian governments. Alabama struggled with its own issues and Birmingham continued to grow. In 1912 Emmet O'Neal began serving as Alabama Governor. He, like his father before him, was president of the state bar association, framer of a state constitution, presidential elector, and governor of Alabama. He ran as a presidential elector in 1884 for Grover Cleveland and in 1896 he supported William Jennings Bryan for president. He was a delegate to the 1901 Alabama Constitutional Convention. He supported white supremacy. He wanted to "purify and elevate the political conditions in Alabama."[1]

Former Governor Jelks at Baltimore Democratic Convention 1912

Former Alabama Governor William Dorsey Jelks "was a delegate to the 1912 Democratic [National] Convention in Baltimore that nominated Woodrow Wilson to the presidency."[2] At that convention Jelks was elected national committeeman from Alabama. While a member of the national committee he undertook to have that body declare itself for the temporary organization of the next national convention on the basis of district and not state sovereignty. Jelks was against the practice of allowing any one person in any large state to vote the whole delegation by majority rule as was done in Baltimore. He was ruled down and the ruling forces in the committee did not appeal to him. So he declined to become a candidate for committeeman again.[3] This was his final public political action.[4]

Woodrow Wilson began serving as the twenty-eighth President of the United States in 1913. Wilson was preceded by William Howard Taft and succeeded by Warren G. Harding. Wilson was re-elected in 1916 and began his second term in 1917. The 17th Amendment to the Constitution (1913) established direct election of United States Senators, as well as a means of filling vacant Senate seats. If a vacancy occurs due to a senator's death, resignation, or expulsion, the 17th Amendment allows state legislatures to empower the governor to appoint a replacement to complete the term or to hold office until a special election can take place. Only 5 Alabama US Senators have been appointed since the 17th Amendment – all Democrats. Francis S. White won a U.S. Senate seat from Alabama when (legislatively appointed) Senator Joseph F. Johnston died. White did not run for re-election. Oscar Underwood defeated three challengers in the 1914 election. He would serve from 1915 to 1927. Alabama ratified the 17th Amendment on April 16, 2002.[5] Also in 1914, Archduke Franz Ferdinand, the heir to the Austrian throne, was assassinated which started World War I.[6]

Charles Henderson was Alabama Governor from 1915 to 1919. He was called by some the "business governor" of Alabama. During his administration the principles of economy and efficiency were his faithful guides. In 1906 he was elected to pubic office for the first time, winning a position on the Alabama Railroad Commission. When he assumed the office of Governor in 1915 the state was deeply in debt. With the outbreak of World War I in 1914 the price of cotton dropped and the state's economy was devastated. Within two years the economy turned around and Alabama began to share the nation's wartime prosperity. Henderson was clearly a representative of the conservative wing of the Democratic Party but with openness to some progressive measures.[7]

World War I, Woodrow Wilson, and the Paris Peace Talks

In 1917 Woodrow Wilson was re-elected President of the United States. In England, King George V re-named the House of Saxe-Coburg, becoming the first monarch from the new House of Windsor. Reasons for the change were that the old continental European empires fell; that Great Britain became a stronger world leader; and there was anti-German sentiment associated with the name Saxe-Coburg. The United States entered World War I and joined with European Allies on April 6, 1917, forming the Central Powers.[8]

At war's end in 1918 President Wilson traveled to Paris. Richard Holbrook wrote "… as Wilson arrived in France in December, 1918, he ignited great hopes throughout the world with his stirring Fourteen Points – especially the ground breaking concept of 'self-determination.' Yet

Wilson, often ill-informed or badly prepared for detailed negotiations, seemed vague as to what his own phrase actually meant."[9]

In her book *Paris 1919* Margaret MacMillan discovered that "Where the Poles tended to bring exasperated sighs, even from their supporters, the Czechs basked in general approval. The Poles were dashing and brave, but quite unreasonable; the Rumanians charming and clever, but sadly devious: the Yugoslavs, well, rather Balkan. The Czechs were refreshingly Western. 'Of all the people whom we saw in the course of our journey,' reported an American relief mission that traveled through the former Austria-Hungary in January, 1919, 'the Czechs seemed to have the most ability and common sense, the best organization, and the best leaders.'"

The Czech delegates to the Paris Peace Talks included Edvard Beneš, who presented their case to the Supreme Council in February of 1919. He was impressive, especially to the American council membership delegation. Beneš did much to build up the Czechoslovak army in Siberia and was recognized as a skilled organizer as well as a Czech freedom fighter. Beneš did most of the presentation to the council. Paired with President Tomas Masaryk, a new Czechoslovak state would emerge from the Paris peace talks and be recognized by the international community. [10]

According to the United States State Department profile information "President Woodrow Wilson and the United States played a major role in the establishment of the original Czechoslovak state on October 28, 1918. President Wilson's 14 Points, including the right of ethnic groups to form their own states, were the basis for the union of the Czechs and Slovaks. Tomas Masaryk, the father of the state and its first President, visited the United States during World War I and worked with U.S. officials in developing the basis of the new country. Masaryk used the U.S. Constitution as a model for the first Czechoslovak."[11] The Austro-Hungarian Empire fell and Prague became capital of an independent Czechoslovakia and Prague Castle became the seat of the first president of Czechoslovakia, Tomas Masaryk.[12] On November 3 World War I ended and on November 12 the last Hapsburg Emperor was overthrown.[13]

Thomas E. Kilby served as Alabama Governor from 1919 to 1923. In 1911 he organized the Alabama Pipe and Foundry Company. Earlier, in

1902 he became president of the City National Bank of Anniston. He benefitted from a brief period of post-WW I prosperity in 1919, but he also inherited large bond indebtedness, and had to deal with postwar inflation and increased cost of state services.[14]

By 1920 the population of Alabama was 2,348,174. Its white population stood at 1,447,031 and its African-American citizens at 900,652. The state remained rural with an urban population of 509,317, rural at 1,838,857. Cotton production in bales was at 718,163 and corn production in bushels was at 43,699,100. The number of manufacturing establishments grew to 3,654.[15]

The journal *Coal Men of America* listed Harold Sanson, Bill Cabaniss's maternal grandfather, as general manager of the Cahaba Southern Coal Mining Company. He held a similar position with Warrior-Pratt Coal Company. He had been in the coal business for 16 years, and was born in East Orange, New Jersey in 1876, according to the journal.[16]

The *Insurance Year Book* of 1920-1921 shows officers of the thirteen year-old Protective Life Insurance Company in Birmingham as W.D. Jelks, President; W.W. Crawford, Treasurer; and Ben Lacy as company secretary. W.G. Harrison was listed as its medical director, and the Cabaniss & Cabaniss law firm listed as company attorney. Directors included in the list were R. Jemison, Jr., Jelks H. Cabaniss, and E.H. Cabaniss. At that time the insurance company had operations in Alabama, Mississippi, and Texas.[17] Another article published in 1920 identified E.H. Cabaniss as a director and general counsel for the Protective Life Insurance Company. It also described him as a Democrat, a Baptist, and a member of the Southern, Roebuck, Commercial and Birmingham Country clubs.[18] Bill Cabaniss – paternal grandson of E.H. Cabaniss and great-nephew of W.D. Jelks – would serve on the Protective board some fifty years later.

WARREN G. HARDING BECAME THE TWENTY-NINTH President of the United States and served from 1921 to 1923. He was a Republican. The twentieth century music era began roughly around 1923.

The politically conscious, anti-romantic generation of musicians that appeared after the First World War was led by Czech composer Bohuslav Martinů (1890 - 1959). He was a pupil of Josef Suk, but he developed fully under the influence of his next teacher, Albert Rousell in Paris, where he lived from 1923 to 1941. After that he moved to the United States, where he became extremely well-known. The final years of his life were spent in Italy and Switzerland, where he died.[1] Music is representative of an era of international political, philosophical, social, cultural, and economic life. The study of music, its timing, its style, all in relation to what preceded and followed it, provides insight into the workings of the international or regional area.

In Alabama, William W. Brandon served as governor from 1923 to 1927. It was said in 1922 when he was running for governor that he was so popular that virtually no one wanted to run against him. And when he left office he was still as popular as when he entered. His modest accomplishments as governor were made possible by the general prosperity of the nation. He inherited a substantial debt from Thomas E. Kilby, his predecessor. But his administration, through a combination of good economic fortunes and strict fiscal restraints, passed on a small surplus to the next governor.[2] Republican Calvin Coolidge became the thirtieth President of the United States on August 2, 1923 at the death of President Warren G. Harding. He was elected on his own in 1924 and served until March 4, 1929. For the most part Coolidge continued the conservative economic and small government policies of Harding. But Coolidge improved on them and reduced the size of the Federal budget and government. This conservative growth period in America followed nineteen years of progressive government which reached its apex in 1919. In the 1924 national election, Calvin Coolidge's Democratic opponent was the highly respected John W. Davis. Davis was Solicitor General and the Ambassador to the Court of St. James in the Woodrow

Wilson administration. Davis, like Coolidge, was a conservative. Davis was the last conservative to run in a presidential election as a Democrat.[3]

University of Alabama in Rose Bowl

In 1926 the University of Alabama football team, the first southern team to be honored with an invitation to the Rose Bowl, defeated the University of Washington on January 1.[4] In 1927 Bibb Graves was elected Governor of Alabama. He would serve until 1931.[5] His alliance with the Ku Klux Klan helped him in 1926 to win election but it tarnished the reputation he later earned as a liberal. Earlier in his political career he allied himself with progressives who supported the policies of reform governor Joseph F. Johnston, and he joined the former governor in opposing ratification of Alabama's 1901 constitution.[6]

Sons of Edward H. Cabaniss and Martha Jelks Cabaniss

Robert Wright Cabaniss (first son of E.H. Cabaniss and Martha Jelks) died on March 31, 1927 when his Navy PN-9 plane crashed near Navassa Island in the West Indies. He was Naval Aviator #36. Cabaniss Field in Corpus Christi, TX was named for him on July 9, 1941. He held the "Order of the Bust of Bolivar," an honor from Venezuela. He was survived by wife Martha Cabaniss of Coronado, California and a daughter, Juliet Harmon Cabaniss, wife of Lt. A.D.A. Crawford, Jr., USNR.[7]

William Jelks Cabaniss, Sr. (the fifth and youngest son of E.H. Cabaniss and Martha Jelks) graduated from the University of Alabama in 1928 with an A.B. degree.[8] The convict lease system ended in Alabama in the same year.[9] The "Hoovercrat Bolt" occurred in Alabama. It was during the bitter and divisive 1928 presidential election between Protestant Republican Herbert Hoover and Catholic Democrat Al Smith that Alabama Democratic U.S. Senator Thomas Heflin and Birmingham attorney and gubernatorial aspirant Hugh Locke supported Hoover. In 1929 an Alabama State Democratic Executive Committee battle for control of the party's machinery took place. Senator Heflin and Judge Locke were ousted as retribution for their parts in leading the bolt.[10] Their expulsion was considered mandatory for the two politicians whose actions placed solid Democrat control and white supremacy at risk.[11]

Herbert Hoover, a Republican, was elected the thirty-first President of the United States and the stock market crashed in 1929. Bill Cabaniss's father, William Jelks Cabaniss, Sr. was hired by the Swann Chemical Company and was trained as an apprentice for six months in office and plant administration in their Anniston, Alabama facility. After the training period he worked in Birmingham where he held several positions between 1930 and 1935.[12] Alabama, though growing in population, was still a rural state in 1930. The state's rural population was 1.9 million and urban 744 thousand. Cotton, still king, reached 1,312,963 bales of output. Corn production was 35,683,874 bushels and manufacturing establishments registered were 2,848.[13]

BENJAMIN M. MILLER SERVED AS ALABAMA'S GOVERNOR during the worst years of the Great Depression, from 1931 to 1935. Miller declared himself a candidate for governor in the Democratic primary and gave opposition to the waning Ku Klux Klan and "loose spending" governor, Bibb Graves.[1] Former Alabama governor William Dorsey Jelks died on December 15, 1931 of a heart attack in Eufaula at age 76 and is buried in Fairview Cemetery.[2]

Nine black youths, later known as the Scottsboro Boys, were arrested on March 25, 1931 in Paint Rock and jailed in Scottsboro, the Jackson County seat. They were charged with raping two white women on a freight train from Chattanooga. The sheriff had to protect them from mob violence that night. Within a month, eight of the nine were sentenced to death. Based on questionable evidence, the convictions by an all-white jury generated international outrage.[3]

In 1933, Franklin D. Roosevelt became the thirty-second President of the United States. William J. Cabaniss [Sr] (28) married Florence Sanson (22) on June 14, 1933 at Church of the Advent in Birmingham.[4] The Tennessee Valley Authority was created to develop resources of the poor Appalachian South, including large parts of north Alabama.[5] In 1934 the Bankhead Cotton Control Act, sponsored by Alabama Senator John Bankhead, Jr., was passed, raising the price of cotton by limiting the amount a farmer could market.[6]

Bibb Graves became Governor of Alabama for the second time in 1935. He served until 1939. During the campaign for his second term Bibb coined the phrase "Big Mules" for his big business enemies. Conservatives in and out of the legislature had vigorously opposed Graves's policies. Graves appointed women to important state government positions and also appointed labor leaders, both actions unprecedented in that era. He refused business demands to use the National Guard to break strikes, something that had been done by progressive governors. He demonstrated strong support for President Franklin D. Roosevelt and the New Deal.[7] Lawrence County native Jesse Owens won his first gold medal on August 3 at the 1936 Olympics in

Berlin, Germany. Owens went on to win four gold medals in Berlin, but German leader Adolf Hitler snubbed the star athlete because he was black.[8] King Edward VIII abdicated in the same year. His brother became King George VI and was the British monarch between 1936 and 1952. Joan Sanson Cabaniss, Bill Cabaniss's older sister, was born on July 7, 1936 in Birmingham.[9] Martha Frazier Jelks Cabaniss died on May 13, 1936 in Birmingham, Jefferson County, Alabama. She was the maternal grandmother of Bill Cabaniss, daughter of J.W.D. Jelks; wife of Edward H. Cabaniss.[10] William B. Bankhead, father of actress Tallulah Bankhead, was elected Speaker of the United States House of Representatives.[11]

In 1937 Franklin D. Roosevelt was elected to his second term. In Alabama a state sales tax was instituted to help fund education[12] and Alabama Senator Hugo Black was appointed by President Franklin Roosevelt to the U.S. Supreme Court.[13] William Jelks Cabaniss, Jr. was born on July 11, 1938 in Birmingham.

Trouble in Central Europe

By September Germany, Britain, France, and Italy signed the Munich Pact, giving Adolf Hitler the right to invade and claim Czechoslovakia's border areas.[14] In less than twenty years since its founding, Czechoslovakia was an operating democracy in central Europe. Among the new nations created in Paris in 1919 Czechoslovakia "was politically and economically the most advanced of the successor states. It was genuinely democratic and had a standard of living comparable to Switzerland's. It maintained a large army, much of whose excellent equipment was of domestic Czech design and manufacture; it had military alliance with France and the Soviet Union."[15] Czechoslovakia had been faithful to the concept of the League of Nations and to the ideals of democracy. Not only did she have an alliance with France, she had great friendships with Great Britain and the United States of America. Yet all of that went for naught in September, 1938 when German Chancellor Adolf Hitler, under threat of war, convinced Czechoslovakia's friends and allies to cede her to Germany.[16] The Munich Agreement allowed Germany to annex areas of Czechoslovakia populated by ethnic Germans and Germany gained control of industrial Sudetenland. In 1939 Germany recognized the independence of

Slovakia, thus eliminating Czechoslovakia. The remaining territories became protectorates. The longer-term effect was the loss of freedom and the eventual communistic system takeover in 1948. Czechoslovakia, created with the aid of American President Woodrow Wilson, would not be free from 1938 to 1989.

Alabama Moves On

On July 2, 1939 William Jelks Cabaniss, Jr. was baptized at the Church of the Advent (Episcopal) in Birmingham, Jefferson County, Alabama by The Rev. John C. Turner. Frank M. Dixon became Governor of Alabama and served from 1939 to 1943. From the Tidewater area of Virginia, but born in California, Dixon was chief executive of Alabama during the years of World War II. A graduate of the law school at the University of Virginia, Dixon married Juliet Perry of Greene County, Alabama. After law school he accepted a position with prestigious Birmingham attorney Captain Frank S. White and his law firm. Dixon managed White's run for the U.S. Senate. He then resigned from the firm to join the fighting in World War I as a volunteer with the Royal Canadian Air Corps. Shot down over Soissons, France, he was seriously wounded. Returning to Birmingham he began his own law firm and entered politics. As a Democratic Party loyalist, he warned against "bolting" the party to vote for Herbert Hoover.[17]

Catherine Hood Caldwell, Bill Cabaniss's wife, was born on March 11, 1940.

Alabama Still a Rural State in 1940

Alabama's population rose in 1940 to 2,832,961. Despite Birmingham's business and industrial growth, Alabama continued to be a rural state with an urban population of 855,941 and rural population of 1,977,020. Cotton production in bales was 772,711 and corn production in bushels rose to 31,028,109. Number of manufacturing establishments stood at a paltry 2,052.[18]

In 1941 FRANKLIN DELANO ROOSEVELT BEGAN HIS THIRD term as President of the United States. Bill Cabaniss's younger sister Florence Pierson Cabaniss, was born on December 18, 1941 in Birmingham.[1] Alabama had new or expanded military bases in Montgomery, Mobile, Selma, and Anniston, and munitions plants in Huntsville and Childersburg,[2] and training of African American military pilots, the "Tuskegee Airmen," was underway.[3]

The light cruiser *U.S.S. Birmingham* was launched, but not commissioned, on March 20, 1942 at the Newport News [Virginia] Shipbuilding and Dry Dock Company by Mrs. Cooper Green, wife of the president of the Birmingham City Commission.[4] On March 24, 1942 a referendum was held in and around Mountain Brook Estates in Shades Valley of Jefferson County, Alabama. Should that area incorporate as a city?

Mountain Brook

Residents in approximately 1,000 homes voted not only to incorporate into a city but also voted to name it Mountain Brook. Because the state legislature was not in session, organizers had to obtain signatures from property owners. Four qualified property owners for every forty acres were required. One year earlier public meetings were held to discuss whether to remain an unincorporated area of Jefferson County, allow annexation into the city of Birmingham, or incorporation. At least six named areas were considered in the new town limits of Mountain Brook – Colonial Hills, Mountain Brook, Mountain Brook Estates, Country Club Gardens, Crestline Heights, and parts of Redmont Park.[5]

Charles F. Zukoski, Jr. was elected the new city's mayor on May 19, 1942. Five city aldermen were elected, one of whom was William J. Cabaniss, Sr., Bill Cabaniss's father. Within another year Cabaniss, Sr. would be serving on the newly commissioned *U.S.S. Birmingham* in the Pacific theatre.

The idea of a planned community in the Shades Valley area of Jefferson County (originally Blount County) came from Robert Jemison, Jr. Jemison believed that many hard-working people wanted a home in "a locality supremely different from the ordinary city lot for the fulfillment of their ideals of a home place."[6] Jemison's plan was quite detailed and highly selective, in not only the homes to be built, but the types of businesses that would be located there. This was being talked about as early as 1926 when Jemison called a meeting of the stockholders of Mountain Brook Estates for August 30 at his development company's office. It took many years before the legal incorporation of the Mountain Brook area.

The financial crisis of the 1930s set back many homeowners and business owners – many lost their homes. But in 1942 the long process of incorporation was finalized.[7] Mountain Brook would become the home of many of Birmingham's wealthiest business leaders and would endure political approbation for any of its residents seeking statewide or national office.

If wealth was notorious, the town's part-time resident, Al Capone, sought little notoriety. Mountain Brook was a convenient half-way point between Chicago and Miami for the famed mobster. Capone either purchased or rented a stone house in English Village on Cahaba Road. Some say his body guards could be seen peering out the upstairs windows with rifles.[8]

World War II and Alabama

In 1943 Chauncey M. Sparks was Governor of Alabama at the height of World War II. Sparks inherited full employment and a surplus in the state treasury from his predecessor. Like so many of his contemporaries, Sparks was an opponent of "federal encroachments on the rights of the states, particularly in such domestic affairs as race relations."[9] The *U.S.S. Birmingham* was commissioned on January 29, 1943 and after her shakedown cruise the ship headed for the Mediterranean on June 2, 1943.[10]

The first oil well in Alabama was discovered on January 2, 1944. The State of Alabama had granted Hunt Oil Company a permit to drill the A.R. Jackson Well No. #1 near Gilbertown in Choctaw County.[11] In the *Battle of Leyte Gulf*, October 23-26, 1944 in the Philippines, World War

II, Cabaniss's father was serving on the *U.S.S. Birmingham* when it was heavily damaged in an explosion of the aircraft carrier *U.S.S. Princeton.* After the battle the *U.S.S. Birmingham* headed for repairs at San Francisco.[12]

Bill Cabaniss, his sister Joan, and their mother, boarded a train in Birmingham for northern California to meet up with Bill, Sr. Bill was six years old. The family was quartered in a Quonset hut at the San Francisco Naval Shipyard (Mare Island) until the *U.S.S. Birmingham* was ready to be re-deployed.[13] The United States Navy, seeing the need for a shipbuilding and repair facility on the west coast during World War II, acquired a private, commercial shipbuilding facility in 1940 and renamed it Hunters Point Naval Shipyard. Later it was renamed Treasure Island Naval Shipyard Hunters Point Annex. Once the *U.S.S. Birmingham* was re-deployed with Bill Cabaniss, Sr. aboard, the family returned by train to Birmingham. Repaired and refitted, the *U.S.S. Birmingham* became part of the engagement in the *Battle of Okinawa* between April 1 and June 22, 1945.

President Franklin Delano Roosevelt died while in office and Vice President Harry S. Truman became the thirty-third President on April 12, 1945. On President Truman's order, the United States bombed Hiroshima and Nagasaki on August 6 and 9, ending World War II.[14] On August 30, 1945 the *Birmingham News* published a picture of William J. Cabaniss Sr., who had been awarded the Bronze Star. The article mentioned that Cabaniss was the assistant executive officer of the *U.S.S. Birmingham* when it was struck by a Japanese suicide plane at Okinawa.[15]

The University of Alabama Medical School moved to Birmingham from Tuscaloosa in 1945[16] and the years between 1945 and 1989 became the Communist Era in Czechoslovakia.[17]

The end of World War II brought prosperity to the United States of America and made Alabama more affluent. According to some historians, as poor white Alabamians made positive economic strides they began to see the federal government less as their savior and more as an enemy of their autonomy. On the national scene, Republicans had most often held the presidency while Democrats consistently controlled Congress. In Alabama, however, Democrats continued to hold the governor's chair and large majorities in the legislature.[18]

In 1947 when Democrat James E. Folsom became Governor of Alabama (1947-1951 and 1955-1959) he challenged the Big Mule Coalition of planters and businessmen that controlled state government, and he attempted to extend the fruits of democracy to blacks and women. Folsom addressed some of Alabama's most pressing problems during his terms in office. His personal weaknesses, however, left him short of promise. And race was quickly becoming the dominant issue in Alabama state politics.[19]

Alabama's Hank Williams signed a recording contract in 1947 with MGM and became a regular on *The Louisiana Hayride* radio program.[20]

Czechoslovakia Ignored Again

Soviet leader Joseph Stalin's agents carried out a coup in Prague in 1948. He replaced Czechoslovakian communist leaders with those of his own choosing. U.S. President Harry Truman, not wanting another war, did not consider Czechoslovakia a big enough issue to justify war. Britain's Prime Minister Winston Churchill had seen the necessity of standing up to Adolf Hitler when the Czechs were forced to give up the Sudetenland in 1938, but no one took up the cause [for a free Czechoslovakia] in 1948. NATO drew a line down the middle of Europe.[21] " … America had no definite military commitment to defend Europe [after World War II]. With successive blows, Stalin made it [an American military commitment] unavoidable. … Czechoslovakia had a mixed government. [General George C.] Marshal considered it part of the Soviet bloc. … On February 1948 he [Stalin] sent his foreign minister, V.A. Zorin to Prague. The next day twelve non-communist [officials] submitted their resignations. After five days of crisis, a new government emerged and the country was a satellite [of the Soviet Union]. The United States Ambassador, Laurence Steinhardt, thought the Czechs might have resisted, like the Finns and the Iranians. He blamed the cowardice of President Beneš and Foreign Minister [Jan] Masaryk [son of Tomas Masaryk]. "But the lack of a forceful American policy was likewise a factor, and tempted Stalin further. On 24 June [1948] Stalin blocked access to the Western zones of Berlin, and cut off their electricity."[22] Others believe that Jan Masaryk "fell to his death from his office window after being almost certainly pushed by communist thugs."[23]

"The initial investigation [of Jan Masaryk's death] by the [Czech] Ministry of the Interior stated that he had committed suicide by jumping out of the window, although for a long time it has been believed by some that he was murdered by the nascent Communist government. (There were others in the country that put it thus: 'Jan Masaryk was a very tidy man. He was such a tidy man that when he jumped he shut the window after himself.') In a second investigation taken in 1968 during the Prague Spring, Masaryk's death was ruled an accident." A third investigation in the early 1990s after the Velvet Revolution concluded that it had been a murder.[24]

February 25, 1948 the Communist Party seized power in Czechoslovakia after a coup d'etat.[25]

Dixiecrats

Democratic President Harry S. Truman's support for an integrated military and other civil rights programs was not favored by Alabama voters. In the post-World War II election, Alabama supported South Carolina's Strom Thurmond. Democrats were losing their grip on Alabama. Thurmond, the Dixiecrat States' Rights Party candidate but running as a Democrat, won in the 1948 Presidential election in the Deep South states of Alabama, Mississippi, Louisiana, and South Carolina. Truman won Georgia. The "Solid South" of Democrats ended. On July 17 the Dixiecrat Convention assembled in Birmingham, with over 6,000 delegates from across the South attending. They selected Strom Thurmond as their candidate. Democratic President Truman was not even on the ballot in Alabama in 1948.[26]

Republicans in Alabama were known as "Post Office" Republicans.[27] The Alabama Republican Party Chairman was Claude O. Vardaman. "For decades the Grand Old Party had existed only to distribute patronage when Republicans held the White House or to furnish delegates at the party's national conventions. These entrenched leaders did not seek out new converts during the late 1940s even as the size of the electorate expanded for the first time since after the Civil War. New Republicans would make a powerful statement when Dwight D. Eisenhower ran for president."[28]

WILLIAM JELKS CABANISS, JR.

President Harry S. Truman took office on January 20, 1949 after winning election on his own. The Korean War began in 1950 and would continue until 1953. The population of Alabama in 1950 totaled 3.061 million people. The ratio of white to black citizens was two to one. The state was still rural with 1.228 million urban residents and 1.833 million rural.[29]

Cabaniss Chickens

On May 21, 1950, eleven-year old William Jelks Cabaniss, Jr. was confirmed at the Cathedral Church of the Advent in Birmingham, Alabama by Episcopal Church Bishop C.C.J. Carpenter.[30] Cullom Walker, a childhood friend, remembers that in the 1950s Bill Cabaniss raised chickens. One day a neighbor's dog killed all of Bill's chickens. "Dad had taken me hunting, and we came back after the trip. We went down to the chicken coop and found this dog killing my chickens. I looked at the dog's collar. It had Charles Gaines's name, a nearby neighbor, on the tag. I was furious. I didn't go to my neighbor, I could have killed the dog right then and there. My dad calmed me down." Cabaniss's father intervened to prevent a bad situation.[31]

Francis Crockard, another boyhood friend, remembers Cabaniss's daring. When Bill was about 12 years old and Francis 14, they went hunting with Mr. Cabaniss and a neighbor. Crockard's father didn't go because it was cold, about 23 degrees. The neighbor was Mr. Alfred Shook. Shook and Cabaniss, Sr., at the campsite were talking to each other about how soft and weak young people were. Crockard told the adults that he and Bill were tough and could prove it. Crockard said that "we told them we would take twenty dollars from them and run naked (in 23 degree coldness) and jump into the nearby lake. We did it, but it was a big mistake. But we got the twenty dollars. But I believe Mr. Cabaniss was scared because he thought we would freeze to death or maybe he was worried about what Mrs. Cabaniss and my [Crockard's] mother would say when they learned of it."[32]

Republicans in the U.S. House and Senate in 1950

"In 1950 there were no Republican [U.S.] Senators from the South and only two Republican representatives out of 105 in the southern [U.S.] House [of Representatives] delegation."[33]

The Swearing In Ceremony
L-R Catherine Cabaniss; Bill Cabaniss; Secretary of State Colin Powell
December, 2003

U.S. Senate Campaign Luncheon
Judge Robert Bork and Bill Cabaniss
Dothan, Alabama 1990

Daughters of Bill and Catherine Cabaniss
Mary and Frances Cabaniss
U.S. Senate Campaign Rally, 1990

L-R: Henry Kabat, Gabriela Kabat, Catherine Cabaniss,
Father John, and William J. Cabaniss, Jr. Others unidentified.
Prague, 2005.

Celebration at the U.S. Embassy Residence, Prague, Czech Republic
Poet James Ragan, Mrs. Ragan & Family with Catherine Cabaniss
July 4, 2004
Cabaniss Family Album Photo

Mr. & Mrs. Zdenek Klezel with Catherine Cabaniss
Reception at the U.S. Embassy Residence, Prague, Czech Republic 2005
Zdenek Klezl Photo

William Lobkowicz at Nelahozeves, Czech Republic
At the time of the Velvet Revolution he was in the Real Estate
Business in Boston, Massachusetts. He returned to Czech Republic afterwards
to reclaim his family's assets.

Bill Cabaniss and President George H. W. Bush
1990

Life-long Friends

L-R: Wilmer Poynor, Walter Evans, Andy Strickland, Walter Shackelford,
Billy Hulsey, Peter Lowe, Lathrop Smith, Bill Cabaniss, Jimbo Smith,
Thomas Boulware, Fred Smith, Adrian Bewley, Corey Jackson

Bob Shepherd

Cullom Walker

Borden Burr

Herb Sklenar, Ambassador Bill Cabaniss, Frank Young
At Meeting of the Birmingham Committee on Foreign Relations
January 11, 2005
Harold Williams, Balch & Bingham Photo

Precision Grinding Fishing Catch
Bill Cabaniss, Fourth from Left
Panama City, Florida, circa 1980

Part Three – Integrity, Politics, and Personal Diplomacy

The personal integrity of William Jelks Cabaniss, Jr. was developed from his childhood. His principled approach to conducting commercial business was well-respected by his commercial peers. At a relatively young age he held seats on the boards of directors of several corporations and charity organizations. His integrity never took a back seat when he entered the Alabama House of Representatives and Senate. His word was solid. His principled and practical approach to politics was and is greatly admired by advocates on both sides of the political spectrum.

RONALD REAGAN ASSUMED THE OFFICE OF PRESIDENT OF the United States on January 20, 1981. The Academy of Country Music selected the musical group *Alabama* from Fort Payne, Alabama as "Vocal Group of the Year" beginning a consecutive five year winner of that award.[1] Bill Cabaniss had served two years in the Alabama House of Representatives by this time trying to "hold the fort" against bad legislation. Former Alabama Republican Party chairman Bill Harris believed that Cabaniss "was frustrated in his first four years in office. Without enough people in the House you cannot get much done. But he impressed people on both sides of the aisle in those first four years. He changed their attitude. He was strategic. It wasn't the bills that he killed or passed, it was the impression he made upon people."[2]

Cabaniss Assessment

The Retirement System of Alabama's (RSA) chief executive David Bronner was well aware of Cabaniss's impact in the state legislature. When Cabaniss came to his organization for information about the real cost of state pension funds, he broke with the typical pattern of questions. Prior to Cabaniss's presence no legislator would ask about cost. "All of a sudden you had a person who cared about the future. Other legislators would ask a question and leave. With tenacity, Cabaniss would go after things he wanted answers to, knowing full well that even if the answer was one he didn't like it would be difficult to convince the Democrats. He was the outsider and the Democrats would say 'Why do you bother with the facts?'"[3]

From House to Senate

Statewide elections in Alabama were coming up in 1982 and Cabaniss began thinking through what he would do. Though frustrated with legislative results and considering dropping out of state politics, he decided that he could better serve Alabama in the state senate and set his plans in that direction. But he was not thinking just of himself. He knew that if the Republican Party was to grow in Alabama new candidates had to be found. Cabaniss knew of a pro-business Democrat in northern Alabama and he approached the man to change party affiliation. But the man's family was so anti-Republican that a change of party would cause family problems. This was another example of the anti-Republican mindset lingering since 1874.[4]

Alabama State Senate Candidate Bill Cabaniss and his Campaign Manager Peggy Balliet
Mountain Brook, Alabama, 1982
Peggy Balliet Photo

Cabaniss ran for the state senate in 1982 and so did Ann Bedsole. They both won in their districts. In the Birmingham area another Republican won a senate district, Spencer Bachus. But Republican candidates across the state did not fare well in the 1982 election. Less than a handful won their elections out of more than fifty candidates. *The Birmingham News* wrote that Alabama Republicans on the morning after must have been saying "Chin up" to each other because "GOP candidates generally took it on the chin Tuesday in county races all over the state. … All [GOP] losers were soundly beaten."[5] Nationally, eight southern GOP Congressional House seats were lost that same year. The loss was not attributed as antipathy toward President Reagan as much as hostility directed at the Republican Party. "When you get into a party contest, Republicans lose," said a strategist.[6]

Reaganomics

President Reagan and his economic plan for the nation – "Reaganomics" – had a tough time in congressional debates because the House was Democratic and the Senate Republican. The national mid-term election of 1982 added almost two dozen more Democrats to the House which was already in the majority. At least the mid-term election losses of the Republican Party were smaller than previous off-year elections for the party of a newly elected president. Both parties could claim some level of victory, citing different factors. Republican losses were less than expected and Democratic gains though not huge were still gains. It was the Republican-led conservative coalition that got Reagan's economic program through that Congress. Rebuilding the coalition and rebuilding the Republican Party were essential to keep Reagan's plan operating.[7]

Oscar Adams, an African American attorney from Birmingham, was elected to the Alabama Supreme Court in 1982 after being appointed to that position by Governor "Fob" James in 1980. The 1982 election was a historical marker, making Adams the first African American elected to a statewide constitutional office in Alabama.[8]

It was an odd political year. Emory Folmar, the Republican mayor of Montgomery, was defeated by George Wallace in his 1982 run for the governor's office. *The Birmingham News* endorsed Folmar over Wallace.[9] But Democratic Speaker Joe McCorquodale was defeated in the Democratic primary by Wallace. Jim Martin was the last Republican candidate for Alabama governor and that was in 1966.

In the State Senate

Cabaniss won his senatorial election and was anxious to get to work in the senate. He planned to chat with Lt. Governor Bill Baxley about committees on which he could serve. Cabaniss wanted assignments on Business & Labor, Commerce & Transportation, and Finance & Taxation. Cabaniss also wanted to act quickly to move a budget isolation measure forcing the Legislature to pass a state budget in the early days of the session. Cabaniss considered it the most important act that the Legislature must do. Cabaniss, Bedsole, and Bachus would become the three Republicans in a Senate of thirty-five members. That there were three Republican senators elected was significant, but they were not the first Republicans elected to the state senate. Leland Childs of Mountain Brook was elected to the state senate in 1966 and holds the distinction of being the first Republican elected since Reconstruction. [10]

Cabaniss believed that the 1982 election was a watershed event in Alabama politics because the so-called "Coalition" took over the legislative arena. It was a coalition of self-interest politics that was pro-union and anti-business. [11] It was enough that the executive branch of Alabama government had shifted from the race-baiting mouthpiece of George Wallace to an anti-business rhetoric when race became less and less an issue in the state. Now the Legislature would lock in its policies based purely on the self-interest of its coalition members and to the ultimate detriment of the economic benefit of the state and its people.

When Cabaniss first entered office in 1978, so did Governor Forrest "Fob" James. A Democrat at the time, James was a businessman like Cabaniss. Cabaniss also had a pro-business friend, if not an ally, in the House in the person of its Speaker, Joe McCorquodale. Cabaniss believed that it was possible to make changes in the way the Legislature operated and make changes in its approach to state economics. But the results of the 1982 election when Democrat Bill Baxley became Lt. Governor, Tom Drake the Speaker of the House, and George Wallace once again governor, things looked dim for any meaningful economic reform. Paul Hubbert, the executive director of the teachers union – the Alabama Education Association – engineered great gains in both the House and the Senate for Democrats. It was going to be an even more formidable hill to climb for the few Republican and Democratic conservatives. Making matters worse was the fact that Governor George Wallace was physically incapable of conducting his office in any efficient manner. The assassination attempt on his life greatly limited Wallace's mobility and removed much of his tenacity and energy to govern as strenuously as he had in earlier years. Wallace may have been weakened but he was not dead. He did need assistance running the state's executive suite. His political friends were there to help.

Re-districting

Prior to the Alabama general elections in November, 1982, a three-judge federal panel was examining the efforts of the Alabama Legislature at redrawing districts in compliance with federal law. This law was based on the 1980 census. The panel cited problems in the reapportionment plan for some districts, including one in Jefferson County and several districts in Alabama's Black Belt. The charge to the state Legislature by the judges was to remedy the cited district problems by early 1983 or face another set of elections for the fall of 1983. The legislative committee assigned to remedy those few situations decided to make changes statewide instead.

The legislative committee's revised reapportionment plan had as two of its goals to keep county lines as boundaries to serve as district lines, and to structure the plan such that re-elections statewide would not be needed. The new plan needed to satisfy the federal panel, the court plaintiffs who had filed suit against the original plan, the United States Department of Justice, and the 140-member state Legislature. The suit was filed, according to *The Birmingham News*, by an un-named "group of blacks" claiming that the original plan did not pay sufficient attention to county lines and other natural political boundaries. Without the suit the federal authorities most likely would not have become involved in the reapportionment debate.[12]

In its effort to provide for re-districting for both the House and the Senate after the 1980 census, the Alabama Legislature acted on October 26, 1981. That plan was objected to by the state's attorney general following the suit made by African American constituents. The attorney general cited an article under the federal Voting Rights Act as reason for the objection. On June 1, 1982 during a special session, the Legislature created a re-apportionment plan that was litigated and held to be invalid. Thus legislators elected that year were to serve only one year of the normal four-year term. It was not until February 23, 1983 that the Legislature again re-districted itself (after the three-judge panel had cited the original flaws). This plan was cleared with the Attorney General in advance of passage and subsequently approved by that three-judge panel in April. Therefore another election was mandated in the fall of 1983 with those elected serving three years in office of the quadrennial. This re-districting plan stayed in force until 1990.[13] The plan did not sit well in Jefferson County and would affect the 1982 elections of Bill Cabaniss and Spencer Bachus.

The re-districting plan called for Jefferson County to lose one Senate seat and three House seats.[14] Although the legislative committee attempted to create an acceptable plan, it also tried to avoid another election. In the end there would be fewer Republicans, if only one, in the heavily dominated Democratic Senate. Spencer Bachus chose to run for the Alabama House in the fall 1983 elections. Both Cabaniss and Bachus won their new elections as did Ann Bedsole in South Alabama. Bedsole noted that in her very first year in the senate, partisanship was high and it was obvious that the Democratic majority was trying to get rid of one Republican during the floor debate on re-districting. Once that issue passed, partisanship began to wane.[15]

ANN BEDSOLE WAS ONE OF THREE REPUBLICANS ELECTED TO the Alabama Senate in 1982, and she was the first woman in Alabama to be elected to that chamber. There was opposition to her Senate membership. Someone said, according to Bedsole, "We just don't want women in the Senate." The remark was made by a senator who was mad with Bedsole simply for being a woman. "There was only one other senator that was disrespectful, but he was disrespectful to everybody. He was a bully. He and [Senator] Larry Dixon [of Montgomery] had some exchanges on the senate floor."[1] But Bedsole said that she expected to be treated equally.[2] When Bedsole showed up in the House in 1979 she found that one of the committees she was assigned to held its meetings in a Men's Room at the State House. It was a change of venue specifically intended to block Bedsole's committee participation. Part jokingly and partly serious, Bedsole said that she felt "honored" to be thought of so much by her male House peers.

Alabama Republicans Gain Momentum

On January 9, 1983 the Alabama Republicans re-elected Bill Harris as state chairman. Harris's opponent, a pharmacist, offered to do the job without pay. But Harris won that election due in no small part to the support of the state's two Republican U.S. Congressmen, Bill Dickinson of Montgomery and Jack Edwards of Mobile.[3] Two days later the recently elected Legislature and the administration of the new governor-elect got an early start on their work. The two big issues that dominated their discussions were the almost depleted state treasury and the possibility of another election for all the members of the Legislature. Although another election cycle loomed over them at this time, the decision would not be made for another month. At any rate the level of funds in the treasury meant that a legislative pay raise seemed unlikely in that session.[4]

Regardless of any large political or economic issue that might have dominated the session of the Legislature, the operations of the state almost came to a halt with news of the sudden death of University of

Alabama football coach Paul "Bear" Bryant. He died of a heart attack. Just two years earlier in 1981 Bryant became college football's winningest coach at that time with 315 victories.[5]

In the summer of 1985 the City of Montgomery received a great gift from Winton "Red" Blount and his wife Carolyn. At a ground-breaking ceremony, the Blounts, flanked by Governor George Wallace and Montgomery Mayor Emory Folmar, all with shovels in hand, broke ground for the new Alabama Shakespeare Festival theatre. Begun in Anniston years earlier, the Blounts acquired the assets of the festival and moved it to Montgomery. Wallace, true to his beliefs, could not hold back and said "I like the way Red gets a job done. He does great things and pays for them himself."[6]

Once the agreement on re-districting was reached and new elections were mandated, most legislators and new candidates began preparing for the November, 1983 election. A Shelby County attorney and farmer, Frank "Butch" Ellis prepared to run in that election as a Democrat even though he knew that his county was gradually turning Republican.[7] In Montgomery County Democratic State Senator Larry Dixon was preparing again to run for office. Dixon's 1982 election was difficult, but he won. In 1983 Paul Hubbert, the AEA executive director, told Dixon one day in the Capitol Rotunda that he needn't bother running again because Dixon would never receive the Democratic Party's nomination for that district.

Hubbert, according to Dixon, said that "I run the Democratic Party and you will not be the nominee." So when Hubbert selected someone else, Dixon switched to the Republican Party. There was virtually nothing held in common politically between Dixon, the liberal Democratic leadership, and their leader Lt. Governor Bill Baxley who practiced traditional Alabama politics. A conservative at heart and a successful campaigner, Dixon took out an advertisement in the local newspaper saying to the voters that "In November you will have a chance to choose your own representative [to the Alabama Senate]. No one opposed Dixon in the 1983 election."[8] Bill Cabaniss deserves some credit for Dixon's conversion. Cabaniss knew that "Dixon has politics in his blood. Emory Folmar and I were going to make Dixon a Republican. But Larry finally saw the light. He was a tough sell."[9]

Dixon recalled that he "first met Bill in 1978. I was a Democrat, not in spirit, but in a pragmatic sense. You just didn't get elected to anything in Montgomery in 1978 as a Republican. Ann Bedsole, Cabaniss, Parker, and Seibels were nice folks. I tried to make up my mind. There were very few lobbyists back then, not many hired guns. But there were those associations that would approach us. I learned that if Bill Cabaniss went to the [House Chamber] microphone, unlike a lot of other folk, I listened to what he said. The way that Bill discussed a topic was the way I understand. He and I had a common way of looking at things. I started spending more time with him."[10] Dixon and Cabaniss had hit it off immediately. Dixon renamed his new friend "Cabanary," calling him by that moniker frequently. "Cabanary" was better name than the one shouted out in Second Lieutenant Cabaniss's first roll call in the Army.

Years later in an interview with a Czech newspaper reporter, Cabaniss said that even he had learned not to correct someone else's pronunciation of his own name. When he was in Army Airborne boot camp at roll call one day the mustering sergeant yelled "KaBANis." Instead of replying "Here, sir," the young rookie officer retorted "It's KAB-in-iss." Needless to say the sergeant couldn't believe that he was corrected by a rookie. "He called me up front, had me get down on the ground and do 20 push-ups. Throughout the rest of the day, it was 'Get down and gimme 20.' At midnight he had me running laps." [11]

Businessman, civil engineer, and Republican Perry Hand of Gulf Shores, Alabama decided that he would enter the fall special election. He would oppose Senator Jerry Boyington of Fairhope representing Senate District 32 in South Alabama. Ann Bedsole, also from South Alabama, was elected to the Senate in the regular 1982 election and would run again but her district was on the western shore of Mobile Bay. Two Republican state senators from South Alabama would be an impressive display of emerging Republican Party strength as was suggested by Bedsole and three other Republicans winning House races in 1978.

Gerald Dial, the Alabama National Guard brigadier general and former member of the Alabama House as a Democrat, was kicked out of his party because of his consistent, conservative record, not to mention his strident independence and outspokenness. When serving in the House between 1979 and 1981, Dial teamed with Republicans Bill Cabaniss,

Ann Bedsole, V.M. Parker and former Birmingham mayor George Seibels on issues beneficial not to special interest groups or individuals but to the state. When the decision to hold the special 1983 election was announced, Dial decided to run for the State Senate from Clay County as an Independent. His opponent was John Casey who had the strong support of his friend George Wallace. Dial couldn't win his county as a Republican because that name was still anathema there. Larry Dixon of Montgomery County, a county with similar ideological opposition to Republicanism, had nothing to lose by running either as an Independent or a Republican since the Democratic leadership guaranteed him no re-nomination.

Prior to the November, 1983 special election, the newspapers across the state published articles informing the electorate of what they might expect as an outcome of the election. Business leaders were hopeful that more pro-business candidates would be elected to office. Sitting legislative leaders and coalition lobbyists wanted the new Legislature to be more responsive to the people. Using traditional Democratic imagery, House Speaker Tom Drake suggested that the new Legislature would consist of "candidates with broad bases of public support – lawmakers who won't be controlled by small groups of rich businessmen ..."[12]

Even Bill Cabaniss, already an elected state senator in the 1982 election, held low expectations for the election of pro-business voices in the House. "There is still some hope that enough senators with business sympathies will be elected that the strength of the [Democratic] coalition could be dulled in the upper house ..."[13] Joe McCorquodale, no longer House Speaker and out of office, was working with a group known as the *Joint Organization for Business Survival*, a name suggesting that too much coalition control had already had a negative effect on businesses in Alabama.

Bill Cabaniss learned on his first meeting with McCorquodale four years earlier, that the former Speaker was not a diehard, anti-business Democrat. McCorquodale was well aware and critical of the liberal-leaning Democratic coalition which represented the other extreme in an unbalanced government. The in-power political alliance consisted of The *Alabama Education Association*, The *Alabama Labor Council*, The *Alabama Trial Lawyers Association*, and the black *Alabama Democratic Conference*. Even McCorquodale believed that these groups were committed mostly to their memberships and not necessarily to the overall good of the state. [14]

The Coalition

The largest of these coalition groups was the *Alabama Labor Council* with 215,000 members in 1982. Its president, Barney Weeks, ruled the organization from 1957 to October, 1983. A strong force in Alabama politics, two-thirds of its endorsed candidates won in elections in the previous year of 1982. The oldest organization was *Alabama Education Association* (AEA) which was founded in 1858. In 1969 its executive director, Paul Hubbert, merged the AEA with the black teachers association which had a combined membership of 35,000 plus 10,000 retired members, 9,000 support personnel members and five hundred student members by 1983. It was viewed as the most powerful of the four coalition members.

The *Alabama Trial Lawyers Association* (ATLA) was founded to speak for plaintiff lawyers. These attorneys, for the most part, represented individuals and not corporations, thereby promoting and benefiting from an anti-business bias and anti-business legislation. This group and the lawsuits brought forth by its membership against small and large businesses in Alabama was the primary impetus leading Bill Cabaniss to seek public office. Founded in 1952 the ATLA came to political lights in 1982 in the contest over a proposed constitutional amendment which would have barred co-employee lawsuits. Such a lawsuit would have broken the back of frivolous and costly lawsuits that forced business to settle complaints rather than go to trial. The trial lawyers, the local juries, the judiciary, and the general anti-business climate of Alabama all contributed to a self-enriching environment at the expense of business. This mode of operations in Alabama actually benefits bordering states. Businesses, particularly large businesses, refused to consider relocating to and building plants in the state of Alabama because of the existing co-employee law suit option. Tort law needed to change if Alabama was to grow.

The youngest coalition member organization was the *Alabama Democratic Conference* (ADC). It was formed in the 1960s as the black caucus within the Alabama Democratic Party because blacks believed that they were not participating equally in the normal politics of Alabama. The ADC would support black candidates or whites sympathetic to black issues. The Democratic Party was, until the 1980s, a conservative party on race but still rather liberal in spending. The 1980s saw a manifested change in the Democratic Party not only in Alabama but in the Deep South where white Democratic candidates were moderates or liberals and opened the party apparatus to blacks. This coalition of whites and blacks made for strong voting blocs.

In the days preceding the 1983 elections, *The Birmingham News* provided voter information such as definitions of the Democratic Coalition membership.[15] Other newspapers in the state did the same because this was to be an even more important election than that of twelve months earlier. Cabaniss felt fairly secure in his run for [re] election in Mountain Brook, and so did Ann Bedsole in Mobile. Both were now well-known fiscal conservatives in a state that had signs of becoming more conservative as compared with the changing Democratic Party faithful who were abandoning conservative positions and embracing moderate to liberal positions. The shift in political ideology was most notable in the Alabama Democratic Party. The national Democratic Party had been liberal and progressive for years and most of the Deep South states were conservative Democrats or nominal Democrats. Alabama, however, had two New Deal Democratic Senators in John Sparkman and Lister Hill from the late 1940s to the 1960s. But rank-and-file Alabama Democrats were conservative in those years. Now in the late 1970s and 1980s, that was changing. So the 1983 special election was another chance to make change, big change.

Coalition Political Power Increasing

Bill Cabaniss witnessed the increasing power of the Coalition, especially the AEA and its leader Paul Hubbert, in the last years of his term in the House and in his first year in the Senate in calendar year 1983. In the 1982 election the coalition threw its support behind Bill Baxley for Lieutenant Governor. As the legislative year began, the coalition called on the Lt. Governor, the senate's presiding officer, to get its bills passed. There were others in the senate who received election support from the Coalition in 1982 who were friends or allies of Baxley whom he appointed to key senate positions. As such the Coalition exercised control of which bills would get presented for passing. "The best way to indicate their [the Democratic Coalition's] power in the Senate," according to Cabaniss, "is they controlled the special order calendar (of bills up for consideration) every day ... The coalition's priorities went bang, bang, bang."[16]

Many bills submitted by the Coalition were passed by the Senate during the year 1983 and except for those killed by the House, became law. Even the most controversial bills were passed. In all of this Baxley said that as long as he held office he would place his friends and allies in key posts, but made little of suggestions that he had ties to special interest groups. The mechanism of the Senate power structure worked quite efficiently. Democratic Senators elected John Teague of Childersburg as Senate pro-tem. Teague contributed to Baxley's campaign as well as acted as a fund raiser. Teague, unopposed in his own election, received funds from the AEA and the Trial Lawyers Association for a total of $7,000.00. He was elected to the state Democratic Executive Committee in 1983, getting his support from those groups plus the *Alabama Labor Council*. The Rules Committee chairman was Baxley's next appointee.

Charles Bishop, a freshman senator from Jasper, was appointed chair of the Rules Committee, the group that actually controlled the flow of legislation by setting the special order calendar. Receiving no funds from any coalition member group, Bishop was reported to have spent $100,000, mostly of his own money he said, on his election campaign. Baxley then placed Hinton Mitchem of Albertville in charge of recommending state spending as chairman of the Finance and Taxation Committee. Like Teague, Mitchem had no opposition in his campaign race but received $500 from the Trial Lawyers Association. More importantly, perhaps, Mitchem contributed $2,000 to Baxley's campaign and worked in Baxley's campaign. There were other appointments made by Baxley to those senators who contributed to and/or worked in his election campaign.[17]

Cabaniss and Bedsole won their seats again and the Democrats maintained control of the 140-member Legislature. But the big surprise coming out of the mandated re-districting election was the victory of sixteen Republicans and eight Independents. In the House two of the five winning Independent candidates were African American. They aligned with the Democrats and the Coalition. The remaining Independents and Republicans, according to Alabama GOP Executive Director Marty Connors (1985-1988), now had "a base strong enough to stop some of the bills" [pushed by the Coalition]. Connors wasted no time in urging the Republican and Independent winners to work together. There was a voter backlash that helped elect the Republicans and Independents, or the backlash simply caused the handpicked Democratic candidates to lose.[18] The Coalition selected the Democratic candidates, a process that produced this backlash and probably set the stage for a larger backlash in 1986.

Gerald Dial of Clay County won a senate seat as an Independent. Already aligned in the House from 1979 forward, Dial knew he could work with Bill Cabaniss. The Lineville, Alabama native defeated Wallace-backed John Casey of Heflin. Newcomer Perry Hand of Gulf Shores defeated Democrat Senator Jerry Boyington of Fairhope. Dial said that the people spoke "loud and clear. They don't want handpicking, and they don't want special-interest groups."[19] Larry Dixon, who in the 1982 election won a senate seat from Montgomery, ran for his own seat again in 1983 but as a Republican and won.[20] Now there would be four Republican senators in the Alabama Legislature and one conservative-leaning Independent. Shelby County elected Democrat Frank "Butch" Ellis to a senate seat. "I ran as a Democrat … but was becoming Republican. There was a group of conservative Democrats in the Senate and I was one of them. We found ourselves aligned with the Republicans. … That's where I met Bill Cabaniss. I knew who he was but we had never met. We became friends immediately and allies on legislation almost immediately. … People like Cabaniss and Larry Dixon had no place to go. Tort reform became a common cause." Ellis said that Cabaniss was the natural leader of the conservatives and that he was the most humble and modest of people. Cabaniss stressed causes.[21]

Holding a House seat for seventeen years was Vestavia Hills' representative Jabo Waggoner. He lost his seat by only seventy-eight votes. Waggoner had been the second most senior member of the House. A powerful politician, artful legislator, and friend of Bill Cabaniss, Waggoner would change his party affiliation in the future. In the twelve months between the 1982 and 1983 legislative elections Democrats lost fourteen seats overall and Republicans gained five. The Independents went from zero to six.[22]

A touch of irony influenced the 1983 election. Just the year before, George C. Wallace was elected to what would be his final four years as governor. His victory in that election was significant because he pulled together a coalition of rural whites and African Americans. The perception held by many Republicans was that their influence rested mainly among white collar voters and the wealthy. In traditional Democratic fashion Wallace appealed to class differences. In his gubernatorial campaign against former Montgomery mayor Republican Emory Folmar, Wallace talked about "Republicans and how all they had to worry about was mowing their beachfront lawns." Blacks gave Wallace ninety percent of their votes.[23] This turnaround by Wallace (with his new supporters) caused famed historian of the South, C. Vann Woodward, to go speechless.[24] Wallace's election may have had the effect of blunting some potential Republican gains in 1982 and had not the Coalition offended the electorate with its "handpicked" candidates the Wallace-effect might have been sustained.

Senate Conservative Alliance

Governor George C. Wallace called a special session of the Legislature within days of the 1983 election. Perry Hand was sworn in just hours before the session opened. That was when he met Bill Cabaniss for the first time. "There were only four Republicans in the Senate – the Four Musketeers of Cabaniss, Bedsole, Dixon and me [Hand]."[25] One could say that sympathetically there were five when counting Democrat Frank "Butch" Ellis, or six including Dial. Ann Bedsole remarked that during her days in the House the Republicans were referred to as the "Gang of Four" – Bedsole, Cabaniss, V.M. Parker, and George Seibels. But she preferred "Gang of Five" because Gerald Dial could always be counted on.[26] The election of the four Republicans to the House in 1978 was the significant point of re-emergence of the Republican Party in Alabama. Because of their meager number they had no choice but to forge alliances with like-minded Democrats, and they did.

But it was a gradual process and Bill Cabaniss was the person to pull together such an alliance. "We decided that if we knew the rules [of the

Senate] we could do anything. I never did learn the rules," said Ann Bedsole. "In my second term we really knew the rules. Bill was the master ... he knew the rules."[27] On conservative issues he showed an amazing amount of leadership. Cabaniss was the de facto leader of the Republican minority all those years and it was the single issue of tort reform that made an alliance on other political issues possible. Ellis believed that Bill Cabaniss was simply a truthful man. Cabaniss built coalitions around causes, not people. There was a time for cloture on a bill that Cabaniss wanted passed but the bill was held up by Ellis. Cabaniss went to Ellis and promised him that if he voted for cloture he, Cabaniss and the other Republicans, would agree to whatever Ellis wanted on another bill. Cabaniss honored his commitment when the time came. Ellis's own party leaders then accused him of following Cabaniss on anything. Ellis replied that he "would follow Cabaniss off the side of a cliff."[28]

Alabama Political Development

African Americans made significant political progress in 1983. Alabama elected five black senators and nineteen representatives to the House: twenty-four in total out of the 140 legislators. The South, particularly Alabama, was making its contribution for equal access to political offices. New York State had nineteen blacks in its Legislature, Pennsylvania 19, Michigan 17, and Illinois 15. By comparison the State of Georgia had nineteen African American legislators but they were out of a body of 236, not like Alabama's 140.[29]

Legislative Service is for the People of the State

The Alabama Legislature, by virtue of the 1901 Constitution, controls much of what local municipal governments can do. Since the re-districting tried to keep political districts within county-line borders the elected legislators from the counties could act as a decision-making body having control over local issues. After the 1983 special election Bill Cabaniss found himself the lone Republican senator in the Jefferson County/Birmingham legislative delegation. His voice was pro-business, not pro-union. Considering the effects of the election on the county's legislative delegation, an editorial in *The Birmingham News* analyzed the new and changed situation. "The cohesiveness and effectiveness of the delegation in representing Jefferson County should be heightened somewhat by the redistricting which made all members of the delegation answerable in larger measure to Jefferson County voters. But effectiveness will still turn on whether the delegation can resolve petty differences and look to the larger issues which confront the county, the City of Birmingham, and other municipalities."[30]

Cabaniss enjoyed working with his legislative colleagues on both sides of the aisle. There were times of frustration and there were times of joy. He had a way of working with people and had a way of working toward compromise. But under no circumstance would he compromise his principles. Cabaniss and the other Republican legislators agreed that personal interests play no part in politics. For Republicans Bedsole, Hand, Dixon, and Cabaniss, along with Democrat Ellis and Independent Dial, pursuing the best interests of the state was fundamental to their service in the Alabama Legislature.

Between 1984 and 1986 Cabaniss was voted one of five outstanding Alabama state senators by his peers. He would continue to be recognized for outstanding service in his second senatorial term. Edgar Welden, one-time executive director and then chairman of the Alabama Republican Party believes that Bill Cabaniss "was probably the most respected person in the Senate."[31]

RSA's David Bronner and his number one deputy frequently received telephone calls or visits from Cabaniss. Cabaniss was trying to dig into the cost of pension plans for state employees with Bronner. Democrats had ways to hide long term costs to taxpayers in their bills. Cabaniss would have no part of that tactic because to him an indeterminate long-term expense was a deep hole with no accountability. Cabaniss kept probing until he got answers. Once he understood what was involved in a bill, its program, its short and long term costs and its potential benefit to the state, he would then attempt to educate fellow legislators. According to Bronner those legislators did not want to be educated. They had their orders from the Coalition and would stick to it. But Cabaniss was "the big picture person" supported by the details of short and long term costs.[32]

WILLIAM JELKS CABANISS, JR.

The Republican National Convention of 1984

In 1984 the Republican National Convention that re-nominated President Ronald Reagan was held at the Reunion Center in Dallas, Texas between August 20 and August 23.

U.S. Senate Campaign, 1990
Catherine Cabaniss, Bill Cabaniss, and former United States President Ronald Reagan

Bill Cabaniss was a member of the Alabama Delegation. Alabama Republican Party chairman, Bill Harris, was Reagan's sergeant-at-arms. Harris eventually relocated to Washington, D.C. and became the national party's official manager for its quadrennial conventions in 1992, 1994, and 2012.[33]

THE TENNESSEE-TOMBIGBEE WATERWAY IN ALABAMA opened in January, 1985. Completed in December of 1984 after twelve years of construction, the waterway provides a shortcut of sorts for commercial river traffic in mid-America to the Gulf of Mexico. The waterway begins where the Tennessee River serves as borders for Tennessee, Mississippi, and Alabama.

The idea of the waterway was considered in the colonial era and surveys were conducted just prior to Alabama becoming a state in 1819. The estimated high cost put the waterway on the back burner until 1938 when President Franklin Delano Roosevelt revived the idea when he proposed the Tennessee Valley Authority. The TVA project made the Tennessee River itself navigable and was an economic success particularly for north Alabama. New Deal Democrats, including Supreme Court Justice Hugo Black of Alabama, took pride in supporting the project. But the development of the Tenn-Tom Waterway did not get underway until 1973.[1]

Democratic Legislative Maneuvering

1985 was also the year that President Ronald Reagan began his second and final term in the White House. In the Alabama Senate one of the main issues for the Democrats was a retirement package for legislators. Alabama was the only state in the union without one. It was all Democrats could think and talk about, but not many were in favor of it. It was standard practice of the Senate to take a regular evening break for dinner before returning to the senate chamber to resume deliberations. Bill Cabaniss, Larry Dixon, and a few other legislators took the dinner break together at a nearby downtown Montgomery restaurant. They discussed the retirement package proposal which had been debated on the Senate floor for most of that day. Suddenly, Cabaniss and Dixon got word that a few Democrats stayed behind in the chamber, took the retirement package bill out of its scheduled order, voted on and passed it with the minimum number of required votes of senators present in the chamber. Cabaniss and Dixon quickly returned to the chamber and Cabaniss took the microphone.

By now Cabaniss was well-known in the State Senate; even his political enemies saw and appreciated his personal comportment and demeanor. He was not a hell-file personality; his was a quiet tone given only to emphasize what is necessary, appropriate, and important. Democrats did not want to argue with him or any of the Republicans. The Democrats always had the votes to carry a bill but they recoiled at answering questions from the mouths of Republicans. This time, however, the stern but mild-mannered Cabaniss went to the microphone and "ate their lunch," according to Larry Dixon.

He spoke against not the bill but against the clandestine and unethical process by which the few Democrats maneuvered to get the bill passed. He spoke for more than one hour while people wanted him to step down and leave the retirement bill alone. He turned and faced Lt. Governor Baxley, saying, "you let this happen, you're not fooling anyone." He would not stop talking until the bill's passage was reversed. The Democrats eventually called on the Alabama Secretary of the Senate to declare that the bill's passage was null and void because there was not an official Senate session active at the time of the call for the vote. Single-handedly Cabaniss got the bill killed. No one else went to the floor microphone to oppose him. No one could.[2]

Just as when Cabaniss was a member of the Alabama House, his Senate office was as physically far away from the Senate floor as could be. Democratic Lt. Governor Baxley placed all of the Republican senators as far from the senate chamber as possible in the Alabama State House offices.[3] When it came time to assemble for voting, Republicans had to make the longer treks to cast their votes or to deliberate. Larry Dixon actually kept his office for twenty-six years. When Cabaniss decided not to run for re-election in 1990 Jabo Waggoner, the former Democrat turned Republican, took over Cabaniss's office and used it for many years. This is how a political minority officeholder is treated by the majority leadership. Cabaniss, Dixon, Bedsole, Hand, and Independent Dial, accepted their "office fate" because they were there to work for the state and not for themselves.

The "Buy American" Bill and the Filibuster

Many political observers believed that Lt. Governor Bill Baxley had his eyes set on becoming Alabama's governor. 1986 was an election year and Baxley had one of his minions submit a "Buy American" bill before the Senate. It was a bad bill according to Larry Dixon. The phrase "Buy American" sounded good but the financial part of the package did not meet muster – at least it did not pass Republican financial scrutiny. The bill required that no state agency could buy a piece of equipment not made in the United States. Conducting his typical research, Cabaniss found that there was only one model of the Ford truck for state use, which fit the constraints of the bill.

But the American-owned manufacturer actually assembled the vehicle in Mexico with Mexican labor. Senator Mac Parsons, a Democrat from the Birmingham suburb of Hueytown, introduced the bill. The Democrats were committed to passing the "Buy American" bill because of Baxley's desire to win the governor's office using what would have been a popular theme. But Cabaniss and his conservative colleagues, five in all, filibustered the bill for two days.[4]

The filibuster ended when the filibustering senators agreed to support a substitute measure. But Parsons opposed any compromise. The bill actually mandated that state and local government purchases have at least fifty-one percent American-made components by 1988. True to his business principles which included a strong sense of competition, Cabaniss's substitute bill encouraged the purchase of American-made goods but only if there was no reduction in quality and the goods were price competitive.[5] Cabaniss had similar experiences between his own Precision Grinding Company and buyers of his products. First of all, he sold no inferior product and if a product was delivered to his customer short of specifications, Precision Grinding would re-work the product at no cost to the customer. This kind of dealing eventually paid off for Cabaniss and Precision Grinding.[6] In like fashion, the State of Alabama as a large purchaser must demand high quality products at competitive prices. "If there were a substantial difference in price, the state or local government could consider quality as a factor."[7] This was simply normal business practice for Cabaniss and other business people, a practice in which state government is unaccustomed.

WILLIAM JELKS CABANISS, JR.

The filibuster was a learning process for many senators. Everyone agreed that "Buy American" was a good concept, but it gradually became understood how complex it would be to implement such a program. In order to explain or to teach the bill's operational and economic consequences, the filibuster was necessary. But it shut down the senate for the week ending on Friday, February 28 and it tied up or delayed much senate work for the previous ten days.

As a minority, Cabaniss, Bedsole, Dixon, Hand, and Dial had to stay awake to keep the filibuster going. They had to trade off time slots with one another. All the Lieutenant Governor had to do when he was tired was to hand over the gavel to another Democratic senator. The Republicans and Independent Gerald Dial "the bulldog" had to stay awake during the standoff because they were few in number. But they were actually encouraged not to quit by some of the Democrats who thought the bill was bad, too, but would not join in on the filibuster. Cabaniss and company were determined to get a reasonable compromise or just kill the bill. Many senators wanted to make amendments to Cabaniss's substitute measure as the only way they would support the bill.

Eventually Senator Bobby Denton, a Democrat from Tuscumbia, spoke out when he realized that as he got into the details of the bill it became more complex. Denton said he was told "that of all the small pickup trucks you can buy, only one is built in America and that is Volkswagen."[8] Cabaniss did his homework in advance of discussing the bill on the floor and before the filibuster began. Chances are that without Cabaniss's homework the bill would never have been challenged and the state and local governments would have been stuck with an impossibly complex bill to implement in practice. It became clear to the entire Senate and to onlookers that Bill Cabaniss was a person not only of high character but of high capability.

No Republican Governor between 1874 and 1986

A Cullman County, Alabama probate judge, Guy Hunt, became the Republican nominee for governor in 1986. Hunt was the party's nominee in 1978 but was defeated. Several people came to Hunt's assistance in preparation for the campaign. Spencer Bachus ran the campaign and enlisted John Grenier to join him. Grenier had not been active politically in more than a decade. They held a meeting attended by Grenier's son Beau, Edgar Welden, and Bill Cabaniss.[9] That campaign year in Alabama contained several interesting episodes of political intrigue for both the Democrats and the Republicans. Bill Cabaniss was campaigning for re-election from his senate district when Luther Strange, a future Alabama Attorney General, encouraged Cabaniss to run for governor.[10]

Cabaniss was popular, but mostly among business people statewide. A Montgomery-based group known as *Taxpayers Defense Fund* recognized Cabaniss as one of the leading senators consistently voting against tax increases. Cabaniss also gained a good reputation in the Montgomery area as a leading spokesman for business interests there "often leading filibusters against bills pushed by organized labor and other groups." In 1986 Cabaniss became the finance chairman of the Alabama Republican Party, member of the State Republican Executive Committee, and the State Republican Steering Committee. He had his finger on the pulse of his party or perhaps Cabaniss himself was the pulse of his party. His popularity was strengthening.

In July Vice President George H. W. Bush came to Birmingham stomping for the re-election of United States Senator Jeremiah Denton. President Ronald Reagan had visited Dothan, Alabama the week before. The two trips by the top two elected officials in the United States gave a signal to many that Alabama was growing in importance to the Republican Party.[11] But in the general election, conservative Democrat Richard Shelby of Tuscaloosa, a member of Congress, narrowly defeated Denton by 7,000 votes. Shelby won by moderating his conservative views and winning support from organized labor and blacks. His biracial coalition won thirty-nine percent of white voters and 93 percent of blacks.[12] Ann Bedsole thought that Bill Cabaniss should have challenged Denton.[13] Cabaniss's rise in popularity, coupled with his significance in leadership positions within the party – and his principled political and personal conduct – probably led him to bypass challenging Denton. But another political challenge faced Cabaniss in 1986.

A Proposal and a Rejection

Sage Lyons contacted Bill Cabaniss one day and suggested that the two meet. Lyons, a Democrat and former Speaker of the Alabama House from Mobile, flew to Birmingham where the two men met for several hours discussing Alabama's political situation. Lyons himself was a man of high accomplishment and well-respected among the people of Alabama. At age 34 he was elected as House Speaker, the youngest in Alabama history. He was known for his integrity and for his ability to provide sound advice to politicians of either party. In 1986 Lyons was considering switching to the Republican Party. The Mobile attorney sensed the shift in mood of the Alabama electorate and believed that he could serve best in the future as a Republican. He wanted to run for governor. In some ways Lyons and Cabaniss were two of a kind. They were respected, honest, and capable people. Lyons wanted Bill Cabaniss to be his running mate as the Republican nominee for Lieutenant Governor. Was Cabaniss interested?

No! Cabaniss believed that he personally was not ready to conduct a statewide race and he certainly had no interest in running on a tandem ticket. It had no appeal for him nor did he think it would be a winning situation for him or Lyons, and on the practical side Cabaniss had no intention of leaving his Precision Grinding business to engage in full-time campaigning.[14] Lyons eventually changed his party affiliation. But the big news that year in Alabama was the action taken by the Alabama Democratic Executive Committee.

Alabama Democrats Implode

Interest group politics in Alabama played a large role in the selection of the Democratic nominee for governor in 1986. Governor George Wallace had planned to retire at the end of his term so four well-known Democrats decided to enter the Democratic primary. They were Lt. Governor Bill Baxley; Attorney General Charlie Graddick; former governor (as a Democrat from 1979 to 1983) "Fob" James; and former Lt. Governor George McMillan. Because general elections for statewide offices in Alabama had been historically perfunctory in electing the Democratic nominee, almost one million Alabamians exercised their voting rights in the Democratic primary. None of the four candidates received a majority. Baxley at thirty-seven percent and Graddick with twenty-nine percent of the votes cast in the June 4, 1986 Democratic Primary would meet again in a runoff three weeks later.

Baxley was the proto-typical liberal Democrat, Graddick was not. Graddick's inclination was conservative and pro-business. The Democratic voters in Alabama had a clear choice in candidates in the runoff election – the status quo or something new. The obvious differences between the two candidates were enough to get the lobbyists and special interest groups very active. Graddick actually encouraged Republicans to cross over and vote for him in the runoff election. Alabama at that time did not have registration by party.[15]

Graddick garnered 8,756 more votes than his opponent. Baxley, the sitting Lieutenant Governor, felt that the election was "stolen" from him and joined a suit challenging crossover votes. Baxley based his challenge on a state Democratic Party rule adopted in 1979 which stated that any person voting in the *first* [emphasis added] primary of another political party shall not be entitled to vote in the Democratic Party runoff. The rule had never been enforced, however. Baxley and his attorney, David Johnson, argued their point before a special panel set up by the Alabama Democratic Party. Johnson asserted that Graddick conspired one year earlier with Republicans to "encourage illegal crossover voting ..." Graddick's attorney, Champ Lyons, Jr. of Mobile (not related to Sage Lyons of Mobile) attempted to change the direction of the proceedings by purporting that the paneled, special hearing itself was nothing more than party big shots attempting to steal the election not from Graddick but from the voters.[16] Ten years earlier Graddick was a Republican and switched party affiliation. It wasn't cool to be a Republican in Alabama since the end of Reconstruction and the Democratic Party in Alabama was simply a mechanism to get oneself elected. But the 1986 Democratic Party runoff election outcome would forever change long-running Democratic special interests.

Political news analysts wrote at that time that a Graddick victory would be suggestive of a new, pro-business era for Alabama.[17] The rest of the summer was spent by a special panel of the Alabama Democratic Party searching to find ways to decertify Graddick and give Baxley the nomination. At summer's end Baxley was certified as the Democratic nominee for governor after more than two dozen suit filings. But how did this Democratic Party decision play in the November general election?

Normally the Alabama general elections were noted for low-voter turnout since everybody knew that the Democratic nominee was always the shoo-in. Between the time of the party decision and the general election, the Coalition and other special interest groups were in a state of confusion. They had to make candidate-support decisions, something unfamiliar to them, particularly in November. What to do? Whom to support? The Alabama State Employees Association's political action committee (PAC) provided equal funding to both runoff candidates, hedging their bets. The Farm Bureau PAC had contributed to Graddick's campaign in the runoff but did not support Graddick's write-in effort when Baxley was "re-picked." The Farm Bureau supported Guy Hunt in the general election and Hunt defeated Baxley by more than 159,000 votes in a turnout of slightly over 1,233,000 ballots cast. Alabama's electorate was fed up with the antics of the Alabama Democratic Party and let them know it.[18] The Alabama Republican Party got a boost.

Keeping Campaign Promises

During all the political turmoil produced by Alabama Democrats in 1986, Bill Cabaniss continued working on one of his campaign promises – ethics reform. The *Tuscaloosa Times* on January 1, 1986 gave "three cheers" to Cabaniss for submitting a bill for the coming legislative session that would create a state ethics commission with real clout. Cabaniss realized that the ethics commission was powerless to enforce any of its own provisions. It had no subpoena power under a twelve-year old act that created the commission. Many believe that the Legislature deliberately made the ethics commission weak and did so by limiting its authority to enforce any rules. Funding was not provided for the commission to hire an attorney. In December, 1985, a Baldwin County circuit judge declared the 1973 ethics statute unconstitutional because the Legislature had failed to set minimum penalties when it was enacted. So, Cabaniss filed a second bill which was designed to render the original or existing 1973 law constitutional by setting penalty violations.[19]

Cabaniss then met with Melvin Cooper, the executive director of the Alabama Ethics Commission and Bill Lovin of Decatur, a past chairman of the ethics panel, to understand the overall situation. As usual Bill Cabaniss sought out the major players and began asking tough questions. David Bronner of the RSA was a keen observer of Cabaniss's business-like methodology. As a businessman within government, Bronner understood how Cabaniss worked. Cabaniss worked with Cooper and Lovin as he did with Bronner. Once satisfied that he understood the situation, Cabaniss made his proposal.

Ethics Reform

At a minimum Cabaniss's ethics bill proposed subpoena power and a full time attorney for the Alabama Ethics Commission. The commission needed its own prosecutor, according to Cabaniss, because the state's Attorney General's office and some District Attorneys had failed to prosecute offenders even when the ethics commission found and documented specific violations.[20] Limits were set in Cabaniss's bill on the dollar amount a lobbyist could spend in the State of Alabama. It eliminated exemptions or escape clauses which formerly allowed some public officials to avoid current ethics laws. The proposal met with little support from within the Legislature. Strong ethics laws would interrupt years of close relationships between special interest lobbyists and legislators.[21] The new bill described a public employee as not just legislators and constitutional officers but anyone at the state or local level who is paid by public funds. Passage of the bill would greatly impact the status quo in state government, which was exactly what Bill Cabaniss wanted to achieve.

Tort Reform

Bill Cabaniss ran for re-election in 1986. Many of the candidates for the Legislature, both Republicans and Democrats, ran on a "pro tort reform" agenda. Tort reform was finally "in" in Alabama after years of anti-business governance. The Alabama Trial Lawyers Association, one of the four members of the Democratic Coalition, for years made sure that tort reform would be difficult to achieve. Their bread was spread with the butter of status quo tort law. During those days Alabama had a co-employee lawsuit problem. Under workers compensation laws throughout the United States, a person injured on the job is provided medical care and weekly compensation until he or she returns to work. The law eliminated the possibility for an injured employee to sue another employee and his employer. But in Alabama there was a quirk in the workers compensation law. Due to an earlier decision made by the Alabama Supreme Court, an employee was allowed to sue not only fellow employees but could sue management from a direct supervisor up to the president of the employing company. It created havoc for Alabama businesses. Instead of fighting suits in courts, businesses found it less expensive simply to settle with the plaintiff out of court. This type of settlement over time opened a floodgate of frivolous lawsuits, and courts and juries almost always ruled against business.

Russell Industries, the Alexander City-headquartered manufacturer of sporting goods and clothing, began moving their factories out of the state of Alabama because of the situation. Neighboring states were benefiting from Alabama law and became recipients of exported Alabama businesses. Boeing Aircraft had a large manufacturing facility in Huntsville. Its top local executive announced that Boeing would not hire another person in Alabama until the co-employee insurance problem was solved. In the 1986 elections, the candidates for governor, lieutenant governor, and speaker of the House, all ran on a platform of tort reform. In what appeared to be a developing win-win situation the Alabama Legislature passed some of the toughest tort reform laws in the nation. But the reforms were never put into effect because the Alabama Supreme Court overturned cases intentionally brought to their attention by Alabama's trial lawyers.[22] Even into the twenty-first century Alabama has the distinction of having the nation's highest payoff verdicts in 2003 and 2004. Alabama, Texas, and California had the highest punitive damages paid out in the same period.[23]

Bill Cabaniss's tireless efforts in the government of Alabama were as a change agent. When elected to the Alabama House of Representatives he was part of a young group of Republican professionals, highly educated, and with the ability to ask the right questions. In the cases of Cabaniss and Bedsole, neither entered politics for personal gain. They were already established in their businesses and settled in their personal lives. They considered public service a high responsibility.[24] Both loved Alabama and they were well-to-do. There are those who use politics for personal gain. This is not to say that others in government did not love their state just as well. A common political tactic is to demean wealthy candidates as vultures and self-serving and neither the state nor its people matter. No one could make that assertion and prove it about Cabaniss or

Bedsole. But in his political future, not only Cabaniss's wealth but his hometown would become targets of the political opposition.

Changes in Anti-Business Bias

An area of importance to Alabama's future that was sorely neglected was the absence of an organized and unified business voice throughout the state. After some combinations and mergers of organizations the situation changed. "Alabama's business associations included the usual state trade associations, plus two umbrella organizations, the Business Council of Alabama (BCA) and the Alabama Alliance of Business and Industry (AABI). These replaced the state chamber of commerce and the Associated Industries of Alabama …"[25]

Unexpected Events

Bill Cabaniss was again voted Outstanding State Senator by his peers in 1987 and by this time he was seriously considering running for the United States Senate. John Claypool, the former Baptist preacher who corresponded with Cabaniss in the late 1970s, came to Birmingham as rector of St. Luke's Episcopal Church, a position he would hold for the next fourteen years. Claypool left the Baptist Church and became a priest in the Episcopal Church in 1986. 1987 was also the year that President Ronald Reagan made his famous speech in front of the Brandenburg Gate in Berlin, Germany on June 12. "Mr. Gorbachev, Tear down this wall."

On February 8, 1988 Vice President George H.W. Bush, a candidate for the presidency, came in third place in the Iowa Caucuses behind Senator Bob Dole of Kansas and television evangelist Pat Robertson of Virginia. Bush's bad showing was a shock to his supporters. The Bush campaign immediately dispatched a lot of their heavyweight supporters around the nation to bring about a sense of calm in the confusion produced by Bush's unexpected Iowa loss.

United States Senator Mitch McConnell of Kentucky was assigned to Alabama, and Bill Cabaniss, since he was the leading Republican state senator, was asked to escort McConnell around the state to meet supporters and to hold press conferences. This short-term political activity with McConnell would be helpful in Cabaniss's future. But there was no time to be lost in meeting with Alabama's Bush supporters because the New Hampshire Primary was eight days away on February 16.[26] George H.W. Bush's recovery the next week was remarkable. Bush led the voting in the New Hampshire Republican primary with 59,290 to Dole's 44,979. Robertson finished behind Jack Kemp and Pete DuPont. "I think you just don't like being told what to do," Bush told New Hampshire voters. "I think you listen, judge, and then decide to do what's right, and I'll never forget it."[27]

The Republican National Convention in 1988 was held in the Louisiana Superdome between August 15 and 18. Bill Cabaniss was elected chairman of the Alabama Delegation. At the convention he cast the Alabama delegation's vote for George H.W. Bush. When casting the vote, with television cameras focused, Cabaniss praised the glories of Alabama by saying that "Alabama is full of surprises; from the white sandy beaches of Gulf Shores and Mobile, to our Shakespeare Festival in Montgomery, to our world class medical center in Birmingham, to our space and rocket center in Huntsville …" a line he would use again in the future.[28] Larry Dixon was a member of the platform committee that year and he had met George H.W. Bush (Bush '41) earlier. "I had talked with 'HW' about a platform idea. Then it dawned on me that Cabaniss had a connection [to HW] like none of the rest of us. [His connection] goes back to Kennebunkport and we had fund-raisers at Cabaniss's house. …"[29]

During the 1988 presidential campaign for George H.W. Bush, Cabaniss served as campaign manager for Alabama's Sixth Congressional District. He also served on the Alabama Republican state Steering Committee. Six weeks before the November general election on September 22, 1988, the *CBS Evening News* program aired a three-and-one-half minute story critiquing a particular television advertisement for Bush's presidential campaign. The *CBS* reporting had to do with Mr. Bush's competency. The program outlined Bush's resume; his position or associations with Richard Nixon, Gerald Ford, and his leadership at the Central Intelligence Agency (CIA). A *Washington Post* article of the day was used in the *CBS* story showing a quote from ex-CIA Director Stansfield Turner who stated that Bush failed to grasp important information while he was CIA Director. Nixon attorney Leonard Garment praised Bush as did Connecticut Republican Senator Lowell Weicker. Presidential historian James David Barber said Bush was a follower and not a leader. The icing on the cake in terms of personal criticism was delivered by Alabama's Democratic Senator Howell Heflin who commented that Bush's footprints were made with Gucci shoes.[30] Bush won the election defeating former Democratic governor of Massachusetts Michael Dukakis. On election night, president-elect George Herbert Walker Bush repeated what he had said nine months earlier, "Thank you, New Hampshire."[31]

Change was in the air. In 1986 Frank "Butch" Ellis ran for re-election to the state senate from Republican-leaning Shelby County and won as a Democrat but he was becoming "more and more comfortable with the Republican philosophy."[32] In 1989 Butch Ellis switched parties. In a media event in Columbiana, Shelby County, Alabama, Ellis and a few other former Democrats serving in county government became Republicans. State Senators Perry Hand of Baldwin County and Bill Cabaniss of Mountain Brook were among supporters attending the event. Alabama Governor Guy Hunt also attended. Ellis said that "We had a mass conversion event. Mike Hill, who was in the House, converted, the Shelby County Superintendent of Education, converted, and a member of the Democratic Executive Committee [converted]. We all converted at the same time. It looked like a revival."[33]

The conversion was long in the making. People like Bill Cabaniss and Emory Folmar worked Ellis constantly. Frank Ellis had a strong Democratic pedigree. His grandfather, Handy Ellis, was once mayor of Columbiana and a state senator. He was also elected lieutenant governor of Alabama and ran against "Big Jim" Folsom for governor in 1946. He lost in the primary. This type of political heritage is difficult to break in a state where memories of 19th century Radical Republican Reconstruction linger. In the 1990 election, however, Ellis drew both Republican and Democratic opposition, but won.

Larry Dixon believed the switch to the Republican Party was indicative of a general understanding that there was a change coming about within the electorate. "These converted Democrats knew that Republicans base our decisions on what was the best thing for the people we represent and the state of Alabama. I don't think Democrats have standards. When there were only four of us [Republicans] in the senate the Democrats liked us, but we were like pets [to them]. As we grew in numbers then the partisanship started. It culminated when Steve Windom was elected [in 1999 as a Republican Lt. Governor]."[34] Republicans were definitely on the move in Alabama.

The United States Senate

In May, 1989, William Jelks Cabaniss, Jr., in a bold and confident move announced his candidacy for the United States Senate seat then held by Democrat Howell Heflin. Heflin had announced in December 1988 that he would run for re-election.[35] Heflin had been well known around the state of Alabama for years. It was just the year before when Cabaniss met Kentucky Senator Mitch McConnell. McConnell had come to Alabama to calm the fears of George H.W. Bush supporters in his loss to Dole and Robertson in the Iowa Caucuses. While escorting McConnell through Alabama Cabaniss mentioned that he was considering making a run for the senate against Heflin.

At his announcement speech on May 17, 1989 on the property of his company, Precision Grinding, Inc., and describing himself as a "progressive conservative," Cabaniss declared that "Alabama is at a crossroads. We have one foot in the future, but one remains in the past. In some parts of our state, Alabama technology leads the world. In others, the old politics still holds us back. It is time for some changes in our state." Cabaniss continued by saying that one of his proudest moments as an Alabamian occurred less than one year before in New Orleans. "As delegation leader [to the Republican National Convention], I had the great privilege of casting our vote for our President George [H.W.] Bush. At the microphone my heart swelled with pride as I told the chairman and the nation that: Alabama is full of surprises; from the white sandy beaches of Gulf Shores and Mobile, to our Shakespeare Festival in Montgomery, to our world class medical center in Birmingham, to our space and rocket center[36] in Huntsville. No one need apologize for Alabama today – we have arrived."

On the day before, a press release issued by Alabama Republican Party executive director Marty Connors stated that Cabaniss would launch his campaign with a fast two day announcement tour.

Cabaniss Campaign Advertisement
Dothan, Alabama 1990

The press release stated that after his opening announcement at Precision Grinding, Cabaniss would make similar announcements in Huntsville, Montgomery, Mobile, Dothan, Auburn, Tuscaloosa, and end in the northwest community of Muscle Shoals in the Tennessee Valley.[37] This was a necessary early start to a campaign that would end in the November, 1990 general election. It was to be an uphill battle not only against a popular figure to Alabama citizens but against a champion of entrenched loyalties to a system of patronage that seemed unending. *The Tuscaloosa News* reported that Cabaniss "… hopes [that] hard work and support from the national GOP will lead to victory in his bid for the U.S. Senate seat held by Democratic Howell Heflin." Even though Cabaniss styled himself a progressive conservative, he said he did not plan to get into a contest with Heflin over who was a conservative.[38]

Freedom Coming to Central Europe

Toward the end of 1989 a sense of freedom had been developing in Central and Eastern Europe since President Reagan's 1987 speech in Berlin and the subsequent destruction of the Berlin Wall. November 17 is the date given as the beginning of the *Velvet Revolution* in Czechoslovakia. Student demonstrations and other popular demonstrations brought down the communist government. The continuous demonstrations in Prague forced the government to resign and a non-communist government was formed, led by playwright Václav Havel.[39]

AT THE BEGINNING OF 1990 ALABAMA'S POPULATION STOOD at 4.04 million people. Almost three million were white and the urban and rural populations were divided at 2.4 to 1.6 million people, respectively.[1] Though statistically an urban state, the political mood of many, if not most Alabamians, was rural. And although Bill Cabaniss was a candidate for the United States Senate he continued to work as a sitting Alabama State Senator, focusing on business issues and ethics of elected officials and public employees.

Public Trust and Ethics

Up until March, 1990 Cabaniss had seen his ethics proposal for the Legislature go down in defeat three times. His new bill would not only provide the Ethics Commission with subpoena powers it would allow it to investigate ethics complaints against public officials even if the complaint was received from an anonymous source. The commission would also have the power to initiate its own investigations but with a unanimous vote of the commission. Cabaniss saw the bill as a safeguard for public and elected officials. The passage of a strong ethics bill was not an indictment of misconduct by any official. According to *The Times Daily*, passage of the bill would help provide a better political environment for the state and build public trust.[2] These were precisely the reasons that Cabaniss entered public life in 1978. He wanted Alabama to change and to build a positive political and business environment. That Alabama would become more attractive to investors and visitors and the old image discarded, was Cabaniss's vision.

William J. Cabaniss, Sr., Bill's father died in 1990 at age 85. Bill's mother Florence had passed away ten years earlier after struggling with pancreatic cancer. Bill's father remarried to Marie Cobbs some years after Florence's death.[3]

Rapid Changes in Central Europe

Internationally, much was being made of the vast and fairly rapid changes taking place in Eastern Europe. Speaking to a joint session of the

United States Congress on February 21, 1990, the new president of Czechoslovakia, elected unanimously by its Parliament, Václav Havel, told his audience and the American public of his and his nation's newly found freedom. "The last time they arrested me, on October 27 of last year, I didn't know whether it was for two days or two years. Exactly one month later, when rock musician Michael Kocáb told me that I would probably be proposed as a presidential candidate, I thought it was one of his usual jokes. … When they arrested me on October 27, I was living in a country ruled by the most conservative Communist government in Europe, and our society slumbered beneath the pall of a totalitarian system. Today, less than four months later, I am speaking to you as the representative of a country which has complete freedom of speech, which is preparing for free elections, and which seeks to establish a prosperous market economy and its own foreign policy. It is all very extraordinary indeed."[4] A few weeks earlier Secretary of State James Baker met with Havel at Hradčany Castle. Havel told Baker that "Czechoslovakia, like a number of other countries, is interested in returning to Europe." But he thought that another Helsinki Conference was needed to end the Four Powers control over a divided Germany. "There can be no divided Germany in a divided Europe, nor a divided Germany in a united Europe."[5] A year earlier Baker met with the Hungarian Foreign Minister, Peter Varkonyi, who told him the "the necessary condition of reforming Eastern Europe was reform in the Soviet Union."[6]

When Václav Havel made his speech to the U.S. Congress, at the core of his message was a paradox, according to former Secretary of State Madeleine Albright. "You can help us most if you help the Soviet Union on its irreversible, but immensely complicated, road to democracy… The sooner, the more quickly, and the more peacefully the Soviet Union begins to move along the road toward genuine pluralism, the better it will be not just for Czechs and Slovaks, but for the whole world."[7] All of Europe began its adjustment to its new political reality.

Campaigning for the United States Senate

Cabaniss continued to work in the State Senate while he hit the campaign trail for the U.S. Senate. The opinions of his friends and business associates about his senatorial candidacy varied. Peggy Balliet, who would begin as Cabaniss's campaign manager and end up playing a minor role, said she and other friends tried to talk him out of it but others wanted Heflin out of office because they felt Heflin was becoming an embarrassment to the state.[8] "Heflin was just a good ole boy who was entrenched."[9] Balliet was unaware that a political consultant from Washington, D.C. would eventually boot her out of her role as campaign manager.

Judy Bewley, manager for Cabaniss's 1978 campaign, knew that it would be difficult to run for a statewide office from Mountain Brook and win, another vulnerability that Heflin would exploit among the electorate. Butch Ellis had similar sentiments. "He couldn't win with a Mountain Brook address so I offered to have a tractor-pull contest and I let him borrow my pickup truck."[10] The tone and tenor of the state, and the populist nature of Democratic political rhetoric, all but prevented Republicans, especially if from Mountain Brook, to get elected statewide. Had Cabaniss's home resided in Montgomery or Selma then he would not have carried the "stigma."[11]

Cabaniss's senatorial campaign finance chairman Lee Styslinger, Jr. believed "It was a shame that Bill picked Heflin to run against. We tried to discourage him but Bill was confident and we had to get out of his way and support him."[12] The dominant reason held by Cabaniss's friends against his entering the race seemed to be his statewide recognition, or the lack thereof. Incumbent U.S. Senator Howell Heflin was well-known across the state and Cabaniss could not make the same claim. Not all of the negative reasoning was with recognition. It was also statistical and psychological.

Alabama continued to think of itself as rural and blue collar, leaning in the direction of late nineteenth and early twentieth century populism. Memories of Republican Reconstruction, though more than one hundred sixteen years earlier, still lurked within the intellectual recesses of a rurally-oriented electorate. It was just a way of thinking, even if you lived in Mountain Brook.

For years since 1874 Alabama Democrats reminded voters of the harm brought by any Republican or any industrial "Big Mule." The Big Mules were not all Republicans, but they were perceived to be wealthy and wealth was always an effective class-divider for Democrats. Therefore, any candidate for statewide office from a wealthy town, a corporation, or from the wrong party, had to realistically feign rural roots in order to get elected.

Peggy Balliet scheduled Cabaniss to speak at a Union Hall in the Roebuck section of Birmingham. She thought it good for him to experience speaking before a room of union-represented workers. Cabaniss, however, was irked, "They're not going to listen to me," but he went anyway. Cabaniss, Balliet thought, did not think they would vote for him, so why bother in the first place. She insisted that union people needed to know where Cabaniss stood on the issues of the day, just like any voter.

A political realist, Balliet believed that Alabama was "not a sophisticated state. It's rural. Blue collar workers could not identify with Bill. They could identify with Howell Heflin."[13] That rural identification was what won elections. In the days of Tom Heflin (Howell's uncle and U.S. Senator), and later in George Wallace's era, a Democratic political candidate always hung everything Republican based on money – silk stockings, expensive cars, the country club. Therefore, said the Democratic candidate to his listeners, "I'm your man." But there was another political reality to campaign management.

Bill Cabaniss had a tough way to go, running against the former Alabama Chief Justice Howell Heflin. Cabaniss was also running against a Democratic state organization with sixty-seven local county organizations that relied on, and were living on, the achievements of Heflin for their livelihood – the *Judicial Article* and all that went with it. Judges in almost every county courthouse in the state were run by Democrats. The 1973 *Judicial Article* was an obstacle to campaign success for Cabaniss. With counties in Alabama run by probate judges, that's where the real power resides.[14]

Reflecting on his first U.S. Senate campaign of 1978 following a few years of implementation of the *Judicial Article*, Heflin said that the local lawyers in every county and the court houses around them "… were my foundation in campaigning and elections and were very helpful. Since we got the probate judges a retirement system, some were active in the campaign, and the circuit clerks and registrars were all happy because the *Judicial Article* had improved their financial condition. People in the [outgoing U.S. Senator John] Sparkman group were also very helpful."[15] But the Cabaniss campaign organization itself also had its own problems.

Cabaniss Campaign Committee Internal Problems

In February of 1988 when Bill Cabaniss and Mitch McConnell were traveling around Alabama to visit with and reassure Vice President George H.W. Bush supporters, Cabaniss mentioned to McConnell that he was thinking of running for the United States Senate against Democratic incumbent Howell Heflin. McConnell then offered to walk Cabaniss around the Washington GOP crowd if he decided to run. After making his decision Cabaniss told McConnell and was subsequently introduced to Senator Bob Dole of Kansas and Senator Kit Bond of Missouri, both of whom were helpful and courteous. Alan Simpson of Wyoming, however, refused to meet with Cabaniss presumably because Simpson's wife and Heflin's wife were close friends. Eventually Cabaniss's senate aspirations were taken on by Senator Don Nickles of Oklahoma. Nickles had the responsibility of working with Republican Senatorial candidates. As the minority party in the late 1980s, Republican senators took great interest in new candidates as a means to gaining the majority. A real dark horse in every sense of the phrase, Cabaniss was much appreciated and admired by the sitting senators. Nickles helped Cabaniss with the nitty-gritty of getting elected and he set up meetings with other senators. But two items of importance dominated.

Cabaniss Told to Please the Republican Establishment in D.C.

Cabaniss was told that he needed to gain credibility with the Washington Republican establishment. That meant that Cabaniss should hire a GOP consultant with an excellent reputation among the establishment to run his campaign. Several consulting firms were suggested and Cabaniss interviewed three of them. He selected Eddie Mahe Consulting. With an associate, Chuck Greener, Mahe traveled to Birmingham to meet with Cabaniss and Lee Styslinger, Jr. Styslinger had always been Bill Cabaniss's campaign finance chairman, including his early Alabama House and Senate races. Together the new team began discussing a campaign strategy which involved quite a number of trips for Cabaniss to Washington for meetings with various Republican Senators. It was Greener who conducted most of the work on the ground. Mahe remained in D.C. Several fund-raising events were planned. Mahe and Greener made clear that Cabaniss needed to meet the sitting senators since he was trying to join them.[16]

That type of thinking had to have been odd for Cabaniss, a person who constantly thought of Alabama and what he could do for its citizens and businesses.

Birmingham Fund Raiser for US Senate, 1990
Bill Cabaniss, Lee Styslinger, Jr., and
Former U.S. President Ronald Reagan

But on that first meeting night at the Cabaniss home, Mahe looked at Styslinger, Jr., and asked "How much money do you have for the campaign?" "Well, not a lot." Mahe pushed. "How much?" Although funding was promised for Cabaniss's campaign by Mahe, Cabaniss self-funded his final television advertisement.

Styslinger was no fan of Mahe. To him Mahe was a typical Washington-type promoter. Though he never mentioned this to Cabaniss, Styslinger was told by Mahe that all the money he needed to raise he could raise in Washington. That never happened, according to Styslinger. Cabaniss and Styslinger raised the money. The national Republican Senatorial Committee donated funds, an effort led mostly by Oklahoma U.S. Senator Don Nickles. There would never be enough money to run against Heflin anyway. It became difficult to raise campaign funding because the Alabama business community did not come to Cabaniss's aid. Many Alabama companies benefitted from Heflin's largesse and did not want to break with him. Not one major corporation in Alabama would commit to Cabaniss.[17] But there were other reasons why fund-raising was difficult.

There is a close connection between early media coverage and a candidate's ability to raise funds. The media can contribute to the making or breaking of a candidate by the way it provides access to its airways or print matter. The candidate and the media need to have a discussion about coverage. It is a two-way street – the candidate needs the media coverage and the media need stories. The media is the main source of information provided to the voting public.

Heflin was well-known across Alabama and had no problem getting media access. But a comparison of media access granted to both Heflin and Cabaniss reveals the fact that the media projects its bias one way or the other. Cabaniss spent approximately $400,000 to start his campaign, but even that amount was not enough to fund an ongoing campaign.

An examination of *The Birmingham News* in the last fifteen days of the senate campaign shows that the Cabaniss name appeared in fourteen paragraphs in the state's largest circulated newspaper. In October, 1990, Cabaniss averaged less than five paragraphs per day in the *News*. His campaign spent less in October – the most crucial campaigning month – than in September. In the first half of October the Cabaniss campaign spent $283,000 and only $177,000 in the last ten days of the month. Without positive media coverage Cabaniss was unable to raise sufficient campaign funding necessary for communicating to voters. Heflin spent $3.5 million on his campaign.[18]

Friends and campaigners for Cabaniss had their own opinions about the consultants. Luther Strange thought that Mahe and Greener did a good job in making the campaign against Heflin. Peggy Balliet thought differently.[19] Like Styslinger, Balliet saw little to no value in bringing in an outside consulting group because all they did was spend money, Cabaniss's campaign money, with no positive campaign results.[20]

Peggy Balliet's husband grew up with Bill Cabaniss. As young marrieds the Balliets and Cabanisses were social friends. Peggy was politically astute; she believed herself to be "street smart" when it came to politics. As a student at the University of Alabama she was part of "The Machine," the student organization that controlled campus-wide elections. Many machine victors eventually became elected Alabama government officials. "I had some knowledge of how things work and how things get resolved. So when Bill made his decision to run the first time in 1978, I volunteered to work on his campaign. ... I coordinated the volunteers." Cabaniss and Balliet shared a common interest. They both thought that Alabama was capable of better government and representation than what it had. But they did not always agree, especially when it came time for Bill's campaign for the United States Senate.

Balliet knew that Cabaniss trusted her "skills about organizing, but he didn't trust me to know other political things." That came true when "I was working at *The Galleria* for the Kidney Foundation running a cooking demonstration for Cordon Bleu."

The retail shopping hub of Alabama is located in the City of Hoover. *The Galleria* was and is the largest enclosed shopping center in the state. Peripheral businesses naturally popped up near the shopping center, and the City of Hoover leaders, through its department of traffic management, made sure that vehicles traveling through the intersection of U.S. Highway 31 and Interstate Highway 459 had clear driving to the shopping magnet.

It was one of Birmingham's *Festival of Arts* salutes, this time to France. Balliet and her friend Sandra Oden were conducting a public cooking presentation at the Mall when Balliet was handed a note that Bill Cabaniss needed to see her now. Cabaniss was in the Mall with political consultant Chuck Greener. When she walked over to meet them this was when she learned that Bill Cabaniss had made a decision to hire the Eddie Mahe group to run his campaign and that she would work directly for them. Balliet was not happy. [21]

She was now Campaign Coordinator, not Campaign Manager. With those Washington types "I was turned off from day one," said Balliet. As far as Balliet was concerned those consultants were nothing but "hot air." Balliet, a stickler for monitoring spending, noticed that spending campaign funds was never an issue for the Washington-based consultants. When they traveled, they traveled first class. The only national help the campaign received was through President George H.W. Bush when he came to Alabama for a fund-raising event in Birmingham. President Bush's visit raised Cabaniss's campaign chest by $500,000. [22]

Vice President Dan Quayle, William Bennett, and Jack Kemp also came to help.[23]

Judy Bewley had a different take on Mahe. Bewley had worked in the past on President Ronald Reagan's campaigns throughout Alabama. She worked on Bill Cabaniss's U.S. Senate campaign as its organizational director. Her job tasked her with traveling to all of Alabama's sixty-seven counties to visit with each Republican county chairperson. She designed what they would do during the campaign for their area.

She understood the professional Washington consultants such as Eddie Mahe and his organization. "He was really good, a plan writer – that's what national guys do. Peggy was great, a detailed oriented person who pushed hard. Mahe was the national guy hired to run the campaign from the National Republican office. He would come and go."

Bewley said that the worst thing that happened to Bill Cabaniss during the campaign was when Heflin made a caricature of him, trying to make Cabaniss look like a rich buffoon. "But my feeling about Bill is that he is such a fine person that I'm not sure I wanted to send him to Washington. If we could get persons elected like Bill, it would be a whole different world."[24]

President George H.W. Bush's fund-raiser speech for Cabaniss was uplifting. Always wanting to include local sites in his presentation, Bush said, "We go back a long way. We first met in the seventies; we've been friends for years. We're so close that not long ago Barbara and I invited ourselves, after we found that for dinner Bill and Catherine were having Ollie's pork barbeque. But you know how it goes. Twenty Secret Service men went over and swept in ahead of us. The good news is that by the time we got there they had big smiles on their faces, and the bad news is, all the barbeque was gone."[25] Bush said of Cabaniss that he was a man of character, a family man – great wife, two great kids. "He values loyalty, and so do I – he worked for me back in 1980. In '88, he cast our first vote at the Republican National Convention. Like me, he's a charismatic speaker." The audience laughed.[26]

President George H. W. Bush
Catherine and Bill Cabaniss
Birmingham Airport, 1990

A Gadsden, Alabama newspaper observed that "Republican U.S. Senate candidate Bill Cabaniss has spent months swimming upstream in his campaign against Democratic incumbent Howell Heflin. Now, he's going to see if a canoe helps."[27] Alabama contains within its borders an extensive river and canal system. Cabaniss worked the rivers not only to garner attention statewide, but to challenge some of the environmental legislation put forward by Senator Heflin. Heflin had criticized President Bush on his environmental record and Bill Cabaniss in turn criticized Heflin's.

At the time that Cabaniss offered the criticism, Heflin had supported a civil rights bill submitted by Senator Edward Kennedy, a bill Cabaniss thought inadequate and unfair, particularly unfair to small businesses. Cabaniss said that he believed "Senator Heflin has grossly misjudged the sentiments and the best interests of the vast majority of the people in Alabama. This vote may make sense in Massachusetts, but it makes no sense in Alabama."[28] But Cabaniss's description of Heflin with Kennedy did not resonate with the Alabama electorate. Heflin had been a good senator for Alabama and no one wanted to cut off the source of any federal benefits.

Bill Cabaniss campaigned in Decatur, Alabama to give a speech at the local Rotary Club. Allen Collins, married to Bill's first cousin, introduced Cabaniss to Barrett C. Shelton, the publisher of the *Decatur Daily*. Collins went to school with Shelton. But Shelton was a long-time Heflin supporter.[29] Collins had told Cabaniss that he could help him with getting support from Shelton. After arriving in Decatur, Collins and Cabaniss met with Shelton before the meeting. They went to a room and talked for ten to fifteen minutes about Howell Heflin.

Collins soon realized that he could not change Shelton. Cabaniss and Shelton rode to the Rotary meeting. Someone told Cabaniss that he was the first Republican that Shelton had ever ridden in a car with.[30] To an outsider, that comment would not make much sense. But memories are long in Alabama about Republican Reconstruction, more than one hundred fifty years later.[31]

Cabaniss's Friday September 28, 1990 campaign agenda entitled "Bill Cabaniss for US Senate" shows a busy day with handwritten changes. The agenda included maps and driving directions. This day's events were in Montgomery. Cabaniss was scheduled to arrive at Brewbaker Junior High School at 7:30 am to speak to Mrs. Voncile Sikes's social studies class beginning at 7:52 am. The session was videotaped for viewing by other classes later. A handwritten notation on the agenda advised that they "may have media coverage."

Once concluded, Cabaniss and his entourage headed for a radio interview on the Don Marwell Show at AM radio station WACV. The interview was scheduled for 9:06 am. Cabaniss arrived six minutes before show time. A press conference followed one hour and forty minutes later. Lunch was scheduled at Martin's Restaurant followed by a visit to the Farmers Market. By the end of the day Cabaniss talked with the president of the *Alabama Council of Association Executives* who was also executive vice president of the *Auto Dealers Association*; took a tour of the county courthouse, and made a visit to an Alabama Power Company facility. In the evening Bill Cabaniss attended a fundraiser dinner led by his old friend Larry Dixon.[32] Campaigning continued with this type of schedule until November.

The "Almost" Debate

Cabaniss and Heflin were scheduled to have a debate on Alabama Public Television, but Heflin pulled out at the last minute. Just days before the election Howell Heflin pulled out of the pre-agreed debate citing "distortions, half-truths and misrepresentations" made by his opponent. *The Tuscaloosa News* charged that the incumbent U.S. Senator from Alabama "has short-changed voters of an opportunity to take full measure of both candidates, unencumbered by the slick images created by publicists. If the incumbent really is so troubled by accusations made by Cabaniss, he has the perfect opportunity – on public TV – to tell his opponent in person." Heflin hinted at a change of heart if incumbent Alabama Governor Guy Hunt would debate his Democratic opponent. Hunt never backed out of having a debate. There was no agreement. But the real issue was Heflin's attempt to link his U.S. Senatorial Campaign debate to the state's gubernatorial campaign. It was a deflection.[33]

Years earlier when Governor George Wallace was running against Albert Brewer, Heflin did not want his chief justice campaign to get mixed up with their gubernatorial election because there had been racial overtones. Heflin said that "we tried to keep out of their fight. It's a fundamental rule that you do not get into somebody else's politics when you're running [a separate and different campaign]."[34] In his 1990 campaign, Heflin apparently changed, or conveniently forgot, his "fundamental rule" and sought safety in a completely different and unlinked political campaign between Republican Guy Hunt and Democrat Paul Hubbert in order to escape facing Cabaniss in a public debate.

Howell Heflin won re-election. Even though Heflin raised more money than Cabaniss, he believed that he won because "the people like me." In an interesting affirmation of the rural mood of political Alabama, Heflin said that "I think basically the people just like [me]. They like my personality. They like my slow, deliberate manner which some of your Republican newspapers refer to as indecisiveness. … I think basically Alabamians are moderate conservatives." Heflin won by sixty-one to thirty-nine percent. Some analysts thought that Heflin's position on the Senate Agriculture Committee was pleasing to farmers. Cabaniss conceded gracefully but refused to look forward to 1992 and a possible run against then-Democratic United States Senator Richard Shelby. After thanking his supporters at the post-election rally Cabaniss then telephoned Heflin.[35]

Dick Morris, a former advisor to President Bill Clinton, later contacted Cabaniss about running against Richard Shelby in the U.S. Senate race in 1992. Cabaniss refused.[36]

Balliet said that "for many years [after the 1990 campaign] there was tension between him [Bill Cabaniss] and me, particularly when in the same room. I needed to tell him so much. I never told him things because I knew he would be hurt. But one night at a dinner party when we were seated next to each other, we looked at each other, and laughed. We both said 'I guess we've got to talk now.' So that was the end. He knew in his heart that those Washington types would misbehave and drain us of everything. I think he realized what was going on after all."[37] Even Heflin allowed that he thought that Cabaniss's campaign received bad advice from outsiders.[38]

Everybody expected Cabaniss to lose the election, except for Cabaniss himself. Perhaps the professional consultants "knew" that Cabaniss could not defeat Heflin. Such professional "knowledge" might have impacted their participation in the campaign. This is an observation that Peggy Balliet could possibly have made. But there were other considerations: some prophetic in nature, some twenty-twenty hindsight.

Tact, Style, Dignity, Respect, Change, Opportunity

Former Alabama State Senator from Mobile, Ann Bedsole, said that it was Howell Heflin who got her interested in politics. "He asked me to serve on the commission to write the *Judicial Article*." Heflin was everybody's granddaddy, according to Bedsole. "It was difficult for me to vote against Heflin and for Bill." Bedsole worked with Cabaniss to broaden his thinking on conservation issues. There was some talk that black Democrats who thought they were not treated well in their own party might jump to Cabaniss. But blacks always vote Democratic. But "people loved Heflin – Bill was too cerebral. He didn't understand that, I didn't understand that."[39]

Marty Connors was executive director of the Alabama Republican Party from 1985 to 1988, and party chairman from 2001 to 2005. As party executive when Cabaniss was running his state senate campaigns,

Connors wrote the press releases. But Connors thought that Cabaniss's United States Senatorial campaign was actually too polished. He likened it to Tennessee's Lamar Alexander's presidential bids in 1996 and 2000. "You've got to get down to eat slop with the hogs," Connors said. "You cannot run a race on issues and not stylings." Noting Cabaniss's ability to bridge interest groups, particularly evident when Cabaniss was in the state legislature, "he is probably one of the top two or three people in the state who you must ask if he's in."[40] The quiet, reserved, and impeccably dressed gentleman from Mountain Brook was, in effect, a kingmaker. Or at least he could give sound advice to an aspiring politician.

Alabama State Senator Gerald Dial said that after the 1990 election Bill Cabaniss talked very little about the campaign. "He took it more personal than he should have. People believed the character assassination put on him by Howell Heflin" was out of order. Dial's perception may have been incorrect, but he noted that Cabaniss put it behind him and moved on.[41]

Perry Hand of Baldwin County worked in the Alabama Senate with Cabaniss. On Palm Sunday in 1990 Hand was stricken with Guillain-Barré syndrome and paralyzed. He did his time in politics and is now chief executive of a Mobile engineering firm. When Bill Cabaniss decided to run for the United States Senate, Hand was asked to do the same by a political operative. "Lee Atwater called me up to D.C. He was playing his guitar, I played. We'll get along fine. We started talking and he wanted me to run against Howell Heflin." Hand was reared in an east Alabama town named Heflin, probably after kinfolks of Howell Heflin and his uncle U.S. Senator Tom Heflin. But Hand asked the perfect question, "Lee, what kind of money are you going to put up. 'We'll see you get plenty of money.' After thirty minutes I told him I didn't think anybody can beat Heflin. I don't think you have enough money, and whoever you put up for that office you better give him a good exit strategy." So Hand left and figured that Atwater could have been talking to Cabaniss at the same time. Then he heard about Cabaniss's plan to run. "I hope he doesn't do that." Hand didn't campaign actively for Cabaniss but did invite him to Baldwin County many times.[42]

Former Alabama Governor Bob Riley said that probably many Mountain Brook politicians wished they lived in a different town.[43] Current Alabama Attorney General Luther Strange said that Alabama is a unique state. It's perhaps a "populist" thing. If you're born in Connecticut or Michigan, making money was an honor and a source of pride. But in Alabama, politicians divide everybody, and being wealthy is seen as not something good. "We've always pitted people against the other. Bill had to face that [in his U.S. Senate race]. But he got through it and that's not an issue anymore."[44] Even as late as 2010 a shift in Alabama popular political sentiment from the 1990s was on the radar.

Campaigning for U.S. Senate from Alabama 1990
L-R: Walter McCullers, Bill Cabaniss at Podium, John Grenier,
Lee Styslinger, Jr.

In an analysis of "Damage Control for Democrats" an article in *The Cook Political Report* suggested that Democrats, by pushing the economy to the back burner for a more socially-oriented legislative agenda, are out of step with the American people. The national face of the Democratic Party was particularly troublesome with House Leader Nancy Pelosi having a forty-four percent negative rating and Senate majority leader Harry Reid with a thirteen percent rating. The article suggested that the Democrats were losing their edge to the Republicans and needed to change. To strengthen its analysis the *Cook Report* looked back twenty years to the Alabama senatorial race between Cabaniss and Heflin. The article noted that Heflin "accused his earnest challenger, Bill

Cabaniss, a businessman from the wealthy Birmingham suburb of Mountain Brook, of being 'one of them silk-stocking boys …' Heflin went on to crush Cabaniss like an overripe chardonnay, 61 percent to 39 percent."

The loss of the U.S. Senate race sent Cabaniss into a period of another loss – a loss of his self-confidence. Anyone who knows Bill Cabaniss could not possibly imagine that such a towering figure through all sorts of adversity would ever lose confidence in himself. But he did. Shortly after the U.S. Senate election, Catherine suggested that the family go south for some time off. Bill needed to relax and unwind. Catherine and their daughters needed to get away also. Campaigning requires a lot not only of the candidate but of the candidate's family.

They went to Key Largo. On the morning after their arrival the girls were ready to hit the beach. It is still warm in November in South Florida. But Bill was still in bed way past noon. Bill Cabaniss is usually an early riser; but here he crashed. Catherine asked Bill, "What's wrong?" Bill said that he had no adrenaline, no energy. "I'm running on an empty tank."

The U.S. Senate race was his fourth race. His only defeat. Even with a supporting family as well as a business he could return to, he was defeated emotionally as well as politically. For more than two years he had put in a 100% effort campaigning for what he considered to be in the public good. Not a self-promoter, Cabaniss had to learn how to promote himself everywhere he went around the state. It was an effort. And he believed that he could win the contest. His waking hours as well as his hours in sleep seemed to be dominated by the campaign and the effort it took to keep going. But through those two years he never thought that he would lose and he certainly did not give any thought to losing his self-confidence. With the election lost, and to his surprise, his self-confidence was lost also.

It took Bill Cabaniss another two years to rebuild his self-confidence and to return to his former self. It was a difficult climb. Others tried to get him to enter other races, but he refused. He had to regain all that he lost within. His interest in elective politics may have waned, but his love of work for the public benefit eventually returned along with his self-confidence.

Since that 1990 election some political observers noticed, later, that "... Democrats, deliberately or not, have shed their working-class image. According to some pollsters, Democrats were increasingly viewed as an elitist, noblesse oblige party that is out of touch with working people – and people [who] wish they were working."[45] The mood of political engagement in Alabama between the years 1990 and 2010 has not gone unnoticed even by disinterested observers.

Alabama was still a small state in terms of population in 1990. No longer rural, the urban population was 2.43 million to 1.6 in the rural regions. Bill Cabaniss would return to full time work at his Precision Grinding Company and remained involved in the advancement of Alabama and the Alabama Republican Party.

Part Four – Statesmanship and Diplomacy

A personal integrity of the highest order never goes unnoticed by friends and foes. William Jelks Cabaniss, Jr. was a friend to virtually everyone. It seemed that everyone wanted to be associated with him. Political operatives wanted him to run for national office; a newly elected governor asked him to help him create his cabinet. It is no wonder that his statesmanship in Alabama public life, his business integrity, and his loyalty to his political beliefs led to his appointment as the United States Ambassador to the Czech Republic.

POLITICAL CHANGE IN ALABAMA WAS ON THE MOVE. Governor Guy Hunt ran for re-election in 1990, defeating AEA head Paul Hubbert. Seen as not a fluke re-election, the Republican Party changed Alabama into the beginnings of a two-party state. John Grenier, the Alabama Republican catalyst of the 1960s, was Hunt's campaign manager.[1] However, *The Birmingham News* headlined that the "GOP proved itself, but only with governor's race."[2] Republican candidates for statewide offices lost, including two of Governor Hunt's appointees. Perry Hand, the former state senator from Baldwin County was appointed Secretary of State but lost in the election.

Golfing at Augusta National
L-R: Corbin Day, Houston Blount, Bill Cabaniss, Lee Styslinger, Jr.
Augusta, Georgia, 1985

No More Elective Politics

In 1992 friends of Bill Cabaniss tried to persuade him to run for the United States House of Representatives. But Cabaniss refused. Perhaps he had his eyes set on the United States Senate where he could probably work better with a fewer number of members.[3] Mike Thompson, a family friend and owner of a heavy duty equipment company in Birmingham, said "Cabaniss never wanted to be in the House. He wanted to be in the Senate."[4] Democrats "Fob" James, Charles Graddick, and Richard Shelby switched parties. The Republican National Convention was held in Houston, Texas at the Astrodome, August 17-20, 1992. In November, 1992 Bill Clinton was elected President of the United States.

"Alabama [U.S. Senator] Richard Shelby, the last of the truly conservative southern Democrats, spent $2.8 million and was re-elected with 65 percent of the vote. Shelby won large majorities from both black (97%) and white (61%) voters. His Republican opponent, Richard Sellers, raised only $150,000, failed to unify the Alabama Republican Party, and lost most of the white independents and Democrats."[5]

In Europe, the new Czech Republic Constitution was ratified on December 16, 1992. It became an independent nation on January 1, 1993.

Bill Clinton took the oath of office as the forty-second President of the United States on January 20, 1993. He served until January 20, 2001.

On January 26, 1993 Václav Havel became president of the Czech Republic as Czechoslovakia splits into two separate and independent nations, Slovakia and the Czech Republic, known as the "velvet divorce." Bratislava is named capital city of the former, Prague becomes the capital city of the latter. President Havel became the head of state of the new Czech Republic and Václav Klaus of the Civic Democratic Party (CDP) became prime minister or head of government just as he had in the free Czechoslovakia government. Klaus's priority was the privatization of the public sector.[6]

James E. Folsom, Jr. became governor of Alabama when Governor Guy Hunt was convicted in court of misuse of public funds and removed from office. Folsom served from 1993 to 1995.[7]

Business in Alabama

In September 1993 Mercedes-Benz Corporation announced that it would build its first North American assembly plant in Tuscaloosa County, in the town of Vance. The factory can be viewed from Interstate Highway 20. On opening day in July 1996 the plant employed 1,500 people. The cost of construction was $300 million and the first M-Class SUV went on sale in September, 1997.[8] Ted vonCannon was brought to Birmingham in the late 1980s from Tennessee. He became the executive director of the Metropolitan Development Board, a privately-funded agency focused on developing businesses in the greater Birmingham area. The MDB worked with companies like Mercedes, Honda, and Hyundai.

Prior to coming to Alabama vonCannon worked in the office of Tennessee Governor Lamar Alexander as commissioner of economic development. vonCannon's biggest accomplishment was in bringing General Motor's Saturn Division to Tennessee. Headhunters in Alabama were looking for a skilled executive to lead the day-to-day work of the MDB.

Edgar Welden, one time executive director and then chairman of the Alabama Republican Party in the 1960s and 1970s, asked vonCannon to talk with the MDB. The Tennessee job was political in the sense that vonCannon's job would be subject to turnover every four years. He told Welden about his reservations and then came for the interview. He took the job that had a board membership of fifty-two corporate executives, mostly of large companies. A senior leader of the board served as chairman for one year. But there was a nine-member executive committee. The board met monthly and the committee more frequently. Bill Cabaniss had been on the board of MDB since vonCannon had been there, but became the one-year chairman shortly after vonCannon arrived in 1988. vonCannon was pleased, at first, at Cabaniss's new role. At their very first meeting Cabaniss said "Show me your books." After the first three hours of grilling, vonCannon thought "I don't know that we got the right guy, he's going to work us out."[9]

Mike Thompson, a former MDB chairman, recalled that Cabaniss held the respect of both Republicans and Democrats in the Alabama Legislature. "My dad [Hall Thompson] said he was a straight-up guy. He was a guy you could count on. He wouldn't lie to anybody. Great friendships. He is a man of huge integrity. … He was always talking business issues to the House and Senate."[10] vonCannon was experiencing Cabaniss's "all business" approach. He thought Cabaniss was an interesting choice since Precision Grinding was a small company and not one of the large businesses in the Birmingham area. But that thought soon faded from his mind. "No chairman before or since had ever been involved with the daily workings of the MDB. Bill grilled us pretty hard. He then told us that he thought we passed muster. We were never over budget, we stayed in the black. I met with Bill once a month at his office and I feared he was going to be a micro-manager. But he wasn't. He was testing me."[11]

In 1994 "Fob" James, who had changed party affiliation, decided to run for governor again. "In the June 7 [primary] balloting, state senator Ann Bedsole of Mobile forced a runoff, but on June 28 [James] defeated her decisively. In the November general election, James ran against incumbent Democratic governor, Jim Folsom, Jr., who had succeeded to that office on the ethics conviction and forced removal from office of Governor Guy Hunt ..."[12]

Karl Rove – from Texas to Alabama

An article appeared in *The Atlantic* magazine in November, 2004 about Karl Rove being called in by the Business Council of Alabama (BCA).[13] By the time of the general election of 1994 all of Alabama's Supreme Court justices were Democrats. There was no political balance in the state's judicial system. Judges in Alabama are elected, not appointed. Part of the continued Democratic dominance in the state's judicial system could be explained, in part, by the passage of the *Judicial Article* in 1973. No one doubted the need for court revision in the 1970s and the results of the 1973 referendum not only changed Alabama's courts but Alabama, in general. Then-Chief Justice Howell Heflin received national attention for the change.

The Alabama judicial model became an unofficial national guide for court management reform. But one of the consequences, unintended or not, of *Judicial Article's* passage was the financial rewards to judicial employees in the form of retirement and pensions. For many, including Republicans and the business community, this was not good. For one thing, it entrenched political power in all sixty-seven counties of Alabama, Democratic political power.

Alabama Supreme Court Justices

A little known fact is that between 1993 and 2004 Alabama led the nation in fund-raising for its Supreme Court candidates. This high-stakes game pitted Alabama's business groups with plaintiff lawyers. Something had to be done. Local judges and juries were awarding verdicts in the millions of dollars for cases that did not warrant it. Alabama had a reputation as "tort hell." It is no wonder that during his time in the Alabama Senate Bill Cabaniss introduced tort reform bills, one after another, as well as ethics reform – the two went together. Every political candidate for the Alabama Legislature campaigned on tort reform in the 1980s, but the courts made their interpretations rendering tort reform ineffective. Again, something had to be done.

According to Alabama businessman Mike Thompson, owner of a Caterpillar Tractor dealership, "Caterpillar never came to Alabama [to build a factory] because of the co-employee lawsuits, heavy unionization, and [a lack of] tort reform. ... Torchmark left for Texas, Caremark went to Nashville. Plaintiffs were 'tort-uring' businesses." That's when Karl Rove was called in to help balance the court, the Alabama Supreme Court.[14]

Rove was hired by the Business Council of Alabama (BCA) in 1994 as a consultant on the Alabama Supreme Court races. Alabama Republicans actually believed that there was no chance of a Republican winning. But, the Republicans did win the Chief Justice seat with Perry Hooper, Sr., an upset.[15]

The Alabama Republican Party was in a slow ascendency in the 1990s and was gaining momentum. It had a Republican governor and there was a rising number of Republican members in the Legislature. Nationally, after two terms of Republican President Ronald Reagan and one of President George H.W. Bush, the Republican Party was strong. But Alabama needed a push, particularly in the makeup of its courts. In Texas, Karl Rove achieved success. Rove came to Alabama and talked with reluctant business leaders – reluctant because business leaders feared retribution if they had a case pending in any state court.[16] That same political reluctance or fear in the Alabama business community might have been a contributor to Bill Cabaniss's senatorial defeat in 1990.

In 1990 Cabaniss needed a direct mail campaign for his U.S. Senate campaign. A Republican Party committee in Washington, D.C. suggested three organizations from which Cabaniss could choose. Cabaniss hired Rove though he never met him personally during the campaign. Some years later Cabaniss and Rove met. According to Cabaniss, Rove said "You're one of the few political campaigns that paid me on time."[17]

The 1994 national elections were significant as they related to Republican victories and growth. "One week after the Republicans gained control of the [U.S.] Senate Richard Shelby of Alabama switched to the GOP, the first crossover since [Strom] Thurmond [of South Carolina] in 1964. Shelby had long behaved as a nominal Democrat, and he gladly joined the new majority in the Senate … I do not believe that there is any future for any conservative Southern Democrat in the Democratic Party … they're marginalized, they're being used and they're not going to really function within the makeup of the House or Senate."[18] Local Alabama politics was not unaffected by the national conservative sweep.

Not only did Republican Perry Hooper, Jr. win Chief Justice, but ten judges in Birmingham defected to the Republican Party, the largest political defection of any state except Texas. In all, Alabama had twenty-three defections including U.S. Senator Richard E. Shelby.[19] When approaching his first re-election campaign, but as a Republican, "Shelby told a reporter that his 'poll numbers are better than they've ever been' and that 'Most people wondered why I didn't do it before.' Shelby did not behave as an ideological purist.[20] Shelby demonstrated his political skill in winning a landslide re-election in 1998 after switching parties."[21]

In the view of famed Alabama historian and former Republican Wayne Flynt, by 1998 "more votes in the Republican primary came from rural areas than from the five major urban counties that had dominated the modern GOP in the state. In both urban and rural races, Republicans tarred their opponents as liberals if they supported their national party and out of step if they did not."[22] But it was Democrat Don Siegelman who won the Alabama governor's race in 1998 and took office in 1999.

Perry Oliver Hooper, Sr. had to wait to assume the Chief Justice's chair. Sitting Chief Justice, Democrat Ernest C. "Sonny" Hornsby, refused to leave his chief justice seat while contesting the results of the election. Hornsby's eleven-month legal suit ended when he lost his court case. Hooper served from October 20, 1995 to January 15, 2001.[23]

The 1994 national general election affected the fortunes of Bob Riley. Riley was "on a plane and read about the 1994 Congressional elections. One line read 'sixty to 70 percent elected had never run for any elected office before.' I had always thought that if you're going to run for office you had to work your way up. That [election] changed my whole perspective. ... My son attended the University of Alabama with Joe Scarborough [a former Florida Panhandle Congressman and TV political talk-show host] who was one of those elected in 1994. [My son said] 'Let's go talk to Joe.' Joe and I became fast friends. Joe said 'If you run for office I will run your campaign.'"[24]

Fob James assumed the office of governor of Alabama, this time as a Republican, in 1995 and served until 1999.[25]

In 1995 the United States-funded *Radio Free Europe/Radio Liberty* relocated from Munich, Germany to Prague.[26] In October, 1998 Czech relations with Iraq and Iran become strained when *Radio Free Europe/Radio Liberty* began new broadcasts aimed at both countries from its Prague headquarters.[27] Even during Ambassador Cabaniss's tenure in Prague from 2004 to 2006 people would tell him how important it was to hear *Radio Free Europe* and the activities of *RFE. RFE* today is still broadcasting to Afghanistan, Iraq, Iran, and Belarus. But there was a time after relocating to Prague that the physical property of *RFE* was threatened by potential terrorist attacks. It took a great deal of effort and discussion between U.S. Congressional committees and authorities of the Czech Republic to eventually build another location outside downtown Prague.[28]

In June, 1996 Václav Klaus was reappointed Prime Minister of the Czech Republic in a minority coalition government following the nation's first general election since independence.[29]

Ann Bedsole, Alabama's first female state senator and Republican gubernatorial primary candidate, was inducted into The Alabama Academy of Honor in 1996.[30]

Howell Heflin's "retirement" in 1996 created an open-seat opportunity for Republicans. In a hard-fought campaign, Republican [Alabama State] Attorney General Jeff Sessions defeated Democratic state senator Roger Bedford 52 to 45 percent. Sessions was a conservative lawyer who had served as U.S. Attorney in Mobile during the Reagan and Bush administrations. [31]

Bill Clinton was re-elected President of the United States in the 1996 general election and took the oath of office on January 20, 1997.

Czech Republic President Václav Havel in October, 1997 urged his nation to fight the 'latent racism' after hundreds of gypsies claimed persecution and sought asylum in Canada and the United Kingdom. One month later the Klaus government resigned following collapse of a coalition amid mounting disquiet over an economic reform program, and allegations of financial corruption. A caretaker administration took over. In November, 1999 the Czech government bowed to internal and international pressure and demolished a controversial wall in the northern town of *Usti nad Labem* built to separate the homes of gypsies from other residents.[32]

Lee Styslinger, Jr. was inducted into The Alabama Academy of Honor in 1998.[33] The stated purpose of the Alabama Academy of Honor is to "bestow honor and recognition upon living Alabamians for their outstanding accomplishments and services." The Alabama Academy of Honor was created by the State Legislature on October 29, 1965. Each person elected to membership is a distinguished citizen of Alabama, chosen for accomplishment or service greatly benefitting or reflecting great credit on the State.

Each year ten members may be elected by The Academy of Honor until its membership reaches one hundred; additional elections will maintain the membership at that size. All living governors of Alabama are automatically members of the Academy.

On October 25, 1968, a nominating committee appointed by Governor Albert P. Brewer in accordance with Act 15 of the Third Special Session of the 1965 Legislature of Alabama selected its first members.[34]

Steve Windom was elected first Republican Lieutenant Governor of Alabama since Reconstruction. He served from January 19, 1999 to January 20, 2003. When Windom was a student at the University of Alabama, he founded in 1968 an on-campus political group called "The Coalition" in opposition to the infamous, and previously unchallenged, campus operation known as "The Machine." Originally a Democrat, Windom switched parties in 1997.[35]

In January, 1998 Václav Havel was re-elected president of the Czech Republic for one more term. Following the general elections in July, Milos Zeman, leader of the Czech Social Democratic Party (CSDP), became Prime Minister. Negotiations with the CDP led to the "opposition agreement" which ensured a full term for the Zeman government.[36]

On March 12, 1999 the Czech Republic became a member of the North Atlantic Treaty Organization [NATO]. And in January, 2000 the Czech CDP renewed its agreement with the Zeman minority CSDP government.

Cabaniss Supports George W. Bush for President

In 2000 Bill Cabaniss agreed to serve as Alabama finance chairman for the George W. Bush presidential campaign. Other members of the finance committee were Luther Strange; Birmingham businessman Mike Thompson, son of Hall Thompson; and Bill Pryor.[37] In the preceding year Catherine and Bill Cabaniss held a fund raising event at their home in Mountain Brook. The host committee included persons eager to support the election of George W. Bush. Some of the committee names were Mr. and Mrs. Ryan deGraffenreid; Mayor of Montgomery and Mrs. Emory Folmar; Mr. and Mrs. Samuel E. Upchurch, Jr.; Mr. Stephen Still; Mr. Drayton Nabers, Jr; Mrs. Judy Bewley; Mr. and Mrs. Luther Strange III; Mr. William Canary, Jr.; Senator Larry Dixon; Mr. and Mrs. Lee Styslinger, Jr.; and Mr. and Mrs. William J. Cabaniss, Jr. Other names were included in the invitation sent out by the committee.

Attending a Book Signing and Honoring First Lady Barbara Bush
L-R: Margaret Barnhart, Kathy Ostrander, First Lady Barbara Bush,
Catherine Cabaniss, Frances Cabaniss Johnson
Front: Laurie Drennen
Kennebunkport, Maine

Special guest at the May 21, 1999 reception was former First Lady Barbara Bush.

In October, 2000 the Czech Republic started up its first nuclear reactor at Temelin which caused an outcry from neighboring Austria. The Czech Republic had not yet been admitted to the European Union, a membership that Austria was now willing to block unless something was done about the nuclear plant.[38]

John Claypool Tribute

The Rev. John Claypool retired and Bill Cabaniss gave the farewell speech at a church family dinner in December, 2000. Although five hundred invitations were sent, 700 people attended. Of the seven hundred attending there were four bishops of the Episcopal Diocese of Alabama and their wives: Furman Stough, Robert Miller, Henry Parsley, and Onell Soto. Claypool, the man whom Cabaniss sought out when his son, Bill Cabaniss III died at age eleven, was now retiring from his pastoral position at St. Luke's Episcopal Church in the Birmingham suburb of Mountain Brook. The former Baptist minister and Episcopal priest and parish rector and the Cabaniss family had become good friends over the years. It was appropriate that Bill Cabaniss, a leader in his church as well as in his community, should lead in giving farewells to his pastoral advisor.[39]

Cabaniss brought to the attention of the farewell gathering Claypool's induction service, some fourteen years earlier. "We should have had some future sense of John's ministry at St. Luke's when the power went off at the church about one hour before his induction ceremony. No lights, no organ, no speaker system, no air conditioning as the procession started down the aisle. Suddenly power came back on and a murmur went through the church 'Here comes John the Baptist.'" Most of all, Bill Cabaniss's farewell recited the spiritual and pastoral dimensions of Claypool's life and ministries: "life is a gift; take courage, take heart, do not be afraid; what breath is to the body, hope is to the human heart; despair is presumptuous; keep the door open to what we don't know; hope is life; the worst things are never the last things; and humility is the doorway to hope." Cabaniss stopped and then proceeded with his favorite – "make us less of what we used to be and more of what we ought to be."[40]

GEORGE W. BUSH BECAME THE FORTY-THIRD PRESIDENT of the United States on January 20, 2001. Birmingham native Condoleeza Rice was appointed National Security Advisor to the president.

Catherine Cabaniss, Secretary of State Condoleeza Rice and Ambassador William J. Cabaniss, Jr.
Birmingham, Alabama 2010
Regions Bank Photo

Street Protests in Czech Republic

The Czech Republic experienced in January the largest street protests since the overthrow of Communism and a strike by journalists led to the resignation of Jiří Hodač as director-general of state television. Hodac was widely seen as a political appointee and accused of compromising editorial independence. In April Vladimir Špidla was elected chairman of the ruling Social Democrats after Prime Minister Milos Zeman stepped down as party boss. Zeman, however, stayed in office until elections were held. And in November the Czech government and Austria's Chancellor Schüssel moved to settle the dispute over the Temelin nuclear power plant by agreeing to tough measures to improve safety and monitor its impact on the environment.[1]

On September 11, 2001 the United States was attacked by terrorists. Marty Connors became chairman of the Alabama Republican Party and served in that position between 2001 and 2005. In November, 2001 Honda Manufacturing of Alabama began production of automobiles in Lincoln, fifty miles east of Birmingham.[2]

In April 2002 the Czech Parliament rejected calls by neighboring countries to repeal post-war Beneš decrees which led to the expulsion of over two and a half million ethnic Germans. In June and July the Czech Social Democratic Party led by Vladimir Špidla topped the polls in elections but won only 70 seats in the 200 seat parliament. Špidla formed a coalition with the centrist alliance of Christian Democrats and the Freedom Union. The Communists were third in the election with 41 seats, their best results since the Velvet Revolution. In December the European Union Summit in Copenhagen formally invited the Czech Republic to join.[3]

Bill Cabaniss wrote a letter to George W. Bush thanking the President for his visit to Alabama prior to the 2002 election. "Laura [Bush] was a big hit in Mobile last Thursday and Friday with Bob and Patsy Riley. And your visit to Auburn this afternoon [October 24, 2002] for Bob Riley and Mike Rogers, will be a tremendous boost to their campaigns for Governor and Congress." Cabaniss hand-wrote a post-script about sending Bush a tape of a John Claypool sermon.[4]

Bob Riley Elected Alabama Governor in 2002

Bob Riley won the election as Alabama governor in 2002. Riley was elected to Congress in 1996 from Alabama's Third Congressional District. A proponent of congressional term limits, Riley left Congress after three two-year terms. While in Congress, the Alabama conservative served as vice chairman of the House Armed Services Subcommittee on Military Readiness. Riley decided to run for the Alabama governor's office in 2002 and defeated Lieutenant Governor Steve Windom and Tim James – son of former Governor "Fob" James, in the Republican primary. In the general election, Riley narrowly defeated incumbent Democratic Governor Don Siegelman.[5]

Riley says he was, at one time, the most non-political person before running for Congress. He ran four different businesses and he and his wife Patsy reared four children. "I remember when I told my father that I was going to run for Congress. He said 'Son, I don't see how you can win as a Republican. Everyone in Clay County wins as a Democrat.'"

Before entering politics, Riley met Bill Cabaniss when Cabaniss was the Republican candidate for the United States Senate. Riley was running a car business. "Having never seen him, when he walked in [to my office] he had a certain bearing, a certain personal [demeanor]. When he walks into a room you know Bill Cabaniss is here. Not being a politician, I was [more] concerned about selling cars." But within a couple of minutes Cabaniss and Riley were talking politics, economics, and the nation. "He really connected with me. … I told my partner at the time that Cabaniss is the quintessential guy." Riley's partner agreed but said, "He's a Republican."

"Bill [Cabaniss] is always ramrod, straight, and totally dignified. We had a bike [motorbike] ride when I was campaigning for governor. We were all going to ride to Montgomery [from Birmingham], 50 to seventy of us. When [my wife] Patsy drove up to our starting point here is this guy [meaning Cabaniss] wearing leather chaps, and a doo-rag on his head, an American flag doo-rag. Patsy then said, 'That's not Bill Cabaniss, is it?'"[6] Cabaniss prepared for that motorcycle ride.

Bill Cabaniss in front of Larry Dixon's home in Montgomery
on motorcycle borrowed from friend Tom Bouleware.

Bill Cabaniss hadn't been on a motorcycle since he was in high school. "This young guy calls me," said Cabaniss. "Why don't you ride in the Riley Rally in Montgomery? We'll get as many motorcycle riders as possible to participate." So Cabaniss went to one of his buddies and asked to borrow his motorcycle. "What for?" "I want to ride to Montgomery for the Riley Rally." "Well," said his buddy, "You're going to have to prove to me that you can ride a bike. You come by Friday night and do some 'lab work'. I've got to check you out." Cabaniss agreed to the lab test and then on Saturday he took a road test, and he passed. One week before the scheduled ride to Montgomery Cabaniss picked up the bike from his buddy, Tom Bouleware, so that he could get used to it.

The plan called for Cabaniss to meet Riley and the other riders on a Saturday morning at the Harley motorcycle dealership in Pelham, Alabama – about ten miles south of Cabaniss's Mountain Brook home. When that Saturday morning came Cabaniss, dressed like Darth Vader, left his home on the borrowed bike. But it was raining. Catherine said "I hope to see you again." Undaunted by the weather, Darth Vader rode off into his re-lived youth. By the time he came to the Birmingham Water Works on U.S. Highway 280, only a couple of miles from his home, Cabaniss stopped to talk with a police officer to ask him what the weather was like between home and Montgomery. "It's raining all the way to Montgomery, in fact it's worse there." "Thank you, officer." Cabaniss moved on and met up with Riley and the other 'Easy Riders' and en masse they rode down to Montgomery for the rally.[7]

Bob Riley won election and began his term in January, 2003. But his transition process got a late start because of an election dispute.[8] The transition process is no small undertaking.

More than 1,000 resumes had been received after the election dispute was resolved, and Riley's team had to fill one-hundred fifty to one-hundred seventy different positions. Not only did cabinet positions need candidates for appointment, but several positions on different commissions that Riley campaigned on needed to be filled with experienced people. Those commissions were a Constitutional Reform Commission, a Tax Reform Commission, and a Commission on Education Spending.[9]

Cabaniss Becomes Alabama Governor-elect Riley's Transition Leader

Bob Riley knew that he wanted Bill Cabaniss to lead his transition team. "There was this universal pride in people knowing Bill Cabaniss, both Democrats and Republicans – his impeccable, immense character, the consummate gentleman." Riley approached Cabaniss about the job and all he asked was "What do you want?" Riley wanted the best people with business backgrounds, if possible, but certainly talented people for his cabinet positions.

Alabama Governor Bob Riley and Ambassador William J. Cabaniss, Jr.
Before the Swearing In Ceremony, 2003
Benjamin Franklin Room, State Department, Washington, D.C.

Of all the twenty-three cabinet members eventually appointed, Riley knew only a few, but was quite pleased with the candidates brought to him by Cabaniss. Riley once told President George W. Bush that he would put his cabinet up against the President's any day.[10]

Riley's cabinet included several former chief executives of major or Fortune 500 companies. One was Drayton Nabers, Jr., former CEO of Protective Life. After Riley asked Nabers about a cabinet position, Nabers went to Cabaniss and asked, "Is he different?" "Different from what?" "Different from other political people," replied Nabers. Cabaniss told Nabers that Riley is different because he might do some unpopular things, but always what is in the best interest for the people of Alabama.

"That's my feeling and that's why I'm supporting him," Cabaniss said.[11] Nabers managed the state's finances and was later appointed to the Chief Justice vacancy in the Alabama Supreme Court. Nabers, also from Clay County, clerked for Supreme Court Justice Hugo Black, another Clay County native. Nabers and Cabaniss attended the Lawrenceville School in New Jersey but were in different classes. Walter Bell became Riley's Insurance Commissioner. Bell was Vice President of Mutual of New York (MONY) living in New York City but in the process of moving to Mobile at the time of the appointment. "Bill just didn't send me one person for each position, he sent two or three and told me to select." [12]

Alabama Republican Party chairman Marty Connors concurred. "If you have Cabaniss as your anchor then you can use that to get other people to follow on, both financial and political people."[13] While serving as governor Riley considered Cabaniss as a sounding board. "He's candid. That's invaluable. He was a source. He had a nuanced institutional knowledge of the Republican Party and the State of Alabama. I don't know the details of his life, but what amazed me is that all the Democrats wanted to be known as a friend of Bill Cabaniss." [14]

Lurking in the Background

Mike Thompson, the Birmingham Caterpillar dealer, met George H.W. Bush on a golf course one time in 2002. Learning that Thompson was from Birmingham, Bush asked "You know Cabaniss?" "Yes, sir." "Well, we have a job for him. And why aren't you raising money for my son?" Thompson and his wife later went to the White House and President George W. Bush, after hearing that they were from Birmingham asked "Do you know Cabaniss?" Not "Do you know *Bill* Cabaniss?" but "Do you know Cabaniss?" "Yes." "Well, I've got a job for him." "What is it?", asked Thompson. "I can't tell you." Something was afoot but Thompson did not know what it was.[15]

There they were, Bill and Catherine Cabaniss, in the White House having dinner with President and Mrs. George W. Bush. A Houston, Texas friend of the Bushes also attended the early fall 2002 private dinner. With just the five of them at dinner Catherine knew that she could begin her education of the President in the appreciation and nuances of fine art. Catherine is a landscape artist.

Months earlier the Cabanisses – along with many supporters of the presidential campaign from the year 2000 – were invited to a big, Texas-styled barbeque on a neighboring ranch in Crawford, Texas. The President held several of these barbeque fests during the summer of 2002. At this particular event that Bill and Catherine attended, the President and others gave short, informal remarks. To Catherine's surprise and amazement the President talked about the art inside the White House. Whatever the President's disposition toward art, Catherine could see that art appreciation was not one of the President's highest priorities. She whispered to Bill that once they returned to Birmingham she would write the President a letter. Bill asked her to forget it and to "please calm down." What Catherine heard could not be set aside in her mind and she told Bill that she still thought that she should at least write. She did. In her letter she offered to walk the President through several Washington, D.C. museums, hopefully to improve his appreciation of art. A few months after the letter was mailed Catherine received a telephone call from a secretary at the White House. "Would you like to have dinner at the White House to talk about art?"

White House Dinner

Once at the dinner, it quickly became clear that the President had his own agenda – and it was not about art. At one point during the evening First Lady Laura Bush quietly turned to Bill and asked if he would be interested in serving in an ambassadorial position. "I'd be honored," Bill replied. Cabaniss understood that ambassadors serve for two or three years and that President Bush and his staff were preparing for the next wave of ambassadorial appointments for 2003 and 2004.

Appreciation BBQ for Supporters
Bill Cabaniss, Laura Bush, U.S. President George W. Bush, Catherine Cabaniss
At a neighboring ranch near the Bush ranch in Crawford, TX, 2002

But the seed was planted and a lengthy wait ensued. It was not until early 2003 that Cabaniss heard anything about the potential opportunity. The White House staff and the Department of State staff were clearly selective in their choice of words when speaking to him. It was two more months after that White House dinner that Clay Johnson called Cabaniss about a "possible" appointment. Johnson called Cabaniss's cell phone as Cabaniss was half-way up his driveway at home. Johnson told him that the President wanted to know if he still held an interest in an ambassadorial appointment. Again Cabaniss said "I'd be honored." Once inside his home Bill told Catherine about the Johnson phone call. "Where are we going?" "I don't know." No appointment had been made and the language and the words used by Johnson were carefully chosen.

It was not until the actual appointment was made that a government official talked as if the appointment were a sure thing, but still in a "what if" mode. The call Cabaniss received in early 2003 simply asked whether he was still interested. Would this tentative mode of conversation ever end in a decision? Yes. That call, followed by another call weeks later, was specifically about an ambassadorial appointment to the Czech Republic.

Not only was a decision made, but now Bill and Catherine Cabaniss knew the country of their assignment. How wonderfully pleased they were with the assignment to the Czech Republic! Cabaniss officially learned of his Czech Republic appointment on October 6, 2003.[16] One of the first persons Cabaniss called was his friend Herb Sklenar. A Harvard Business School M.B.A., Sklenar was at one time chairman and chief executive officer of Birmingham-based Vulcan Materials. He is also of Czech heritage. Sklenar's immigrant father settled in Omaha, Nebraska. Herb Sklenar attended high school with investor Warren Buffet and famous college football coach Homer Smith. Sklenar was helpful in providing background information about the Czech Republic.[17] After the appointment was officially disclosed to Cabaniss, the State Department began the background checks. The ambassadorial training process began soon, preceded by an appearance before the Senate Foreign Relations Committee. With their preparation complete, the Cabanisses were anxious to get to their assignment.[18]

Prior to Cabaniss's arrival in the Czech Republic, Václav Havel ended his ten years [two five-year terms] as president, and Václav Klaus, the former Czech Prime Minister was elected President on February 28, 2003 and sworn into office on March 7.[19] Cabaniss continued in his role of advising Alabama's governor about cabinet appointees, other appointments, and state financial issues.

Amendment One

Alabama Governor Bob Riley initiated his Amendment One/Tax Plan, a promise made during his gubernatorial campaign. Uncharacteristically not Republican, Amendment One called for not only a tax hike but included some strong fiscal accountability measures. The voters killed the Amendment. But Bill Cabaniss had been on board with it and assisted Riley in developing and promoting the Amendment, a measure they believed Alabama needed to return to fiscal health.[20]

Republican Party chairman Marty Connors was livid at even the thought of raising taxes, which is what Amendment One would have done. According to Connors, Riley rolled out the Amendment One tax plan without the knowledge of the Republican Party. It was a $1.2 billion tax proposal. Cabaniss sided with Riley and they created a group endorsing Riley's plan, a group calling itself "Real Republicans." But the Republican Party rejected the plan, too. Connors and the party's steering committee rejected Amendment One nineteen to two. The executive committee of the party numbered 120 members, but 100 members didn't show up for the meeting. The voters rejected the Amendment, handily. But, [Connors] gave him a pass because Cabaniss is loyal, a soldier, and he went along with Riley. "Cabaniss is a soldier and when asked to go to war for his leader, he will."[21] The underlying story of *Amendment One* centered on a clash of principles within the Alabama Republic Party.

Within months of assuming office, Governor Riley was informed by his finance director, Drayton Nabers, Jr., that the state's budget was in worse shape than originally thought. The so-called "Rainy Day Fund" was unfunded. It was at zero. Increases in costs of insurance benefits for teachers and state employees were not helping. In all, Riley believed that he had to reverse his campaign pledge of "no new taxes" and submit a plan to the Legislature to raise taxes to the tune of more than $1 billion. That broken pledge or broken principle was replaced by the reality of saving the state's services for its constituents. The proposed package by Riley contained several reform measures in cutting the rising costs of public employee health insurance, changes in teacher tenure and closer control and oversight of education spending. Already, a tax hike was not a Republican principle. Earmarks, not necessarily Republican, had always been used for requiring state income taxes to be spent on teacher salaries, for example.

Riley's package, to be known as *Amendment One*, demanded that none of the taxes would be earmarked. Riley's House floor leader and later Speaker of the Alabama House, Mike Hubbard, said that the "no earmark" demand was one of two reasons that worked against the bill. The "politics makes strange bedfellows" motif also kicked in. Paul Hubbert, the powerful Democrat head of the Alabama Education Association (AEA), and Bill Canary, the chief executive of the Business Council of Alabama (BCA), supported *Amendment One*. That was prior to the referendum being placed before the public.

Another irony was that the people most likely to benefit from *Amendment One's* passage, meaning the lower middle class and people living in poverty, voted against the bill.[22] Professor Emeritus Wayne Flynt of Auburn University and state historian, shares the belief that the people who would have benefited most from passage of Amendment One did not vote in its favor. Flynt understood why Bill Cabaniss stood by Governor Bob Riley on the tax hike. Yes, Cabaniss is loyal. But Cabaniss was doing what he thought was right for the people of Alabama. Many voters, Flynt opined, did not know that some of the leading proponents of the measure would be the ones most taxed. The tax burden would have financially impacted the upper income people more than others, and yet they were the ones who voted for the measure.[23] After the voter defeat Governor Riley began other cost cutting and reform measures and began to move the state forward. Bill Cabaniss was one of his closest advisors.

November 13, 2003 – Alabama Chief Justice Roy Moore was removed from office for defying a direct Federal Court Order to remove a monument of the Ten Commandments from the Alabama Judicial Building site. William Pryor, Alabama State Attorney General, a Republican like Moore, prosecuted the case and Moore was removed from office. Governor Bob Riley appointed Drayton Nabers, Jr. to fill the Chief Justice vacancy.[24]

On the national scene it was reported that the United States Ambassador to the Czech Republic, Craig Stapleton, was stepping down in order to advise President George W. Bush on his 2004 re-election campaign. The same report, an Internet blog, reported that William Cabaniss, Jr., an Alabama businessman, had been nominated to replace Stapleton. The blogger asserted that though Cabaniss was not a "Pioneer for Bush," the nomination was political payback. According to the Center for Responsive Politics, a group that tracks campaign contributions, Cabaniss and his wife had contributed $35,050 to Republican candidates since 1999.[25]

Within days of the nomination announcement by The White House, the Birmingham area was a buzz of excitement. The Very Reverend Paul Zahl, then dean of the Episcopal Cathedral Church of the Advent in downtown Birmingham, wrote of the nomination in his "Dean's Bulletin Board." Sounding more like a political reporter than a preacher, Zahl wrote "Cabaniss, who declined comment Wednesday, is CEO and chairman of Precision Grinding, Inc. … His political history, which can be a key factor in picking ambassadors, is that of a loyal Republican and friend of the Bush family well before the GOP grew into its current prominence in Alabama politics."[26]

Cabaniss sat before the Senate Foreign Relations Committee on September 30, 2003 and gave an account of himself.

At the hearings, Mr. Cabaniss testified that "Since graduating from college and my days in the United States Army, I have been compelled by three interests: public service, community affairs, and business. Much of my professional life has been dedicated to building Precision Grinding, Inc., a small metal grinding company, into a successful steel plate processing and metal machining business." He stated that he eventually ran for and won seats in the Alabama House and Alabama Senate and that he had served on numerous boards such as Junior Achievement and the Boy Scouts.[27]

Wayne Flynt received a call from Bill Cabaniss. Flynt had spent time in the Czech Republic over several different periods and had once taught at the International Baptist Seminary in Prague. Flynt said that Cabaniss reached out to him to ask him his perspective on the Czech Republic, particularly its youth, the drug culture, and other areas of concern. "It was typical of Bill" to seek the opinion of others even though he had already been briefed by the State Department. In Flynt's view there are several well-educated entrepreneurial leaders in Alabama who are genuinely interested in Alabama's future. Although at opposite ends of the political or ideological spectrum from Flynt, he believes that people like Herb Sklenar, former CEO of Vulcan Materials in Birmingham; Ann Bedsole, a financier and former state legislator from Mobile; Mike Warren, former CEO of Energen, Inc. and CEO of Children's of Alabama in Birmingham; Bill Smith, CEO of Royal Coffee in Birmingham; and Bill Cabaniss all have an unselfish eye toward making progress for all of Alabama. Those are the leaders who understand how to make Alabama competitive and have worked their professional careers toward those types of goals.[28] Flynt said that Cabaniss may not have been an effective retail politician, but he has always been the perfect diplomat. "He does not care what part of an ideological continuum a person lives and works in. He is adept at learning the point of view of others, at making friends, and at making alliances for the good of the whole."

Flynt was not at all surprised at Cabaniss's appointment as Ambassador to the Czech Republic. It was natural.

Cabaniss Takes Oath of Office

On December 9, 2003, and flanked by family and friends, Cabaniss took his oath of office as administered by United States Secretary of State Colin Powell, with all the seriousness of an ambassador's responsibility to his host country and to his own. Soon Catherine and Bill Cabaniss returned to Birmingham and prepared to leave for their new home in Prague.[29]

WILLIAM JELKS CABANISS, JR. UNDERSTOOD THE HIGH responsibility of representing the United States and its President in his new assignment. The Czech Republic is pro-American, pro-free market, and is a democratic nation. Cabaniss knew that and he wanted to promote that relationship as much as possible. He noted those sentiments and facts in his confirmation hearing in September, 2003.

Cabaniss stated that the United States' "excellent relationship with the Czech Republic is rooted deeply in our historical ties. We share a common bond as people whose love of liberty was forged in the struggle to attain it. The Czechs are now successfully completing their transition to an open society that began in the 1960's [sic] with the Prague Spring and continued in the 1970's [sic] with the dissident movement, Charter '77. The Revolution of late 1989, just days after the fall of the Berlin Wall, was truly inspiring."[1]

Prague
"Prague has emerged as a crown jewel of central Europe—a vibrant center of culture and thought that attracts students from around the world." This declaration about Prague resides on the homepage of the Internet-based website of New York University Prague.[2] On June 24, 2004 Ambassador William J. Cabaniss, Jr. delivered an address to the third graduating class of NYU Prague. He told the class that it was his pleasure to be with them and that he congratulated them for the successful completion of their studies. He saluted their parents and grandparents for their support.[3] The NYU Prague course of studies was a calling card for any student interested in world affairs, art, culture and politics. Who could turn down an offer so well presented?

NYU Prague advertised that many of their courses are taught by leading dissidents of the Velvet Revolution, foreign ambassadors, and noted writers. Promoting Prague, the university's website shares that "NYU Prague students engage in this environment via co-curricular programming that includes attendance at global conferences in the city and a dynamic lecture series hosted at the NYU Prague Institute for

Democracy, Economy, and Culture. Internships are widely available, and in past semesters students have written for Czech magazines and worked with the public relations and fundraising arms of the Archa and Ponec theatres and the Prague Philharmonic Orchestra."

Prague is a beautiful city. It is a city of both Gothic and Baroque churches and medieval synagogues. It is a city of contrasting architectural styles, of ancient castles and modern day shopping malls. In the early days its natural geography made it a center of central Europe, and the town's outskirts formed a crossroads through which trade was conducted and armies would pass. It became a new home for settlers, especially for Germans and displaced Jews. The historic center of Prague – the Czech word *Praha* means "threshold" – had five quarters: Hradčany, the Castle District; Mala Strana, the lesser quarter; Staré Město, the Old Town; Nové Mesto, New Town; and Josefov, the Jewish Quarter.

Beginning in the early seventeenth century, Czech religious liberty was suppressed by the Hapsburg Empire for one hundred fifty years. Jesuit missionaries in their attempt to convert the population probably caused a rise in Baroque architecture and music during this same period. Rapid industrialization began in the mid-1800s – a railroad was built and operated between Prague and Vienna. Czech culture began to recover during the mid-1800s, inspiring the construction of monuments like the National Theatre and the National Museum.

The movie *Amadeus*, which had its first showing in the United States on April 5, 1985, was produced by Czech native Milos Forman. Set during the productive years of Wolfgang Amadeus Mozart, Forman filmed the movie in Prague, Kroměříž, and Vienna. Some of the scenes were recorded in the Count Nostitz Theatre known today as the Estates Theatre in Prague. Mozart personally conducted the premier production of his *Don Giovanni* in this theatre. [4]

On October 28, 1918 an independent state of Czechs and Slovaks was declared in the wake of the fall of the Austro-Hungarian Empire at the end of World War I. For the next twenty years Czechoslovakia would flourish in the arts, literature, industry, and trade. In 1938 the Nazis occupied Bohemia and Moravia and in 1948 a communist coup d'état combined to end the Czech and Slovak short period of freedom for the next forty-one years.[5]

The U.S. Ambassador's Residence in Prague

Petschek Palace or Petschek Villa, as it is affectionately known, is the Residence of the U.S. Ambassador in Prague.. Otto Petschek, the patriarch of one of the wealthiest families in the country, built the edifice in the late 1920's, during the brief flowering of the first republic of Czechoslovakia. The Petscheks were a German-speaking Jewish family, and their wealth was in large part from coal mine holdings and banking.[6] Upon completion of construction the family moved into the new home in the winter of 1929-1930. In 1934 Otto Petschek died.[7]

The Nazi threat of 1938, particularly toward Czechoslovakia, caused the family to flee to the United States. When the Nazis occupied Prague they seized the house until 1945. During that time, the house became the residence of the head of the German occupying army. The Soviets were the next residents when they drove out the Nazis. The next resident was a communist Czechoslovak army general and his staff. Amazingly, little damage was done to the Residence during all those years. Indeed, Prague suffered little destruction during World War II.[8] According to Cabaniss, the word on the street at that time was that Adolf Hitler wanted to place his art in the Petschek home; therefore, the German Army did not destroy the home.

In 1945 United States Ambassador Laurence Steinhardt leased the Residence from the Czechoslovak Ministry of National Defense on a year-to-year arrangement. Eventually the Ministry turned over the property to the City of Prague, but the city government was either unable or unwilling to maintain the property as called for in the terms of the transfer agreement.[9]

On July 20, 1948 the United States Government, through Ambassador Steinhardt, purchased the property. The deteriorating relationship between the U.S. and the communist government of Czechoslovakia saw the assets of the property frozen for several decades. It was during the communist period, especially in the 1980s when the Residence was frequently visited by Czech dissidents at the invitation of U.S. Ambassador Bill Luers and his wife Wendy to participate in meetings or social events. Václav Havel was arrested once when only two blocks from the Residence on his way home from one of the U.S.-sponsored events.[10]

Deputy Chief of Mission in Prague

Kenneth Hillas was the Deputy Chief of Mission (DCM) at the American Embassy in Prague. The Ambassador's position is known also as the Chief of Mission. Cabaniss met Hillas in Washington, D.C. months prior to his arrival in Prague. Already in service as DCM, Hillas was in Washington attending a DCM conference in 2003. Cabaniss had only been nominated at this time, but not yet confirmed. Sensing a positive result from the Senate Foreign Relations Committee, the two had some time to prepare for Cabaniss's arrival in Prague.

Normally a newly appointed ambassador is given a choice to select one of three potential DCMs. Hillas was already serving under Ambassador Craig Stapleton when Stapleton resigned to return to Washington to advise President Bush on the re-election campaign in 2004. Stapleton's departure automatically made Hillas the "acting" ambassador or *charge d'affaires ad interim* in Prague. Hillas was a career diplomat, not a political appointee. Nonetheless, he was acting ambassador when he and Cabaniss met for breakfast in 2003. Hillas's term was three years which at the time of their meeting had not expired – he had eighteen months remaining. But the two men hit it off well and Hillas was asked to continue as the new Ambassador's DCM.[11]

While Cabaniss was still in his pre-credentialing period, DCM Hillas thought of a way to meet "unofficially" with high level Czech government officials. Technically, until an Ambassador had been officially credentialed by his host nation, he could not meet with anyone in a diplomatic role. Hillas, however, knew that Czech Foreign Minister Cyril Svoboda loved to attend musical performances at the National Symphony. One evening Hillas took Cabaniss to a Czech National Symphony concert in the hope of a chance encounter with the Foreign Minister. Such an encounter would innocently introduce the new American Ambassador to a high ranking government official. Intermission presented their best opportunity. Seeing the Foreign Minister at a glance, Hillas quickly introduced Cyril Svoboda to Bill Cabaniss. But, no. It was Cyril's twin brother Josef, the Czech Finance Minister. Hillas believes that in his eagerness to have his new Chief of Mission meet a government official, he mis-interpreted the face of one brother for the other. Hillas noted that "Svoboda" is the Slavic word for freedom.[12]

Officially Received as U.S. Ambassador

On January13, 2004 Ambassador William Cabaniss presented his credentials to Czech Republic President Václav Klaus.[13] Within days of credentialing, he flew to Baghdad with Foreign Minister Cyril Svoboda.[14]

U.S. Ambassador William J. Cabaniss, Jr. and Czech Republic President Václav Klaus, January, 2004 Credentialing

In an interview with Ian Willoughby of *Czech Radio 7- Radio Prague*, Cabaniss was asked about his first weeks as Ambassador. "It was a tremendous opportunity to be invited to travel with Foreign Minister Svoboda, and to attempt to help the Czech companies who were also travelling to Baghdad to meet the different people in the Provisional Authority, to try to qualify for some of the contracts to rebuild the oil fields and refineries in Iraq."[15] Cabaniss knew that several of the Czech companies had originally built many of the oil fields and refineries in the 1980s. Who best to renovate them than those companies that built them in the first place? And Cabaniss was indeed the best person to travel to Iraq with those Czech business leaders. As a successful businessman himself, Cabaniss knew how to bring different parties together for their mutual benefit.

In the same interview, Cabaniss was asked about the possibility of President Klaus being invited to Washington. "Your predecessor here in Prague, Craig Stapleton, disagreed with the Czech President, Václav Klaus, about the [Iraq] war, and there has been some question as to whether Mr [*sic*] Klaus will be invited to Washington during George Bush's current term. Do you know anything about that invitation, will it come?" Cabaniss said that he hoped that the invitation would come but "that the invitation has to come from the White House. … I'm just not in a position to speculate on that, at any time." A clear statement, not only about the decision-making authority of the White House, but perhaps a message to the public that the American Ambassador represents the President of the United States and that this ambassador would not put his president in a bad situation by speculating on the chief executive's decision-making.

Prior to Cabaniss's arrival in Prague, it was known that there was a strained relationship between Klaus and Stapleton. Klaus became President in early 2003 and Stapleton left office that fall. Hillas was acting ambassador after that. Cabaniss might have been aware of the relationship between Klaus and Stapleton. But it is characteristic of Bill Cabaniss, regardless of prior histories, to seek amicable relationships not only with business partners, but political opponents. So it was natural for Cabaniss to seek out Klaus, and Klaus was possibly more eager to get on a good footing with the new ambassador. In any case, the relationship proved fruitful over time.[16]

Bill Cabaniss's first few days in Prague were covered by the *Prague Post* and the Czech weekly *Respekt*. Noting the headline "CABANISS, NE CANNABISS!!!," *Post* reporter Alan Levy asked him when he had "first discovered that his ancestral family name could carry a certain countercultural cachet in post-1960s drug society." Cabaniss said that he didn't even know what the word meant until he was well into his thirties. "My generation had escaped the drug culture. We were more into smoking and drinking … I did a little of each."[17]

The Prague Post reporter wanted to know much about Bill Cabaniss and his life, including his courtship of Catherine. The article provided some detail about Cabaniss's commuter courtship between Vanderbilt University located in Nashville, Tennessee to Sweet Briar College in the mountains of Virginia – a twelve-hour, 500 mile commute from Friday evening to Monday morning on the return. Cabaniss's business and political careers received attention, and especially the Kennebunkport connection to the Bush Family was noted. As Ambassador, this was the first time that Bill Cabaniss had been to Prague. In 1995 Catherine

Cabaniss visited Prague on an art tour by the Birmingham Museum of Art. Cabaniss told Levy that "I venture to predict that the spring weather will see her sitting out with her easel on the Letná plain."[18]

The American Chamber of Commerce in Prague (AmCham)

The American Chamber of Commerce in the Czech Republic, led by Weston Stacey its chairman, is known as *AmCham*, and on St. Patrick's Day, 2004 Cabaniss was its guest speaker. Knowing that the audience was mostly interested in his history, he recited his college, military, business, and political background. He especially wanted *AmCham* members and guests to know that he was associated with the Birmingham Area Chamber of Commerce, the Birmingham Metropolitan Development Board, and the National Association of Manufacturers. In other words, as a business owner and developer himself, he was one of them. It was appropriate in his ambassadorial role to cite the Czech business environment in relation to neighboring nations.

At the same time that Ambassador Cabaniss was pushing for reform in the Czech business arena, New York banker Jack Stack, CEO of Ceska Sporitelna Bank in Prague, through his great leadership, was instigating major reform in the Czech banking industry. In addition, Stack's wife, Patty, made a major contribution to the Czech community while serving as president of the International Women's Association of Prague (IWAP).

Cabaniss said that foreign investment had been one of the two motors of Czech economic growth since 1999. The second was domestic consumption which had been boosted by the better wages paid by foreign investors. He did not ignore the fact that inward foreign investment had fallen between 2002 and 2003 – from $8.4 billion to $2.5 billion, respectively. Looming larger than the investments themselves was the need to complete the reform process that began in the 1990s after the Velvet Revolution. Cabaniss reassured his audience that part of his job when meeting with Czech ministers was to emphasize the continuation of government and political reform.

The cost of employment at that time in the Czech Republic was higher than in Hungary and Poland. There was much that *AmCham* could do to encourage positive business change. Aware that *AmCham* had a large number of Czech members Cabaniss reassured them that the objectives of *AmCham* were intended for the benefit of both U.S. and Czech businesses.

Cabaniss said that the Embassy would continue to support efforts to increase the transparency of government business and reduce corruption. He cited work by the Czech Ministry of Justice drafting a bill to be presented to Parliament on conflicts of interest by public officials. The U.S. Embassy would be urging progress on that effort.[19]

The political environment in the Czech Republic can be characterized as fragile because it has a coalition-type of government like most European nations. For the almost three years that Bill Cabaniss was the U.S. Ambassador in Prague, the Czech national government had four different prime ministers.

First Meeting in Havel's Personal Office, 2004
Former Czech President Václav Havel and
U.S. Ambassador William J. Cabaniss, Jr.

Former Czech President Vaclav Havel and
U.S. Ambassador William J. Cabaniss, Jr.
U.S. Embassy, Prague, Czech Republic 2004

Ambassador Cabaniss's DCM, Kenneth Hillas, after serving out his term in Prague, was transferred to Warsaw, Poland and served as the DCM to Ambassador Victor Ashe, former Mayor of Knoxville, Tennessee. Cameron Munter, DCM to Ashe, then transferred to Prague under Ambassador Cabaniss.

The office of the Czech presidency, with a term of five years, provides a level of continuity. President Klaus, as head of state, and his office provided the necessary continuity during those political leadership changes.[20]

During the initial eight weeks on the job Ambassador William J. Cabaniss, Jr. covered a lot of territory, both literally and diplomatically. On March 23, 2004, Cabaniss delivered an address to the European Banking and Financial Forum. The theme of the businessman-ambassador was that the United States is not only a technology power house, it is a major contributor to the development of innovative financial instruments that facilitate the movement of capital from savers to productive enterprises.[21]

Letter Home

Bill Cabaniss wrote to his friends back home. His April 28, 2004 email began with a summary. "I will try and give a snapshot of our first three and a half months in the Czech Republic beginning January 9th when we flew into Ruzyne Airport with 12 inches of snow on the ground.

U.S. Deputy Chief of Mission Kenneth Hillas, daughter Adriana, Barbara Hillas , and
U.S. Ambassador Bill Cabaniss, Prague, 2004

We were met by U.S. Deputy Chief of Mission Kenneth Hillas and his wife Barbara, and Rhonda Krizova of the U.S. Embassy. For the next eight weeks, snow was on the ground – quite cold, but beautiful." One of the Cabaniss daughters, Mary Cabaniss Ballard, arrived two days later from Seattle and Catherine's sister Jean Caldwell arrived from Atlanta. They stayed ten days and helped "Catherine get settled." Other early visitors from the states were Robert Hanson who was serving in the Peace Corps in Romania, and Bill Bru from Mobile, Alabama, an early Prague real estate investor, and his wife Annabel. Dr. Douglas Hyland came soon after with an art group from his New Britain (Connecticut) Museum of American Art. Other early visitors were Jeanne and Ross Hamilton of New York; Stuart Bohannon from Tryon, North Carolina; Katherine Houston and Dr. Ted Ongaro travelled from Boston. Katherine Houston made a presentation to Czech women of her beautiful porcelain fruits and vegetables which she has been making for many years.

A reception was held for the Fulbright Program with music provided by Mark Ludwig's Terezin Chamber Music.

There were also visitors from Maine: Gail and Charles "Chuck" Alling [author of the book *A Mighty Fortress: Lead Bomber Over Europe*], Becky and Gil Perkins, Ann and Elliot Speers, and Betsy and "Spike" Heminway.

The letter stated that after Cabaniss returned from Baghdad he traveled to Stuttgart, Germany for meetings with European Military Commanders on the reorganization of the North Atlantic Treaty Organization (NATO). This was followed by speeches to various groups and introductory meetings with then Prime Minister Špidla, President Klaus, Czech Cabinet Ministers, members of Parliament, and business leaders. There were other meetings with the people who work within the Embassy, both American and Czech citizens. There were eighty Americans who were career foreign service people, and 130 Czech citizens.

Fourth of July, 2005
Saluting the Colors
U.S. Embassy, Prague, Czech Republic
L-R: Czech President Vaclav Klaus, U.S. Ambassador William J. Cabaniss, Jr.,
Czech Prime Minister Jiří Paroubek
United States Marine Corps Embassy Detachment Color Guard

The Embassy and the Residence are in separate locations in Prague. The Residence is where the Ambassador and Mrs. Cabaniss lived and is used for receptions and other functions by the Ambassador and others on staff. Soon after their arrival in Prague, the Cabanisses held a reception for all Embassy personnel and then another reception for ambassadors stationed in Prague from other nations. Cabaniss once held, in 2005, a breakfast at the Residence for Czech business leaders and Microsoft founder Bill Gates. There were also lunches, not only with business people, but with Czech Parliamentarians. Cultural receptions and concerts were frequent events. Catherine had coffee meetings with Czech women, artists, and wives of Embassy personnel. Ambassador Cabaniss and Catherine welcomed Gail Andrews, Director of the Birmingham Museum of Art; Margaret Livingston, former Board Chairman of the Birmingham Museum of Art; and Dr. Jeannine O'Grody, Chief Curator of the Birmingham Museum of Art; in June, 2004. The purpose of their visit was a lecture by Dr. O'Grody on "The Art of Leonardo: The Da

Vinci Code Deciphered." Following the lecture was a piano recital by LaVona Rushton of Birmingham.

One of Many Art and Social Gatherings with Czech Women
Front L-R: Lenka Duskova, Iva Drebitko, Pavla Kalousova, Eliska Collidge, Catherine Cabaniss
Second Row L-R: Marilyn Wyatt, Katerina Krylova
Others unidentified
Cabaniss Family Archive Photo

In his April 28, 2004 letter, Cabaniss mentioned not only his travel and meetings but such activities as the Embassy's monitoring of and assistance in the extensive U.S. trade and investments in the country. He mentioned U.S. efforts through the Embassy to encourage reforms in commercial registry, bankruptcy laws, and corruption. Cabaniss told his readers that "We work hard at persuading Czech government leaders of the importance of creating the best business and investment climate in Europe."[22]

The Cabaniss Team Approach

The team approach by Bill and Catherine Cabaniss was evident in their work. Catherine was interested in discovering the Czech art scene. An artist herself, she met many Czech artists and visited their studios in Prague and in other towns. The Art-in-Embassy Program installed a beautiful exhibition of New York artists in the Residence which also included paintings by two Alabama artists – Beverly Erderich and Amy Pleasant.

Catherine Cabaniss and Barbara Hillas, the wife of Embassy DCM Kenneth Hillas, traveled one day to Železný Brod to visit the widow of Stanislav Libenský, Jaroslava Brychtová. Libenský was the premier glass maker-artist in the Czech Republic who had died two years earlier. Corbin and Dodie Day, friends of the Cabanisses, gave a Libenský sculpture to the Birmingham Museum of Art.[23]

Catherine Cabaniss and Artist Lenny Aardse
Attending the Exibitiion of Adela Matsova at
Museum Kampa

Catherine was introduced to Meda Mladek, founder of Museum Kampa, by an American Embassy staff member. Ms. Mladek then introduced Catherine to the Czech art community and she visited the U.S. Residence for many art events.

Madame Meda Mladek
Founder, Museum Kampa, Prague, CR
Photo: Cabaniss Family Photos

Cabaniss remarked once that "Our experience in the Czech Republic was joyous. With my background in business and politics, and Catherine in art, we were a joint venture. We had receptions and she would bring in people from the art community around the Czech Republic. She would invite them to the Residence for artistic and social gatherings. In the basement of the Residence she set up her shop – she painted while over there. Catherine couldn't sell her art, obviously, but her work would be in Czech art shows. Through her I met a lot of Czechs that I would never otherwise have met."[24]

Ambassador William J. Cabaniss, Jr. meets Dagmar Havelova
U.S. Embassy Reception, Prague, Czech Republic 2005

A week prior to writing his first letter home to friends, Bill and Catherine drove to Ostrava on the eastern border with Poland. Comparing Ostrava with Birmingham, Cabaniss described Ostrava as a town in transition of downsizing from a steel-making and coal mining economy by attracting more diversified businesses. While there the Cabanisses met Mayor Evžen Tošenovský, who developed Ostrava's Center of Integrated Rescue System of Moravia-Silesian Region. This was an operation where fire, police, and emergency medical services were joined under one operational roof serving a population of one million.

Cabaniss wrote that he was impressed by the character of the Czech people who, since coming out of forty years of Communist rule, have established since 1989 a democratic form of government and a market-driven economy. "It's certainly an honor for us to represent the United States in the Czech Republic."[25]

The Embassy

The Cabaniss team approach extended to employees of the Embassy, both American Foreign Service persons and Czech staff. According to Deputy Chief of Staff Kenneth Hillas "With every ambassador there is a little bit of re-orientation [by staff with the new ambassador]. Ambassador Cabaniss was more engaged, he was like a sponge, he really wanted to understand." There are several major areas of responsibilities which Embassy personnel manage. For example, there are consular duties covering citizenship, deaths, welfare and whereabouts; issuing visas for tourists and business people, for immigrants; and property issues.

Bill and Catherine Cabaniss with Staff at U.S. Residence in Prague

Embassies are run along typical business lines such as finance, personnel, and information technology. But there is also a political section, an economic section, and a security office. There is, of course, public diplomacy dealing with cultural and educational issues, and a press attaché and media relations staff. This U.S. embassy had onsite representatives from the U.S. Federal Bureau of Investigation; legal attaché; representatives from the Commerce Department; Department of

Homeland Security; and the Foreign Agricultural Service. Some embassies have Secret Service personnel.

An Ambassador, though the President's personal representative, is employed by the United States Department of State.[26]

The Visa Situation

One of the major items calling for Cabaniss's attention after arriving was the visa issue. Czech Republic citizens who wanted to travel to the United States for personal or business reasons found the process quite challenging. In many ways the requirements for obtaining a visa were humiliating. The visa issue had a history.

In the 1980s the U.S. Congress passed visa-waiver legislation allowing citizens from nations such as Germany, France, the United Kingdom, Spain, and Italy to obtain a tourist visa to come to the U.S. for a 90-day period. But countries such as Czechoslovakia, Hungary, Poland and other former Iron Curtain Soviet satellites were not included in the visa waiver. Because they were under communist rule in the 1980s they were excluded, but the legislation had not been updated since the fall of the Iron Curtain in 1989.

It was next to impossible for an American Foreign Service officer to conduct a two- to three-minute interview with a visa applicant and determine whether that applicant would actually return to his or her home country after the 90-day period. Applicants had to present their financial information so that a determination could be made whether he or she had sufficient funds to return to their home country after the visit to the United States. To Ambassador Cabaniss the process was a major impediment to good U.S.-Czech relations.

At virtually every meeting Cabaniss had with Czech government officials, the topic of visa obstacles was brought up. Much lobbying of the U.S. Congress by Polish, Czech, and Hungarian groups was conducted. But it was the President of Poland who lobbied American President George W. Bush on the problem. The Polish president, who was on good terms with Bush, would always raise the question of American visa policy.[27]

Once when Ambassador Cabaniss was in Washington he went to the Department of Homeland Security and spoke with people who directly dealt with the visa situation in European nations. "I was amazed to find out that the ambassadors from Poland, Hungary, and other countries, had ... given information which helped Homeland Security. Ironically, they had not heard from the Czech Ambassador [to the United States]. So I called Ambassador Kolar, who had just been in the United States for a few months and had been a good friend of mine in the [Czech] Department of Foreign Affairs. I gave him the name of the person [in Homeland Security] and suggested that he meet with him to resolve the situation."[28]

According to a group known as the Congressional Research Center, the George W. Bush administration began in 2005 to provide countries interested in joining the Visa Waiver Program (VWP) with "roadmaps" to aid the countries in meeting the program's criteria. Some of the countries complained that since the "roadmaps" did not contain milestones or time tables, it was difficult to measure the amount of progress made toward fulfilling the criteria for VWP membership. There were 13 "road map" countries some of which were Bulgaria, Cyprus, Czech Republic, Hungary, Poland, Romania, and Slovakia. Eight of those countries have been admitted to the VWP. The issues surrounding the "road maps," were the focus of an event held by the Heritage Foundation on February 8, 2006. The event, held in Washington, D.C., was entitled, *"Fighting a More Effective War on Terrorism: Expanding the Visa Waiver Program"* The featured speakers were Ambassadors Petr Kolar of the Czech Republic, John Bruton of the EU, Janusz Reiter of Poland, and András Simonyi of Hungary.[29]

American ambassadors are cautioned by the State Department not to get involved in consular affairs. An ambassador is the highest-level representative of the President of the United States and therefore is encouraged to stay clear of day-to-day, normal embassy transactions. For Bill Cabaniss that is like asking him to ignore the details of his company's machine shop's procedures when machining steel plate for a customer. For a company CEO as well as an ambassador, decisions must be made concerning involvement in the details of operations.

But Ambassador Cabaniss received telephone calls, emails, and letters from families whose sons and daughters had received visa rejection notifications. Their visa requests were for travel to visit friends and family for weddings and various other events in the United States.

For fear of their never returning to the Czech Republic the Foreign Service Officer rejected their visa requests. Cabaniss asked his Consul General to review many of these cases. In some cases, the decisions were reversed. Cabaniss said "I invited the different political leaders, including the Prime Minister at that time, to come to the Embassy and I would give them a tour through the consul section. This gave them a first-hand view of what [Czech citizens] had to go through in order to get a visa."[30] It was a two-way street.

After seeing the reasonable care that the Embassy consul staff took and the seriousness in which they examined visa applications, a change of attitude in Czech leadership began to emerge. But the problem was not totally resolved. Czech leaders received many letters from their constituents about how they were treated in the U.S. Embassy. Many had hurt feelings. The visa issue was a reason for strained relations between the U.S. and the Czech Republic.

Ambassador Cabaniss communicated closely with other United States ambassadors in three Central European nations. Every six months Ambassador Bert Walker from Hungary, Ambassador Chris Hill and later Ambassador Victor Ashe from Poland, and Ambassador Ron Weiser from Slovakia, would meet on a rotation basis in their respective embassy residences to compare similar challenges and solutions.

U.S. – Czech Relations

Bill Cabaniss emphasizes that the relationship between the Czech Republic and the United States goes back to the period after World War I. President Woodrow Wilson and Czech President Masaryk worked together during peace talks. Wilson is revered for helping bring into existence the new nation of Czechoslovakia in 1918. In 1928 a monument was erected in Prague honoring Wilson. The statue is situated across from the main train station. In 2002 a memorial to Masaryk was placed on Embassy Row in Washington, D.C. The people of this central European nation have always been pro-American, freedom-loving, and believers in a free market system of commerce. Despite their loss of independence in 1938 and later difficulties, the Czech and Slovak people have maintained their zest for freedom and independence.

On May 1, 2003, the Czech Republic joined the European Union.[31]

Fourth of July

Ambassador Cabaniss invited Czech President Klaus to speak at the U.S. Residence for the 2004 Fourth of July celebration. Klaus began his address with "I am honored to be asked by the Ambassador of the United States, this time by Ambassador Cabaniss, to say a few words here on this very special occasion as a representative of the Czech Republic. ... I can assure you that for the last [few] years the 4th of July has been a firm and fixed point in our annual calendar of events. In the past we were forced to remember other events." Klaus continued by reminding the audience that July 4, 2004 was also the 15th Independence Day in a free Czech Republic. In no way did he want the world to forget who "helped us to get rid of the oppressive communist regime."[32]

In his short address President Klaus covered a lot of international political ground. He wanted his audience to know that he participated in the funeral of former American President Ronald Reagan. It was Reagan's action, according to Klaus, that helped end communism in his country. Three days earlier Klaus was in Istanbul at a NATO summit, and in May, 2003 the Czech Republic became a member of the European Union.

Sounding somewhat cautious, Czech President Klaus explained that they joined the EU because "we wanted to participate in the – in principle positive – European integration process. Believing that the current form of the EU presents a problem, it presents an opportunity also." But he wanted to assure the American Ambassador and America that "the Czech Republic will not forget the importance of the transatlantic cooperation and will not let anyone weaken our friendship with your great country."[33] This address was indicative of not only a pro-Western, free-market inclination of the Czech people, but a pro-American policy.

In his remarks on July 4, 2004 to a gathering of Czech leaders and citizens, American Ambassador Cabaniss said that the United States is "a nation of many different people from every corner of the world, including from the Czech lands. They came because of religious freedom; deliverance from political oppression, and opportunities denied them at home." He cited common goals and visions shared between Czechs and Americans and provided examples. "The Moravian Brethren came to the U.S. in the mid 1700s looking for religious freedom. They opposed slavery, established hospitals, and in 1792 started a school that became the sixth oldest college in our country, the Moravian College in Bethlehem, Pennsylvania." Cabaniss also mentioned that Ray Kroc's grandparents came from Stupno near Plzeň. Kroc was born in Chicago and was the developer of the McDonald's worldwide hamburger franchise.

Cernan received the Czech Republic's Highest Peace Time Award
U.S. Ambassador William J. Cabaniss, Jr., and
Czech-American Astronaut Eugene Cernan.

American Astronaut Eugene Cernan, the last man to walk on the moon, was born in Chicago of parents with Czech and Slovak ancestries. In American politics the longest serving congressman was Adolf Sabbath who was born in Pisek. A Governor of the State of Illinois of Czech heritage was Otto Kerner. Madeleine Albright, from Prague, became the first female Secretary of State of the United States.

Exchanging Books
Former U.S. Secretary of State Madeleine Albright and
Ambassador William J. Cabaniss, Jr.
Lillis Werder Photography and
The American Friends of the Czech Republic

The number of Czech-Americans is countless. George Halas, the once player-coach of the Chicago Bears also played in the 1919 Rose Bowl football game. John Havlicek led Ohio State University to three consecutive NCAA college basketball finals and won eight National Basketball Association titles with the Boston Celtics. Ambassador Cabaniss made note of the fact that all of these Czech-Americans believed in a society and a system of government "that treated everyone equally and gave everyone a chance to rise as far as their God-given talents could take them."[34]

A Scheduled Week in July 2004 for the Ambassador

Bill Cabaniss remarked at one time that when he was Ambassador he had never been "more scheduled" in his life. In the last week of July in 2004, in the first year of his diplomatic life, his Deputy Chief of Mission, Kenneth Hillas – a career diplomat – took his annual leave. Not that the Ambassador was incapable of conducting his own business. Mr. Cabaniss met at 9:00am with Czech Foreign Minister Cyril Svoboda for one hour followed by a thirty minute press meeting at 10:30am. Since this day was a Monday – July 26 – he attended his weekly POLMIL (Political-Military) meeting in a sound-proof room. After a two hour "thank you luncheon" for various vendors at the Residence, Mr. Cabaniss met with a group of medical students.

A 4:00pm visit to Strahov Monastery (Strahovského kláštera) ended at 5:30pm. Ambassador and Mrs. Cabaniss then had a private dinner with the Embassy Group. Early on Tuesday morning the couple attended a Czech language training session at the Residence. This was followed by two separate meetings before the noon time break. Later in the afternoon the Ambassador attended the "Sister City Symposium" at the [Woodrow] Wilson Center in Plzeň with Ted vonCannon, the Executive Director of the Metropolitan Development Board in Birmingham. A Reception in the early evening was held at the Residence and a late dinner with Czech Senator Outrata began at 7:30pm.

Over the next five full days, Cabaniss made a day trip to Plzeň with vonCannon; held three morning press briefings; hosted at the Residence a Czech Art Exhibition known as "Dialogue;" attended a cocktail party at Schwarzenberg Palace; more language training; a brown bag lunch; small business receptions, an overnight trip to Český Krumlov to attend several events; and a tea party hosted by Catherine Cabaniss held in the Residence. On Sunday the schedule allotted time for attending church services between 11:00am and 12:30am. The Cabanisses and the Hillases usually attended Saint Clement's Anglican Episcopal Church. The Rev. John Philpott was the church's rector, or pastor/chaplain.[35]

The Czechs, Americans, and Iraqis

A few days before Christmas, 2004, Ambassador Cabaniss was interviewed about the situation in Iraq as that reforming nation prepared for elections. Reporters wanted to know if the elections would be the "coveted" turning point in lowering the level of violence there. Cabaniss responded by saying that "The elections are another step in the process of returning the country to the administration by the Iraqis themselves. The first turning point was the removal of Saddam Hussein, the second was the installation of the interim government, and the elections are the third step." The Czechs were already training Iraqi police and reporters were concerned whether or not this Czech effort measured up to Poland's two thousand soldiers. Was the United States pleased with the Czech contribution to security?

Ambassador Cabaniss told reporters that the U.S. was very satisfied with the support it had received from the Czech Republic. He reminded his audience that it was the Czech specialized nuclear, biological and chemical (NBC) unit that went into Kuwait years earlier under a U.S. request to neutralize and clean up the hazards. During the Iraqi hostilities the Czechs set up their mobile military field hospital in the Iraqi town of Basra. It was at this time that the Czech medical team found young children with heart problems. That Czech field hospital army unit was from Hradec Králové.

Three weeks before this December 22, 2004 interview a group of fifty Iraqi judges was in Prague for training. The plan at the time called for the Czech Republic to provide legal training to two hundred Iraqi judges, a process that contributed to the building of a legal state in Iraq.[36]

While Czech doctors were treating both military personnel and Iraqi citizens, they discovered that many Iraqi children had a congenital heart problem that caused them to die prematurely. They knew that this condition could be corrected fairly easily, if they could only get these children to a hospital in Prague.

Arrangements were made to transport six to seven Iraqi children at a time with this heart defect to Prague for corrective surgery. Many Iraqi children received life saving medical treatment because of this humanitarian effort by the Czech Republic.

**Ambassador Cabaniss with Iraqi Fathers
And their Children in Prague**

Honored in Alabama

Ambassador William J. Cabaniss, Jr. was inducted into the Alabama Business Hall of Fame and the Alabama Academy of Honor.

At The Alabama Business Hall of Fame Induction
Bill Cabaniss and leadership team of Precision Grinding, Inc. at induction ceremony.
L-R: Dan Griffin; Andy Cunningham; Joe Wilson; Bill Cabaniss; Jim Quinn; Jerry Quinn;
Miles Cunningham; David James; and Junior Coffee
Precision Grinding, Inc. Photo

Other members of the Alabama Academy of Honor Class of 2004 were Hall Thompson, Catherine Johnson Randall, Cameron McDonald Vowell, and William Michael Warren, Jr.[37] Warren, one-time chief executive officer of Birmingham-based Energen Corporation, retired from that position and became CEO of Children's of Alabama. Warren, a good friend of Cabaniss, began and led a building program that expanded the size and scope of the medical center. Birmingham has transformed itself over the past forty years from a center of steel manufacturing to one of the best medical centers in the United States. Catherine and Bill Cabaniss both received honorary degrees awarded in May, 2007 by Birmingham Southern College. The Cabanisses were honored because of their service to their local community, the state, and the nation.

Law and Order

The American Bar Association and the United States Agency for International Development (USAID) began an organization in Europe known as the Central and Eastern European Law Initiative, or CEELI, after the fall of the Berlin Wall. The law center was placed in Prague for the purpose of bringing in the rule of law for those nations formerly behind the Iron Curtain. Lawyers, judges, politicians, and other legal-related professions were brought to Prague for weeks of training by lawyers and judges from the United States who gave their time *pro bono*.

During Ambassador Cabaniss's tenure in Prague, judges were brought in from newly freed Iraq. "We held receptions for the Iraqi judges at the Residence. It was very emotional seeing that most of those judges from Iraq were in harm's way by people who did not want any laws to be put in place. Most of those judges were in their sixties and seventies. They were brave people. There was no guarantee that they would survive." During one of the receptions given at the Residence, two judges, one a Kurd, one a Shiite, each wanted to give a speech. Cabaniss said "I think it was the Kurd. He was a big guy. But during his [translated] speech he broke down and cried in front of everybody. He thanked the United States for its involvement [in Iraq]." Cabaniss says that he still gets emotional when recalling that particular reception. There were other compelling moments for Cabaniss.

Liberation of Plzeň Remembered

On May 6, 1945, the town of Plzeň and most of western Czechoslovakia were liberated by American troops. General George Patton's Third Army was the liberating unit. Since Czechoslovakia continued its post-World War II existence under communist rule, it could not celebrate nor even recognize the historic event in the spring of 1945. But after the Iron Curtain was lifted in 1989 the 45-year lapsed celebration began in the open.

The year 2005 was the 60th anniversary of the liberation of Plzeň and Ambassador Bill Cabaniss was not about to miss it. Cabaniss tells the story of when representatives of President George W. Bush attended the celebration. Not only the Ambassador but the U.S. Secretary of Veterans Affairs, Jim Nicholson, accompanied by the Czech Army attaché, attended. More than 100 American soldier-survivors attended - some on crutches, some in wheel chairs.[38] In the center of town was the celebration platform flanked by a Czech Army Band. Several former Czech Army and U.S. Army soldiers made speeches. Ambassador

Cabaniss made a speech after being introduced by his friend, the mayor of Plzeň, Miroslav Kalous.

Ambassador Cabaniss in Army Uniform on Motorcycle
U.S. Embassy Grounds
Prague, Czech Republic 2005
Men in background are Czech citizens in U.S. Army uniforms and members of
The American Car Club

Approximately 40,000 people attended the event which began with a parade. There was an American Car club, a group made up of Czechs not all from Plzeň, who had maintained American vehicles for all of the years following the end of World War II. In the parade were army jeeps, trucks, other military vehicles and machinery. For forty-five years these vehicles were hidden in country barns, garages, dense fields, and anywhere out of sight of the communist government. Some were buried, others were placed in haystacks. After 1989 all of these vehicles were "freed" and refurbished.

As Cabaniss and Nicholson watched the parade from a hotel third-floor outdoor balcony, they thought they saw a platoon of American soldiers marching their way. It was not until they heard them speak, in Czech, that they discovered the soldiers were not American. American uniforms were maintained also for all those years. There were so many vehicles in the parade Cabaniss said "you would think that the U.S. Army had invaded the Czech Republic." Nicholson, a Vietnam Veteran, asked "Where the hell did they get our vehicles?" Cabaniss replied that "they're not our vehicles." There were more than 200 cars, tanks, and other vehicles in the parade. Some of the vehicles had been retrieved from battlefields during World War II, some bought at auctions.

Plzeň Monument
Catherine and Bill Cabaniss, 2005

The Patton Museum in Plzeň is named after American Army General George Patton. The museum's website states in part that there are more than one thousand exhibits from private collections on display. One section of the museum depicts the final air-raid campaigns in Western Bohemia and the bombing of the Škoda plants.[39] Authentic film and photographic moments lay out the final combat operations of World War II. The museum also contains documents, newspapers and magazines from the period of the totalitarian regime from the years 1948 to 1989. These documents are placed symbolically in a barred cage. These documents provide a statement about the efforts of the communist regime to obscure facts about the liberation of Plzeň by the United States Army.[40]

While the Ambassador was in Plzeň, his Deputy Chief of Mission, Kenneth Hillas, visited Moravia. During World War II a number of American military airplanes were shot down in that area. In the Battle of White Mountain, the Germans shot down B-24s and B-17s. There are many American graves there. The United States occupied southern Bohemia and Moravia while the Soviets occupied Prague and regions east of Prague.

Though discouraged by the communist government, Czech citizens in the face of real hostility, quietly and discreetly maintained American gravesites during the Cold War era. For these actions they were denied employment. Hillas said that one woman every year, during the same time period that American Army General Patton moved into Bohemia, goes to an American gravesite to place flowers.[41]

Czech Life

Ambassador Cabaniss believes that the Czech Republic has more golf courses than Hungary, Slovakia, and Poland combined. Bill and Catherine Cabaniss had a favorite driving range outside Prague. Golf is good for tourism but the Czech people have taken up the sport also. American football is evident there. Cabaniss was asked once to throw out the first ball rather than a kickoff at an opening game. But he did kick the ball, right into the hands of an opposing team player. The player gave the ball to Cabaniss and said "It was a good onsides kick but it went to the wrong person."[42] American Country-Western music is big in the Czech Republic as well as in much of Central and Eastern Europe. According to Kenneth Hillas, music was not considered political during the communist period in Czechoslovakia. Western rodeos and branding events are common fare in the Czech Republic and Poland. It is not unusual to witness Czech and Polish cowboys in 10-gallon hats. Rodeos took off and became popular beginning with the end of the communist period.[43]

Ambassador William Jelks Cabaniss, Jr. completed his service in the Czech Republic on September 23, 2006 and returned home. He joined the American Friends of the Czech Republic (AFoCR) in 2007 as that organization's executive vice president.[44] In Alabama politics Cabaniss's friend, Bob Riley, was re-elected as the state's governor. Overall, the Alabama Republican Party continued to make electoral gains.

International Cooperation in the Arts

In April of 2007, less than one year after Bill and Catherine Cabaniss returned to Birmingham, a "Salute to the Czech Republic" was presented by the Birmingham International Center. Cabaniss believes that the best way to foster and promote understanding among people is to invite them to your own country. Many Czech citizens were inspired to come to Birmingham for the celebration, including Czech President Václav Klaus. In the Birmingham Museum of Art the Hascoe Collection of Czech art from the state of Connecticut was exhibited. President Klaus officiated at its opening. That evening a dinner was held at Birmingham's Summit Club in honor of President Klaus. The other guests of honor at this Ambassador's dinner were the Czech Ambassador to the United States Peter Kolar and Mrs. Kolarova.

U.S. Embassy Residence Reception
Catherine Cabaniss and Jana Outratova
Prague, Czech Republic 2005

Also held during the "Salute to the Czech Republic" was International Women's Day organized by Iris Gross, Director of the Birmingham International Center. The award for her lifetime devotion to the arts and the founding of Museum Kampa in Prague, was made to Mrs. Meda Mladek who attended the "Salute to the Czech Republic" in Birmingham.

Fourth of July Celebration
U.S. Embassy Residence in Prague
Catherine Cabaniss and Louise Beer
Prague, Czech Republic 2005

Charles Bridge, Prague 2005
L-R:Lenka Bryndova Kodytek, Ambassador Cabaniss, Arjana Suskova,
Catherine Cabaniss, and artist Čestmír Suška
Cabaniss Family Album Photo

Famed Czech sculptor Čestmír Suška, his wife Arjana and their son
Andrew, visited Birmingham for six weeks. Suška created sculptures at
Robin Wade's Foundry and they were exhibited in the garden of the

Birmingham Museum of Art. Arjana presented puppet shows at Birmingham schools and hospitals, and Andrew, a pianist, studied at the Alabama School of Fine Arts during his visit.

Bedřich Kocman, printmaker at the University of West Bohemia in Plzeň, exhibited his work at Space One Eleven. Founded in 1986 in Birmingham by Ann Arrasmith and Peter Prinz, Space One Eleven is a visual arts foundation that provides professional opportunities for artists. Part of its mission is to create a forum for public understanding of contemporary art.[45]

Epilogue

IN THE FALL OF 2006 BILL AND CATHERINE CABANISS LEFT Prague for Alabama. His ambassadorial appointment expired. He served his nation honorably and with distinction. His public service, however, continues. No longer does he officially represent the Government of the United States of America. But he continues to serve nationally and internationally. This book is an introduction to William Jelks Cabaniss, Jr. Although widely respected in political, social, and charitable circles in Alabama and Washington, D.C., Cabaniss was also well-known by the leadership community in the Czech Republic. But to the general public Cabaniss is virtually unknown. Hopefully this book will cause other historians, particularly historians of American and European politics, to delve more deeply into Cabaniss and his effect not only on change in Alabama politics, but his service in the international diplomatic sphere.

Indeed, Cabaniss was a "party man" in domestic politics, but he was and is always a person endeavoring to do the right thing. Some post-Ambassadorial endeavors of Mr. Cabaniss provide examples of his ongoing contributions for the public benefit. William Jelks Cabaniss, Jr. has become associated with the *American Friends of the Czech Republic* (AFoCR). Its website (www.afocr.org) states that "Founded as an American private non-governmental organization, American Friends of the Czech Republic fosters closer ties between the United States and the Czech Republic in the areas of business, trade, culture, education, diplomacy, and security. It enhances understanding, friendship, and respect between the peoples of the two countries, while educating U.S. government leaders, media and other opinion makers about the goals and aspirations of the Czech people. Nationwide in scope, AFoCR is the voice of the American constituency that supports the Czech democracy." Cabaniss serves the organization as its Executive Vice President.

The leadership of AFoCR includes Fred Malek, Chairman; Thomas A. Dine, President; Robert Doubek, Secretary; and Director Officers Phillip M. Kasik and Lillis Werder.

Mr. Cabaniss is also active in fund-raising efforts within the *Václav Havel Library Foundation* (VHLF) headquartered in New York City. "The Václav Havel Library Foundation was established in 2012 to honor, preserve, and build upon the legacy of President Václav Havel. ... On September 7, 2012, VHLF Board Chairman Craig Stapleton convened the first meeting of the Václav Havel Library Foundation's Board of Directors. At that meeting, the Board nominated and approved [former Czech] Ambassador [to the United States] Martin Palouš to be President of the Foundation." (www.vhlf.org) Stapleton preceded Bill Cabaniss as U.S. Ambassador to the Czech Republic.

In addition to Stapleton who chairs the VHLF Board of Directors are Wendy Luers, Vice-Chairman; Joseph Balaz, Treasurer; Martin Palouš, President; Milton Cerny, Geoffrey R. Hoguet, John Shattuck, Count Riprand Graf Arco-Zinneberg and William J. Cabaniss, Jr.

An International Advisory Board provides valuable support for the VHLF. It is chaired by former United States Secretary of State Madeleine Albright and co-chaired by former U.S. First Lady Laura Bush and Dagmar Havlova (Havel's wife). Advisory Board members are Fred Malek, Daniel Arbess, Thomas Dine, Carl Gershman, Vartan Gregorian, Stephen Grand, William Luers, William Shipsey, Jan Švejnar, Lise Stone, and Paul Wilson.

Currently, only the United States holds the distinction of having presidential libraries. The Václav Havel Library, located in Prague, is the first presidential library of another sovereign nation.

Bill Armistead. Chairman of the Alabama Republican Party beginning in 2011. As a college student in the 1960s he worked for John Grenier in his efforts to reform and restructure the Republican Party in Alabama. Interviewed on October 18, 2013.

Peggy Balliet. Campaign manager for Cabaniss's two successful runs for the Alabama Senate in 1982 and 1986. Coordinator for Cabaniss's run for the United States Senate in 1990 against incumbent Senator Howell Heflin. Interviewed on May 24, 2012 in Mountain Brook, Alabama.

Dick Baruch. A football friend and fellow student at the Lawrenceville (NJ) School. He was quarterback and Bill Cabaniss played center. Both planned to play football for Princeton University. Baruch went to Princeton University but did not play football. Cabaniss went to Vanderbilt University and played football only one year due to a knee injury.

Ann Bedsole. One of four Alabama Republicans who ran and won (along with Cabaniss) in the state elections of 1978. Interviewed on January 4, 2012 in Mobile, Alabama.

Walter Bell. Bell was named by Gov. Riley as Alabama's chief insurance regulator in January 2003. He had retired from Mutual of New York (MONY) as executive of its Diversity Marketing Group and returned to his home in Mobile, Alabama. Bill Cabaniss while serving as Governor Riley's transition manager recommended Bell. After serving his state as Insurance Commissioner Bell became CEO of Swiss Re America Holding Corporation in 2008.

Jerry Bernstein. A good friend and classmate at the Lawrenceville (New Jersey) School. He would organize Sunday open houses and his father would send salami and pastrami from Binghamton, New York.

Judy Bewley. Bill Cabaniss's campaign manager for his first run for the Alabama House in 1978. Continued to work on all of Cabaniss's campaigns and active in the national Republican Party. An early supporter of Ronald Reagan. Interviewed on May 29, 2012 in Mountain Brook, Alabama.

Winton Malcom (Red) Blount. Postmaster General of the United States from 1969 to 1972 under President Richard Nixon. A Montgomery businessman and founder of Blount International, Inc. In 1964, Blount was appointed by President Lyndon B. Johnson to the National Citizens Committee for Community Relations, to advise the White House on the enforcement of the new Civil Rights Act of 1964. In 1952 he served as chairman of Alabama Citizens for Eisenhower. "Red" supported Cabaniss in his political campaigns. Blount had asked Cabaniss to manage his campaign for U.S. Senate against incumbent Democratic Senator John Sparkman in the early 1970s. Cabaniss had no time to manage this campaign early in his business career. George W. Bush came to Birmingham for six months to help Blount's campaign.

David Bronner. Executive Director of the Retirement Systems of Alabama. Interviewed on February 14, 2012 in Montgomery, Alabama.

George H.W. Bush. The 41st President of the United States of America. He campaigned for Cabaniss in the 1990 election bid for a U.S. Senate seat from Alabama. Catherine and Bill Cabaniss rented a cottage in Kennebunkport, Maine which was located in the same neighborhood as the Bush family.

George W. Bush. The 43rd President of the United States of America. Bush appointed Cabaniss chairman of his Alabama Finance Campaign Committee when he first ran for the presidency in 2000.

He appointed Bill Cabaniss as Ambassador to the Czech Republic in 2003.

Laura Welch Bush. The First Lady of the United States from 2001 to 2009. Catherine and Bill Cabaniss were invited to The White House for a dinner in 2002. At this dinner it was Laura Bush who asked Bill Cabaniss if he would be interested in serving as a U.S. Ambassador. It was Catherine's interest in the President's "understanding" of art that created the dinner invitation.

Catherine Hood Caldwell Cabaniss. Bill's wife and partner for many years and the mother of their three children (Mary, Frances, and Bill III, (deceased)). She is a landscape artist and has exhibited her work around the world. While in the Czech Republic she spent much time with the Czech art community. Interviewed on March 14, 2011 and February 15, 2013 in Mountain Brook, Alabama.

Edward Harman Cabaniss. Bill's grandfather who was both a businessman in the eastern part of Alabama and later an attorney in Birmingham. He was a business partner with William Dorsey Jelks in east Alabama before moving to Birmingham to practice law. He founded a law firm that still operates today. He was also briefly an elected state senator.

Florence Cabaniss Parnegg. William J. Cabaniss. Jr.'s sister (Mrs. Hannes Parnegg).

Frances Caldwell Cabaniss Johnson. Cabaniss's daughter (Mrs. Kenneth Steele Johnson, Jr.).

Joan Cabaniss Harrison. Cabaniss's sister (Mrs. T. Randolph Harrison, Jr.)

Mary Caldwell Cabaniss Ballard. Cabaniss's daughter (Mrs. David Ballard)

Robert Wright Cabaniss. Cabaniss's uncle who was U.S. Navy aviator number 36. He lost his life in a Navy plane crash in 1927. He was a United States Naval Academy graduate.

William Jelks Cabaniss (Sr.). Cabaniss's father and a successful businessman in Birmingham, Alabama. He was listed in America's *Who's Who* in 1964-65. He retired as chairman and chief executive officer of Southern Cement Company.

William Jelks Cabaniss III. Bill and Catherine Cabaniss's son who tragically passed away on August 26, 1979 at age eleven from an aneurism.

Henri Cabaniss. The father of the American branch of the French Cavanis family. He came to America on the ship *Mary and Ann* from England on July 23, 1700. The spelling of the family name changed or mutated over the centuries to various forms like Cabanet, Cavinot, Caviness, and Cabaniss. See Appendix A.

Florence Pierson Sanson Cabaniss. William J. Cabaniss, Jr.'s mother, Mrs. William Jelks Cabaniss.

Frances Caldwell Bennett. Catherine Caldwell Cabaniss's sister. A highly successful advertising executive in New York City for many years. She developed the effective Volkswagon television commercials of the 1970s. She married Dr. Claude Bennett, a former president of the University of Alabama-Birmingham, after a chance meeting at a dinner party in the Cabaniss home.

William J. Canary. The executive director of the Business Council of Alabama (BCA), a successor organization to Alabama's chambers of commerce. The BCA presented Cabaniss with its annual business achievement award in 2010. Interviewed on January 3, 2013 in Montgomery, Alabama.

Miroslav Cernik. Served as manager of the U.S. Residence in Prague, Czech Republic. He was in charge of all diplomatic and private events.

John Claypool. The famous Southern Baptist minister, later an Episcopal priest, wrote the book *Tracks of a Fellow Struggler* based on the death of his daughter when she was only eight years old. Bill wrote him a letter after the Cabanisses experienced a similar tragedy. He later became rector of St. Luke's Episcopal Church in Birmingham, Alabama – the Cabaniss home church at the time.

Marie Cobbs. William J. Cabaniss, Sr.'s second wife. He married Marie after Bill's mother passed away.

Marty Connors. Former executive director and chairman of the Alabama Republican Party. Interviewed on March 14, 2012 in Hoover, Alabama.

Francis Crockard, Jr. A childhood friend of Cabaniss and a fellow student at the Lawrenceville School in New Jersey, although at overlapping times. Crockard is chairman of General Machinery, Inc. in Birmingham, Alabama and still a close friend. Crockard is also a first cousin of Mignon Smith, the Alabama Republican and National Committeewoman in 1956 and 1960. Interviewed on February 28, 2012 in Mountain Brook, Alabama.

John Crowell. The first delegate of the Territory of Alabama to the United States Congress from January 29, 1818 to March 3, 1819 and a member of Congress from the State of Alabama's first congressional district from December 14, 1819 to March 3, 1821. He was brother of Matilda Crowell Jelks, J.W.D. Jelks's sister-in-law.

Andrew Cunningham. One of the two brothers who came to work with Bill at Precision Grinding Co. Cabaniss later sold his company to Andy and his brother Miles. Andy came on board six years after Miles bringing an expertise in Information Technology that helped transform Precision Grinding Co. Interviewed on November 14, 2011 in Birmingham, Alabama.

Miles Cunningham. One of the two brothers who came to work with Cabaniss at Precision Grinding Co. Cabaniss later sold his company to him and his brother Andy. Interviewed on November 14, 2011 in Birmingham, Alabama.

Gerald Dial. Alabama Republican State Senator from Lineville in Clay County (a former Democrat and Independent Alabama legislator), and Army Reserve Brigadier General. Dial and Cabaniss, two former Army Rangers, found common ground in working together in the Alabama legislature. Interviewed on February 14, 2012 in Montgomery, Alabama.

Larry Dixon. A Republican member of the Alabama Senate, elected in 1982 along with Cabaniss and two other Republicans. Dixon retired from Alabama politics in 2010. Elected initially as a Democrat, he served in the Alabama House of Representatives from 1978-1982. Dixon and Cabaniss became not only political colleagues but good friends. Interviewed on October 9, 2012 in Montgomery, Alabama.

Frank Ellis. Elected to the Alabama Senate from Columbiana in Shelby County, first as a Democrat then as a Republican. His conservative leanings made him and Cabaniss politically compatible in their days in the Senate. Interviewed on February 7, 2012 in Columbiana, Alabama.

Wayne Flynt. Distinguished University Professor Emeritus, Auburn University, Auburn, Alabama. Dr. Flynt is an honored historian of Alabama. Although at opposite ends of the political spectrum, Flynt and Cabaniss sought agreement and worked diligently for better education standards – and its appropriate levels of state funding – for Alabama public schools. Interviewed on November 26, 2013 in Auburn, Alabama.

Bill Gates. Co-founder of Microsoft Corporation. Cabaniss hosted breakfasts with Gates and Czech business people in the U.S. Ambassador's Residence in Prague.

Rick Graber. Succeeded Bill Cabaniss as U.S. Ambassador to the Czech Republic. He was nominated by President Bush and was sworn in by Secretary of State Condoleezza Rice in Washington, DC on September 14, 2006.

John Edward Grenier. The developer or creator of the modern day Alabama Republican Party. Changing its persona from "Post Office" Republicans to "real" conservative Republicans Grenier appointed party chairmen for each of Alabama's sixty-seven counties beginning in 1962. A visionary, Grenier saw that national Republicanism was shifting from the Northeast to the South and Southwest and worked to make sure the shift actually occurred. See Mignon Smith.

John Beaulieu Grenier. Chairman and Chief Executive Officer of the law firm of Bradley Arant Boult Cummings LLP in Birmingham, Alabama and son of John E. Grenier. Interviewed on May 17, 2012 in Birmingham, Alabama.

Douglas Hale. Elected to the Alabama House of Representatives in 1970 from Huntsville. Hale and Bert Nettles were the only two Republicans to serve in the state legislature for the four-year term 1970-74.

Perry Hand. Elected to the Alabama State Senate in 1983 as a Republican along with Bill Cabaniss, Ann Besole, and Larry Dixon. Interviewed on January 5, 2012 in Mobile, Alabama.

John Murdock Harbert III. An Alabama businessman and founder of Harbert Corporation, a large international construction firm. He and Eason Balch viewed the Alabama State Supreme Court as heavily one-sided in its decision-making. The court was very anti-business and consistently overturned tort reform bills enacted by the State

Legislature. Harbert and Balch thought it best to call in Karl Rove & Company to help launch a campaign to help the Alabama electorate ensure a balanced court. Alabama is one of the states where justices are elected and not appointed.

Bill Harris. Former executive director and chairman of the Alabama Republican Party. Interviewed on October 22, 2012 in Washington, D.C.

Václav Havel. Novelist, poet, playwright, political dissident, and the tenth and last President of Czechoslovakia. Havel was elected President of Czechoslovakia in 1989 when the Berlin Wall came down and was elected President of the newly formed Czech Republic in 1993. Cabaniss met him in 2004 after Havel no longer held office.

Howell Heflin. The Alabama Democratic politician who was at one time Chief Justice of the Supreme Court of Alabama and successfully changed Alabama's court systems by modifying the *Judicial Article* of the state's antiquated 1901 constitution. As a candidate for the U.S. Senate, Cabaniss opposed him. One could say that Cabaniss was "out-campaigned" by Heflin who used ingrained Alabama cultural beliefs (anti-business, anti-wealthy people, and a general distrust of Republicans) as fundamental campaign tools.

S. Richardson (Dick) Hill. The second president of the University of Alabama-Birmingham (UAB). An educational visionary, he was an endocrinologist and was persuaded in 1954 to leave Harvard University to lead UAB's first Division of Endocrinology and Metabolism. A personal friend of Catherine and Bill, Hill passed away on July 4, 2003.

Kenneth Hillas. The Deputy Chief-of-Mission at the U.S. Embassy in Prague, he and his wife Barbara met Catherine and Bill upon arrival in Prague in January 2004 at the airport, in the snow. Interviewed on April 13, 2013 in Mountain Brook, Alabama.

Paul Hubbert. A long time Alabama politician and a Democrat. One of his major accomplishments was facilitating the merger of the all black Alabama State Teachers Association with the Alabama Education Association. Once merged Hubbert, the AEA's leader, converted the AEA from an apolitical to a powerful political organization that dominated Alabama legislative politics and the state Democratic Party for more than four decades.

Joseph William Dorsey Jelks. The father of Governor William Dorsey Jelks and great-grandfather of Bill Cabaniss. Killed in June of 1862 presumably in the Battle of Seven Pines outside Richmond, Virginia; he formed the Alabama Dixie Eagles rifle company and was a captain in the Third Alabama (Confederate) Infantry Regiment that became a unit of the Army of Northern Virginia.

William Dorsey Jelks. Democratic Governor of the State of Alabama from 1901 to 1907. At the end of his term in office, he was the longest-serving governor in the state's history. He governed when the infamous 1901 Alabama State Constitution was passed into law. Jelks was a businessman's governor having left office with a surplus in the State Treasury. After leaving public service Jelks founded Protective Life Insurance Company in Birmingham, Alabama. Jelks was Ambassador Bill Cabaniss's great uncle.

Clay Johnson. A classmate at the Phillips Academy of George W. Bush and a roommate at Yale University. At one time he was President Bush's White House assistant and Director of Personnel. Successful in the direct mail business he became Director of the Office of Management and Budget. He was Chief-of-Staff for Texas Governor George W. Bush. A telephone call from Johnson to Bill Cabaniss began the journey toward the ambassadorial post in the Czech Republic.

Václav Klaus. The second President of the Czech Republic. Cabaniss presented his ambassadorial credentials to Klaus in Prague on January 13, 2004.

Wanda Kleinsmith. Succeeded Connie Parish as Executive Assistant to Ambassador Cabaniss.

Zdenek Klezl. A medical doctor, he provided assistance to a Cabaniss friend who suffered a stroke in Prague and remained in a Czech hospital for three weeks under Dr. Klezl's care.

Rhonda Krizova. She met Catherine and Bill at the Prague airport in January of 2004 upon arrival in the Czech Republic. She was a staff member of the U.S. Embassy.

William Lobkowicz. At the time of the Velvet Revolution he was living in Boston, Massachusetts with his wife Sandra and their three children. He worked in real estate. He and his family returned to the Czech Republic to claim his family's assets which were appropriated by the Nazi-led and communist-led governments. The family assets included valuable paintings, real estate, several breweries, and castles.

Wendy Luers. Founder of The Foundation for a Civil Society, a foundation that funds annually The Chalupecky Art Award for a Czech artist under the age of 35. She serves as Vice Chairman of the Václav Havel Library Foundation.

G. Sage Lyons. A former Democratic Speaker of the House (1971-1975) who in 1986 tried to persuade Bill Cabaniss to run on a statewide ticket with him; Lyons would switch parties and run for governor and Cabaniss for lieutenant governor. Cabaniss declined.

Joe McCorquodale. Democratic Speaker (1975-83) of the Alabama House of Representatives when Republican Bill Cabaniss entered the House in 1979.

Walter McCullers. Partnered with Bill Cabaniss in Precision Grinding business for twenty years. He was a former U.S. Marine drill instructor. Interviewed on March 19, 2013 in Hoover, Alabama.

Dick Morris. He visited with Bill Cabaniss in Birmingham in 1991 in an attempt to persuade him to run for the U.S. Senate seat held by Richard Shelby. Cabaniss declined.

Cameron Munter. Succeeded Kenneth Hillas as Ambassador Cabaniss's Deputy Chief of Staff (DCM) in Prague. Subsequently, he became U.S. Ambassador to Pakistan.

Drayton Nabers. A former Chief Justice of Alabama, lawyer, former chairman of Protective Life Corporation, author, and lay evangelist. Nabers provided legal assistance to Cabaniss in acquiring the assets of what would become Precision Grinding, Inc. Interviewed on March 8, 2013 in Birmingham, Alabama.

Bert Nettles. A native of Monroeville, Alabama. He was the first Republican elected to the Alabama House of Representatives since Reconstruction, in a special election held in 1969. He was elected to a full term in 1970.

James L. Noles, Jr. A local Birmingham attorney and author of many books on military history. He wrote a book about the *U.S.S. Birmingham*, a light cruiser on which Cabaniss's father served during World War II.

Gary Palmer. Founder of the Alabama Policy Institute located in Birmingham. The author utilized the published research and opinions of the API on Ethics and Tort reform in order to understand the practical implications of proposed legislation whether enacted or not.

Connie Parish. The Executive Assistant to Ambassador Cabaniss at the U.S. Embassy in Prague, Czech Republic.

V.M. Parker. Along with Cabaniss, Bedsole, and Seibels, he ran for the Alabama House of Representatives in 1978 as a Republican and won from the Mobile area.

Daniel Pierson. He formed Southern Cement Company of Birmingham with Bill Cabaniss's maternal grandfather, Harold Sanson.

Colin Powell. A former United States Army General and Secretary of State under President George W. Bush. He swore Bill Cabaniss into his ambassadorial office in December, 2003.

William Holcombe Pryor, Jr. Alabama Republican State Attorney General from 1997 to 2004. Best known for his decision in 2003 calling for the removal of Republican Alabama Chief Justice Roy Moore, who had disobeyed a federal court order to remove a Ten Commandments monument from the Alabama Judicial Building. He later received an appointment from President George W. Bush as a judge on the eleventh circuit U.S. Court of Appeals. He served on the Alabama Bush Campaign Committee in 1999-2000.

Ronald Reagan. The 40th President of the United States of America. He campaigned for Cabaniss in his bid for the U.S. Senate seat in 1990. Reagan traveled to Alabama for a fund-raising reception and speech on behalf of (Governor-to-be) Guy Hunt and Cabaniss.

Condolezza Rice. Succeeded General Colin Powell as U.S. Secretary of State. Cabaniss was U.S. Ambassador to the Czech Republic for one and one-half years under Secretary Rice. Rice and Cabaniss are Birmingham, Alabama natives.

Bob Riley. Republican Governor of the State of Alabama from 2003 to 2011. Prior to his election as governor he was a member of the U.S. House of Representatives from Alabama. Cabaniss was transition team leader for Riley immediately following the 2002 election. Interviewed on November 5, 2012 in Homewood, Alabama.

ROMEO or **R**etired **O**ld **M**en **E**ating **O**ut. Ambassador Cabaniss and close friends keep in touch by having lunch bi-weekly. ROMEOs include Lee Styslinger, Jr.; Harry Brock, Byard Tynes, Cooper

Hazelrig, Gene Moor, Carl Bailey, Stan Mackin, Bill Reed, Tippy Bickerstaff, and Miller Gorrie.

Karl Rove. Owner and operator of a direct mail company at the time Cabaniss ran for the U.S. Senate. He was chief political advisor to U.S. President George W. Bush. Rove provided Cabaniss with an excellent direct mail campaign even though Cabaniss lost the election. Rove's company also played a pivotal role in Alabama state politics earlier by assisting Republicans in educating the public on the need of voting in a politically-balanced Alabama State Supreme Court.

Florence Pierson Sanson. Bill Cabaniss's maternal grandmother, a native of New Jersey.

Harold Sanson. Bill Cabaniss's maternal grandfather and founder of the Cahaba Southern Coal Mining Company of Birmingham. He and Daniel Pierson formed Southern Cement Company.

George Seibels. Along with Cabaniss and Ann Bedsole of Mobile, he ran for the Alabama House of Representatives in 1978 as a Republican and won. Seibels and the other Republicans can be viewed as the beginning of the end of Alabama's one-party system. He was a delegate to the Republican National Convention in 1972. Seibels represented Jefferson County in the Alabama legislature from 1978 to 1990. He was mayor of Birmingham from 1967 to 1975.

Richard Shelby. For many years a U.S. Senator from the State of Alabama – initially as a Democrat then Republican. The political pollster and Republican activist Dick Morris tried to persuade Cabaniss to run against Shelby in 2004.

Jirina Skopek. Catherine and Bill Cabaniss attended the State Department's "charm school" after Bill received the ambassadorial appointment. Mrs. Skopek was the Czech language instructor at the State Department.

Mignon Smith. Served as Alabama's First Young Republican Committeewoman and selected as the Alternate Delegate at Large to both the 1956 and 1960 National Republican Conventions. Working to promote a two-party system in Alabama in 1953 led her to take on leadership roles in Alabama with the then almost non-existent Republican Party to provide voters with a true democratic selection process. She was largely responsible for encouraging John Grenier to become active in the Alabama Republican Party in the 1960s.

John Sparkman. An Alabama Democrat, he served in the U.S. House of Representatives and the U.S. Senate from 1937 to 1979. He died in 1985 at age 86. Alabama businessman "Red" Blount campaigned against Sparkman in the early 1970s and lost. Bill Cabaniss was asked to be Blount's campaign manager in Jefferson County. Unable to devote full time to the campaign, reluctantly Cabaniss declined.

Weston Stacey. For approximately ten years the leader and President of the American Chamber of Commerce, or *AmCham*, in Prague, Czech Republic, with 400 members, 50% Czech and 50% American corporate representatives. He and Ambassador Cabaniss worked closely in supporting economic development in the Czech Republic.

Craig Stapleton. Cabaniss's predecessor as U.S. Ambassador to the Czech Republic. He ably assisted Cabaniss during the transition period. He subsequently served as U.S. Ambassador to France.

Steve Still. A shareholder in the Birmingham, Alabama-based law firm of Maynard, Cooper & Gale PC, he serves as Chairman of the firm's Governmental and Regulatory Affairs Section. He is a longtime friend of Ambassador Cabaniss, and he is the writer of the Foreword to this biography.

Luther Strange. An attorney and lobbyist, he was elected as Attorney General of the State of Alabama in 2010. He, along with Cabaniss, was a member of the Alabama Campaign Committee for George W. Bush in 1999-2000. Cabaniss was his campaign chairman for

Attorney General in 2010. Interviewed on February 15, 2012 in Montgomery, Alabama.

Lee J. Styslinger, Jr. A close friend, and Chairman of Altec Corporation, he served as finance chairman for all four of Cabaniss's political campaigns. Interviewed on December 21, 2011 in Mountain Brook, Alabama.

Michael L. (Mike) Thompson. A member of the Alabama Campaign Committee for George W. Bush in 1999-2000 and one-time chairman of the Business Council of Alabama (BCA). Interviewed on December 21, 2012 in Mountain Brook, Alabama. He is Chairman and CEO of Thompson Tractor Company.

Margaret D. Tutwiler. A former Under Secretary for Public Diplomacy and Public Affairs at the U.S. State Department and was the U.S. Ambassador to Morocco from March 2001 to 2003. At the time of Cabaniss's bid for a seat in the Alabama House in 1978 she wrote Cabaniss a three-page letter on yellow legal paper detailing how he should conduct his campaign. At that time Tutwiler worked for the Alabama Republican Party.

Theodore vonCannon. Former director of the Metropolitan Development Board of central Alabama. Prior to relocating to Alabama in 1988 he worked for economic development policy in Tennessee under then-governor Lamar Alexander. vonCannon and Cabaniss worked together bringing businesses to the Birmingham area. Interviewed on February 1, 2013 in Vestavia Hills, Alabama.

George C. Wallace. Four-time governor of Alabama. During Wallace's third term he was physically unable to run the office of governor on a daily basis. It was also a time in Alabama politics when "self interest" among politicians was dominant and the anti-business climate of state government was high and expanding.

Bert Walker. Former U.S. Ambassador to Hungary who served during the same period as Ambassador Cabaniss. They became fast friends.

Cullom Walker. A childhood friend of Cabaniss and owner of Empire Pipe and Supply Company in Birmingham. An avid hunter, Walker and Cabaniss are still close friends. Walker's great, great, great-grandfather was Judge William Swearingen Mudd, who, with the Elyton Land Company, founded the City of Birmingham, Alabama in 1871. Interviewed on February 28, 2012 in Mountain Brook, Alabama.

Edgar Welden. Former executive director and chairman of the Alabama Republican Party and former Alabama Republican National Committeeman. Interviewed on March 20, 2012 in Birmingham, Alabama.

William C. Westmoreland. The United States Army General known for his leadership during the Vietnam Conflict was also the commencement speaker at Vanderbilt University in 1960 at Bill Cabaniss's graduation. Westmoreland inspired the ROTC graduates to consider the military as a career.

Appendices – Historical Lines

Family heritage accounts for much in a person's life. The Cabaniss family history and the Jelks family history provide a framework for viewing more than one strand of Americana. Henri Cabaniss came to the Virginia Colony in 1700. A French Huguenot, Henri had no choice but to escape France and make a life in the New World. Before Henri Cabaniss arrived, Williams Rookings, a forerunner in the Jelks family, came to the Virginia Colony with his wife eighty years earlier. Both Rookings and his wife were indentured servants.

THE FAMILY HISTORY OF WILLIAM JELKS CABANISS, JR. originates on the European Continent in France, and in the British Isles. A litany of family surnames precedes his birth. Bill Cabaniss's historical paternal family surnames are Mann, Rookings or Rukins or Ruckins, Nicholson, Jelks, and Cabaniss. His maternal lineages are Pierson and Sanson. In all cases those families removed themselves from their traditional homeland for resettlement in the English colonies in North America. His earliest known American ancestors were probably William Rookings and his wife Jane Baxter. Both arrived in Virginia in 1619 during the reign of James I (1603-1625) as indentured servants to William Barry.

After completing their seven-year contract William and Jane were released from indentured service and given 150 acres of land in 1625, located in James City County. Their son, William Rookings, Jr., married Ann Nicholson and they had three children: William (III), Jane, and Elizabeth. His birth date and place of birth are unknown, but he was born probably after the term of indenture of his parents in Virginia. William, Jr. fought in Nathaniel Bacon's army against the colonial Virginia government. He died while in prison.[1]

Richard Jelks in 1666 was an indentured servant to John Bromfield in Virginia. Jelks was released from his contractual obligation in 1676, the same year when Virginia enacted laws to enslave Indians, igniting Nathaniel Bacon's "rebellion." Bacon was displeased with the Indian policies of Virginia governor Berkeley.[2] Although it is not known when Richard Jelks married, he married one of the daughters of William Rookings, Jr. – Jane Holt or Elizabeth Rookings. One of their sons was William Jelks, born between 1675 and 1687.

The city of Bristol, England kept records of those signing indentures prior to departure for the American colonies. Transcriptions of those records published in Baltimore in 1967, reveal the following: "Richard Jelke-Destination Virginia." A separate transcription of those records, although showing a different surname adds the following: "21 November 1666, Richard Folkes, of.... bound to John Bromfield for 7 years in

Virginia." The original register of indentures kept in Bristol has been examined and confirms the reading "Jelkes," not "Foulkes."[3]

The phrase "the Lord is bountiful" is the origin of the name Jelks. Although it is an English surname it is of French and Breton origin. The early French version, *Ledecael,* morphed over the years into *Gicquel* and currently is spelled *Jezequel.* The modern day English version of the name is found in Devon, Cornwall, Yorkshire, and East Anglia. The Breton followers of William the Conqueror, or King William I of England, settled those areas of England after the Norman Conquest of 1066. Several spelling versions live on as Jewell, Juhel, Joule, Jockle, Joel, Jiggle, Jekyll, Jelk, and Jelks. Surnames in England became a necessity when taxation was introduced. Richard Juel witnessed a document in 1247 in the register of Bedfordshore Assizes during the time of English King Henry III (1216-1272).[4]

Another part of Bill Cabaniss's American paternal line in the seventeenth century is Thomas Mann II. He was born in the Timberneck area of Gloucester, Virginia in 1666. He married Bridgett Hooker. Another was William Nicholson, Jr. [or II], who though born in Ireland in 1670 probably settled in Virginia before the end of the seventeenth century. He settled in Norfolk County, Virginia and became a wealthy landowner. The last of Cabaniss's ancestors to arrive in the colonies in the seventeenth century was Henri Cabaniss. Along with more than 200 other French Huguenot refugees, Cabaniss, his wife and small child, arrived at Hampton, Virginia in 1700. Of those ancestors on William J. Cabaniss, Jr.'s paternal side, only Henri Cabaniss is known to have come to the New World to find religious freedom. The Rookings, Jelks, Nicholsons, and Manns appear to have sought opportunities better than what they had experienced in Ireland or England.[5] The Piersons, on Bill Cabaniss's maternal side, left England clearly for religious freedom.

Abraham Pierson [II] was born in 1613 in Yorkshire, England and emigrated to the colonies in New England in 1639 during the reign of King Charles I (1625-1649) of the House of Stuart. He was well educated, having studied and graduated from Trinity College-Cambridge. Once in America he moved around, first living in Boston and Lynn, Massachusetts in 1640, then he relocated to Southampton on Long Island where he stayed until 1647. From there he moved again to Branford in Connecticut and finally to Newark, New Jersey. He married in 1642 a woman named Abigail [surname uncertain, either Mitchell or Wheelwright] whose parents were from Lincolnshire, England. He died in 1678.[6] Before Abraham left England he was ordained, probably by an Anglican bishop.[7]

The French Reformed Church (1559)

The first synod of the French Reformed Church was held on May 25, 1559 in Paris. This meeting was followed by persecutions and the issuance of an edict prohibiting heretical (non-Catholic) worship. Thirteen years later in 1572 thousands of French Huguenots (Protestants) were slain in what became known as the St. Bartholomew's Day Massacre.

The Protestant Reformation affected France in the early 1500s and was relatively quickly embraced by the intellectuals, nobility, and professionals. The contrast between this new reformed religion and Roman Catholicism provided them with the hope of religious and political freedom. The Huguenot Church experienced steady growth in membership and by 1559 had at least fifteen of its churches present at its first meeting or synod. The official ecclesiastical discipline adopted by the synod mirrored that of the Reformed Church in Geneva. Similar reformed churches in Germany and Scotland adopted similar disciplines, and the churches took on a more democratic ecclesiastical life than found in the Roman Catholic Church.[8] But during the 1560s tension between Catholics and Huguenots grew to such an extent that Catholic leaders began to organize mobs to intimidate and even kill French Protestants.

Prince Henry of Navarre (Henry IV) led Huguenot forces against the Catholic League at the Battle of Ivry in Normandy, resulting in a decisive victory in 1590.[9] In 1594 when Henry IV was crowned, he became the first [House of] Bourbon king of a France that was neither a unified nor a modern state. Variations in language and culture were wide and the Protestant Reformation effected another division along sectarian lines.[10]

When the Protestant King Henry converted to Catholicism in 1593 religious battles between the Catholic League and the Huguenots ended. His conversion was a politically astute move and was based on reunifying France by and eliminating all political opposition and the winning of Paris.[11] Henry then made the Roman Catholic Church the state church by issuing the *Edict of Nantes* on April 13, 1598. Notable was the fact that the Edict granted equal rights to Protestants.[12]

The Edict allowed Protestant enclaves to remain, but the Edict also disallowed Protestant congregations to develop in Paris. Even though Catholic churches were restored by the former "protestant" King Henry, the Pope in Rome and the French Roman Catholic clergy were not satisfied with the strength and the enforcement of the Edict. Eventually Cardinal Richelieu in 1629 would annul all of the political clauses contained in the Edict.

Revocation of the Edict of Nantes (22 Oct 1685)

On October 22, 1685 in France the Edict of Nantes was revoked, triggering renewed persecution of Huguenot Protestants, this time forcing Huguenots to flee France for the Swiss Cantons, the Netherlands, Ireland, and England. But the massive exodus from France did not occur immediately in the year of the Revocation. Most fled in 1687 to England after James II issued his Declaration of Indulgence.[13] In the year 1689 Parliament passed the Act of [religious] Toleration.[14] The Dutch Republic or the United Provinces became the most popular destination for fleeing Huguenots. The United Provinces had become a homeland for the Protestant faith and was relatively easy to get to from France. William of Orange, in the United Provinces, was a protector of Protestants and was integral to a Continental network of refugee resettlement operations. The Huguenots were industrious workers, mostly bourgeoisie, business-oriented people, and not agricultural workers.

The Huguenots were the source of a vibrant French economy. Ironically, the Catholic King Louis XIV decreed that Huguenots could not leave France yet his anti-Protestant policies forced their exodus and the underpinnings of the French economy gradually began to fall apart. Protestant clergy had a choice to convert to Catholicism or they could leave France, but not with their children beyond a certain age. Once England appeared to be a safe haven, the Huguenots left France in large numbers. Scotland was a destination initially but when Huguenots discovered that the markets in Scotland were weak compared to English markets, England became their destination. Over the years the French Huguenots assimilated into English culture never to return to their homeland. In 1688 William of Orange would invade England and change not only the way English government operated, but engaged in a Nine Years' War with France.

The Glorious Revolution (1688)

Parliament became the head of government in England. By agreement William of Orange and his wife Mary, both having claims to the English throne, became co-monarchs in 1689, after William's 1688 invasion. No longer would the two responsibilities of head of state and head of government lie jointly in the monarchy. Nonetheless, the monarchy would still exert its influence in the long tenure of post-1688 transition. In 1694 after Mary's death, William of Orange became King William III and was the sole English monarch until 1702. William III was the first monarch of the House of Orange. The Glorious Revolution in England affected not only English politics but the colonial political environment as well. In Virginia there was an economic gap between the gentry and other white people. Even though Virginia sold itself as the colony where the poor could work themselves out of poverty, the poor were deemed subservient to the ruling class. But the effects of the revolution of 1688 changed the dynamics of English and colonial politics, and governance.

With the throne acting as a governmental executive, and Parliament as lawmakers and the superior branch of government, rank and file citizens were witnessing a major change in how government would operate. Once colonial leaders understood how the monarchy would operate under the new political arrangement, they recognized the emergent supremacy of Parliament. A new relationship between England and its colonies would have to be worked out over the next few decades, but clearly a shift toward some level of populism was in play, and it would not be reversed. For those settlers already in Virginia, and for those who would come after 1688, a political basis for continual change was in the air.[15]

French Huguenots and the Business of Escape

In 1699 the Virginia colony provided for religious tolerance even though it had a preference for the established (Anglican) church. This tolerance opened the door for victims of religious persecution from around the world. Even though many, if not most Huguenots migrated to Ireland and England through the Netherlands, by 1700 "almost one in every five Berliners was a French Huguenot, living in a French 'colony.'"[16]

On July 23, 1700, after thirteen weeks at sea, the ship *Mary and Ann* arrived at the mouth of the James River with a new group of Huguenot immigrants.[17] Other Huguenots arrived later the same year at the same port. It is a wonder that these particular Huguenots arriving in Virginia in 1700 and 1701 ever made it out of Europe in the first place. Henri Cabaniss was on that first ship.

Ship 'Mary and Ann' Land at Hampton 1700

In 1700 when the ship *Mary and Ann* anchored off Hampton in colonial Virginia, the two hundred and seven passengers were met and welcomed by then-Lieutenant Governor Francis Nicholson. King William III of England had requested the Virginia colonial government to provide French Huguenots with all aid possible. Knowing the inhumane treatment of Huguenots by the French, England was prepared to receive them. Over time, however, the increasingly large numbers of Huguenots in England placed stress on relief agencies. Although some Huguenots made England their permanent home, others could not assimilate. England had to do something. Huguenot leaders and British authorities worked together to form a solution to England's "refugee problem." British America was a good place to relocate those Huguenots who wished to make a new life. So William III called on the Virginia government to make provisions for and to receive the new emigrants in their resettlement.

Cabaniss Family Lineage

The Cabaniss family line is clear and unmistakable in its American beginnings. Henri Cabaniss (Cavinis)[18], his immediate family, and more than two hundred other Huguenot immigrants sailed the Atlantic Ocean from Gravesend, England, arriving at the mouth of the James River in Colonial Virginia. The Huguenot experience in catholic France was more than difficult and their eventual exit from France was fraught with seemingly unending legal and physical obstacles.

While in France and shortly after the revocation of the Edict of Nantes in 1686, the Cabaniss family, under duress, relocated to Switzerland. There was already a large group of Huguenot refugees living in one of the western Cantons. But the Cabaniss family did not stay there long and headed for Rotterdam. More than seventy other refugees went with them. It was there that the family made its way to London, a voyage funded by another Huguenot, the Marquess de La Muce. After making preparations for approximately two years, about 205 or 207 Huguenots boarded the *Mary and Ann* and left England for the Virginia colony. As planned, de La Muce was in charge of the refugees. He was assisted by a Monsieur Charles de Sailly. In a letter to the Lords of Trade Virginia Governor Francis Nicholson wrote on August 12, 1700, that

"The 24th of last month, I had the good fortune of receiving his Ma'y's [Majesty's] Royal Commands of March ye 19th, 1699, sent me by your Lord'p [Lordship], concerning the 1700 Marquis de la Muce, Mons'r de Sailly, and other French Protestant Refugees; and I beg to leave to assure yo'r Lord'p, that as I have, so I wil endeavor to ovey them (they were on board the ship (Mary and Ann, of London, George Hawes, Commander, who had about a 13 weeks passage, and the 23rd of the last month arrived at the mouth of this river), and upon receipt of them, I immediately went down to Kickotan, to give directions in order to their coming hither, some of wh. Came on Sunday in the evening, the rest the next day. I wrote to Colo. [Colonel William] Byrd and Colo. [Benjamin] Harrison to meet them here, w'ch they did, and we concluded that there was not settling them in Norfolk nor whereabouts, because esteemed an unhealthful place, and no vacant land, except some that is in dispute now betwixt us and No. [North] Carolina; So we thought it would be best for them to go to a place twenty miles above the falls of the James River, commonly called the Manakin Town. ..."[19]

Manakin Town

Henri Cabaniss and his family settled in an area between the Monacan and Powick creeks, both of which flowed into the James River north of the fall line. Conditions were poor because the settlers arrived too late in the season to plant crops for the winter food. Many died as a result of poor to no provisions and complaints were filed with the King, describing the terrible conditions in which they lived. But Henri Cabaniss and his small family would not stay at Manakin.

The thirteen week voyage across the Atlantic had its own troubles, mostly man made. Captain Hawes, it was reported, abused the passengers and short changed them of their provisions. Once settled near the James

River fall line, de Sailly attempted to form a government of the community. Settlers were refused permission to exit without approval from the new local authority. When a second ship of refugees arrived and settled in the same area, de Sailly refused them provisions unless they took an oath of allegiance to local justices that he had appointed. Complaints were filed against de Sailly. Henri Cabaniss, however, left his settlement and moved to an adjoining plantation. There he was able to provide for his family and himself. But why was Cabaniss part of the last wave of Huguenots to leave the Continent for England, and then from England to the Virginia colony, in particular?

There is some information about Henri Cabaniss but very little about his time living in France. He was born in 1655 and some historians speculate that he was born and reared in Lasalle, Gard, France. That would place his home near the south of France, west of Avignon, southwest of Lyons and Geneva. It can be assumed that his family lived a life relatively free of persecution as Protestants living in Catholic France.

Indeed, they would be living under the protective of the Edict of Nantes of 1598 under French King Henry IV. Though a Catholic nation, certain rights were accorded Protestants, the Huguenots. It is not known what business Henri's family business may have worked or if they were farmers. It is safe to assume that in 1685 when Henri was thirty years old and the Edict of Nantes was revoked, his life would have changed. Under the Revocation rank and file Huguenots were not allowed to leave the country, although Protestant clergy were allowed to convert to Catholicism. A period of terror commenced. France was not the place to be. Henri Cabaniss lived geographically close to some Protestant Swiss Cantons. There was a route of escape.[20]

It is probable that Henri Cabaniss, when between the ages of 33 and forty-one, was unmarried and sustained himself economically by serving the armies of William III. One historian wrote that the Cabaniss family fled to a Swiss Canton shortly following the Revocation, then they traveled through Rotterdam to get to England. There is no record of dates of movement. But one fact is outstanding, at the end of the Nine Years' War – which included a signed treaty between William (and an Alliance) and France – there was no need for a large military. Plans were in the making to disband the military, but William III had a fondness for the Huguenot fighters and felt an obligation to resettle them. During wartime a continental network of resettlement managed to move the Huguenots from France, but once the war ended there appeared to be little to no need for the resettlement network.

It is presumed that Henri Cabaniss was part of the last wave of Huguenot refugees to arrive in England and then resettled in the Virginia Colony. That last wave consisted of four ships of refugees that arrived in Virginia from July of 1700 to 1701. Cabaniss, his wife (he was married by then) and a young child, were listed on the manifest of the first of the four ships to arrive at Hampton.

When the war ended there was no need to keep a large military and so Parliament had to act to reduce the size of the military. Many Huguenot military volunteers feared abandonment. The Nine Years' War ended in 1697 with the signing of the *Treaty of Ryswick*. There was already conflict between William III and Parliament but the discussion of military disbandment was economically and militarily a necessity. After the war many French Protestant refugees remained on the Continent. In France itself, even after the *Treaty of Ryswick*, Protestant oppression arose and a new wave of Huguenots fled for England and the Swiss Cantons.

IN ENGLAND, UPON THE DEATH OF KING WILLIAM III in 1702, Queen Anne began her reign which would last until 1714. She was the second and last member of the House of Orange to sit on the English throne. Not only was she Queen of England; she was Queen of Scotland until 1707 when the monarchy would be one under the nation named Great Britain.[1] By this time the small Jamestown settlement of 1607 had expanded into the one-hundred year old and more geographically settled Virginia Colony, a colony with a vibrant tobacco economy and a colony of laws.

Henri Cabaniss (1ˢᵗ generation)

Henri Cabaniss claimed a parcel of land on May 1, 1708 on a headright basis.[2] In 1709 he was granted a "body of land," 200 acres in all, in Henrico County, Virginia.[3] The headright claim read in part that "Upon the petition of Henry Cabiness [sic], these are to be certified that there is due unto him two hundred acres of land, for the importation of himself and Mary [Marie] his first wife, with Magdalene his second wife and Magdalene her daughter into this Colony, the same being legally proved in open court."[4] Magdalene, if she was indeed Henri's second wife, was a widow with her daughter of the same name. In 1710, according to other records, Henri married Mary Harrison.[5]

It is believed that Henri's first wife Marie died shortly after arriving on American soil. Together, Henri and Marie had one son, Henri [Jr.] and they were the three persons listed on the manifest of the ship *Mary and Ann* when it arrived in Hampton in 1700. Henri Cabaniss and Mary Harrison [or Magdalene] had two sons, Matthew and George. Variations in historical records give no hint, for example, that Mary Harrison and the widow Magdalene, were the same person. And since we learn from Henri's Will that his wife Mary is to be its executrix (as is pointed out below), another scenario becomes possible. Mary Harrison had to be Henri's third wife and Magdalene died without issue of that marriage.

What is verifiable is that Henri Cabaniss fathered three sons – Henry, Jr., Matthew, and George.

Henri lost any wealth he might have accumulated in France. As a Huguenot it can be safely assumed that he fled France precisely because of his religious convictions. In 1720, at the age of sixty-five, Henri Cabaniss died leaving little to his survivors in terms of highly valued assets. His undated Will was presented in court and probated on August 9, 1720 at Merchants Hope in Prince George County, Virginia.[6] According to that Will, Henri stated that he was weak and sick in his body but that he was in "perfect sense mind and memory." He knew his life was nearing its end and made his "Last Will and Testament … first and principally I commend my Soul into the hands of Almighty God, who gave it, begging pardon for my sins." Henri bequeathed to his young son, Henry [son of first wife Marie] "my Silver Shoe Buckles and Old Sword." To his youngest son George, he left a "Gold ring." And to his son Matthew, Henri bequeathed "my largest Gold ring, and my Silver hilted Sword." He named his wife Mary Cabanis [as spelled in the Will] and Francis Epes "my whole and sole executrix and executor of this my last Will and Testament."[7]

Henri Cabaniss could have been a goldsmith, but he could have been a banker as well. Whatever he did, he persevered until the end of his life. He worked. The detailed inventory of his assets leads one to conclude that he was not a wealthy person at the time of his death, nor was he a person of agriculture. His Will made no mention of land ownership – despite the content of earlier court records – nor could he have been a farmer. A listing of the tools of the trade was insufficient to infer farming or planter status.[8] The swords might indicate his background in a military organization. Beyond a goldsmith's business, interest in silver hilted swords could be valued souvenirs of possible service in the military of William of Orange during the Nine Years' War.[9]

The geographical importance of Virginia to the development of the United States can never be overstated. Its importance as the adopted homeland of immigrant families from 1607 forward is the grounding for building a great new, independent nation. For the descendants of those original families, it provides their historical basis in the New World. Great risks were taken by all settlers. Ninety-three years after the founding of Jamestown, Manakintown was a frontier area, an outpost of the original colony and it was located only seventy miles up-river above the falls of the James River. The landowner expected the Huguenots to provide a level of protection of that frontier. Though the threat of Indian attacks had minimized over those years, it was still a frontier area and threats of attack were real. When Virginia was divided into counties, some were very large geographically. As areas of counties were being settled, new counties were formed out of the original, and new local governments were formed.

The American Revolution and International Changes

In 1779 Virginia disestablished the Church of England (Anglican Church) as the official state church. In central Europe Emperor Joseph II issued in 1781 his Edict of Tolerance granting political and religious rights to religious minorities. By 1783 the territory of the original thirteen states was ceded by Great Britain to the new American republic.

The Commonwealth of Virginia established freedom of religion in 1786 and the Constitution of the United States was adopted on September 17, 1787 by the Constitutional Convention meeting in Philadelphia. Later, on November 28, 1787, France issued their Promulgation of Edict of Toleration.[10] A new understanding of freedom was sweeping worldwide and the new nation of the United States of America would become the vessel carrying the concept of freedom around the world. Many scholars have argued that the decade of the 1780s marks the beginning of the modern era in world history.

Given the different successes of the American Revolution and the French Revolution, a new and different world was emerging. It was during this era that the British had a self-sustaining industrial economy and the United States had developed world markets in cotton and tobacco. A longer period of struggle would have to transpire if the modernity's potential was to be unleashed. In Europe the Napoleonic War would delay the real implementation of modernity with its new resources of science and technology, finance and management, and capital growth.[11] In the United States, eager to expand within its own borders now that she was free from her former mother country's dominance, she would continue to encourage settlement westward on the

North American continent. The Cabaniss families – no less than the Rookings, Manns, Nicholsons, and Jelkses – took advantage of national policies implemented to grow America.

Matthew Cabaniss (2ⁿᵈ generation)

Matthew was born about 1712 in Prince George County, Virginia. In 1734 he married Hannah Clay whose father was Colonel Thomas Clay also of Prince George County as well as Surry County. Hannah Clay was the great-granddaughter of Henry Clay, the notable statesman from Kentucky. It is with Henri's second son Matthew that William Jelks Cabaniss, Jr. locates his ancestral lineage.

A grant of land, three hundred forty-seven acres, was made to Matthew in 1734 in Amelia County, Virginia. Nine years later he acquired four hundred more acres in the same county. [12] Unlike his father Henri, Matthew was a member of the Baptist Church. It is believed that Henri was a member of the Reformed Church in France, the same church of the Huguenots where Marquis de la Muce – an organizer of the Manakintown settlement for the Huguenots refugees – was a member. Matthew might have been the first politician in the Cabaniss family – he certainly was public-minded. Matthew fought for the validity of non-Anglican Church clergy and the rights of the people in Amelia County, Virginia. On May 12, 1780 Matthew presented a list of his concerns in the form of a petition. He called for the dissolution of vestries and for their election by a free vote of the people.

Vestries were made up of the gentry and whenever a vacancy occurred in a parish vestry, its remaining membership selected a replacement. Matthew called for any regularly ordained minister to have the power to issue marriage licenses. He called for the recognition of dissenting ministers as lawful clergy and for the legal removal of any doubt as to their validity. He also petitioned for the good people of the state [of Virginia] to be apprised of their just rights. Less than one month later the court, on June 7, 1780, deemed his petition reasonable and ordered it to be presented. There could have been a number of underlying reasons for Matthew's petitioning of the local government.

Matthew Cabaniss was owner of a vast amount of land and he might have been a planter. But he probably was not a gentleman, a member of the ruling elite. Traditional English ways were difficult to break even in Colonial Virginia, and the mere presence of a gentry implied an aristocracy or at minimum a stratification of society. Local Virginia governments – counties – experienced many forms of gentry-domination which gradually became "subtly concentrated and institutionalized." Most offices in the county courts as well as in the parishes (political divisions within a county), were held by ruling elites.[13] This practice had to be broken as Virginia and the emerging United States of America were refining the definition of personal freedom and individualism.

On January 2, 1789 the Georgia colony was admitted to the union as a state. Its claimed land mass spread from the Atlantic Ocean to the Pacific. The new Constitution of the United States went into effect on March 4, and on April 30 General George Washington became the first President of the United States. In France the storming of the Bastille occurred on July 14.

Matthew Cabaniss's Will of June 6, 1789 was probated on August 5, 1790 in Nottoway County, Virginia. Much of his land in Amelia County was deeded to his sons beginning in 1768. Matthew and Hannah had twelve children.[14] Their seventh child was George Cabaniss.[15]

George Cabaniss (3rd generation)

George Cabaniss was born in Amelia County, Virginia approximately 1744. In 1797 President George Washington completed his second and final term in office and John Adams became president in March, the year that George Cabaniss (a son of Matthew Cabaniss) at age fifty-three moved to Georgia after leaving Virginia for Rowan County, North Carolina. George and his father both served in the Revolutionary War.[16] By Congressional Act of April 7, 1798, the United States formed the Mississippi Territory out of the State of Georgia. The Mississippi Territory was the land above the thirty-first parallel consisting of what are today the states of Mississippi and Alabama.[17]

The year 1800 was the beginning of America's Second Great Awakening (1800-1840). George Cabaniss had become a large landowner in Jones County, Georgia.[18] He married twice, first to a Miss Carter. He married Palatea Harrison in 1776,[19] a granddaughter of Benjamin Harrison. George Cabaniss was granted land in Oglethorpe

County. He moved to Greene County in 1799, and eventually settled in Jones County where he died in 1815. A Baptist, George Cabaniss was a thrifty person who became wealthy as a planter. George and first wife, Miss Carter, had one child, Matthew. George and Palatea had ten children. Their fifth child was Elbridge Gerry Cabaniss.[20]

Non Cabaniss-surnamed ancestors of William J. Cabaniss, Jr., such as Thomas Mann III, lived between 1718 and 1782, probably in northeastern North Carolina. Thomas III's father and grandfather – both bearing the same name – lived in the Timberneck area of Gloucester, Virginia, on a peninsula between the James and York rivers. At some period during his lifetime Thomas Mann III relocated to the Halifax-Edgecombe-Bertie-Nash counties area in North Carolina, the Old North State. He married Elizabeth Denton who was born in 1725. The date of their marriage is unknown. Their daughter Penelope Mann, born in 1752 in Nash County, North Carolina, married John Nicholson.[21]

The Nicholson family in America began with William Nicholson, Jr. (or II)[22] who was born in Ireland and died in Norfolk County, Virginia in 1727 or 1728. He married Alice Smith and one of their sons, Lemuel Nicholson, born in Norfolk in 1715, married Ann Wright. Lemuel and Ann died in Halifax County, North Carolina. Their son John Nicholson was born after 1740 in Edgecombe County, North Carolina. It was Mary Nicholson, the daughter of John and Penelope, who married Robert Jelks.[23] In the first United States Census in 1790, John Nicholson was listed as a "Head of Family" in Edgecombe County. The census stated that Nicholson had four free white males under the age of 10 year, 3 females under the age of ten, and 10 other females in his household.[24]

Robert Jelks was the great-grandson of Richard Jelks, the American family patriarch. In 1723 William Jelks, born sometime between 1675 and 1687 to Richard Jelks and Jane Holt, purchased land in Southampton County, Virginia, the county of his birth. He was a resident of Isle of Wight County, Virginia. Southampton County borders North Carolina. One of their sons, Etheldred [or Ethelred], was born about 1720 in either Surry County or Southampton County, Virginia. Etheldred married Phyllis [surname unknown] and their son was Robert Jelks.[25] Robert Jelks was married first to a woman unnamed, according to documents. His second wife was Mary Nicholson and it is from this marriage that the

Jelks family line and the Cabaniss family line inter-marry. Robert Jelks died and was buried in Russell County, Alabama.

THOMAS JEFFERSON BECAME THE THIRD PRESIDENT of the United States on March 4, 1801. He was a member of the Democratic-Republican Party and served two full terms in office. The Louisiana Purchase was transacted in 1803 and in 1804 Thomas Jefferson began his second term. In 1809 James Madison became president. In 1810 the United States annexed West Florida from Spain. The 1812 war between Britain and the United States ended in a stalemate, a situation that nonetheless guaranteed America's independence. Part of the War of 1812 was the Creek Indian War (1813-14) which was fought mostly within the boundaries of present-day Alabama. This was the war that made Andrew Jackson a military hero as he led U.S. forces against the "Red Stick" Creeks.[1]

Elbridge Thomas Gerry, 5th Vice President of the United States

Elbridge Gerry lived between July 17, 1744 and November 23, 1814. In 1810 he was elected governor of Massachusetts after several attempts at running as a candidate in the Democratic-Republican Party. During his second term the Massachusetts legislature reorganized the state's senate districts, thus the neologism "gerrymandering." He lost re-election but was asked by President Monroe in 1812 to be his vice presidential running mate. Gerry served as a member of a diplomatic delegation from the new United States to France but was treated poorly in that assignment by his political detractors. Personally and politically, Elbridge Gerry was a class act. Although he initially opposed the idea of political parties he developed friendly and long-lasting relationships with colleagues on both sides of the political divide – Federalists and Democratic-Republicans.

He was one of the original signers of the *Declaration of Independence* and the *Articles of Confederation*, but he refused to sign the *United States Constitution* because in its original form it contained no *Bill of Rights*. But once the constitution was ratified and Gerry became a member of the first United States Congress he involved himself in the writing and passage of the *Bill of Rights*. He advocated individual and state liberties. He died eighteen months into his term as Vice President of the United States. Gerry is the only signer of the *Declaration of*

Independence who is buried in Washington, D.C.[2] When did the name Gerry enter the Cabaniss family-naming tradition?

Elbridge Gerry Cabaniss (4ᵗʰ generation)

George Cabaniss, son of Matthew and a grandson of family patriarch Henri Cabaniss, apparently thought highly of the person and accomplishments of Elbridge Gerry by naming one of his sons after him.[3] Elbridge Gerry[4] Cabaniss, born in 1802, married Sarah Ann Chipman on January 27, 1827 and they had ten children. After studying law at Yale Law School in 1823 he settled in Forsyth, a new town in the newly created county of Monroe in Georgia.

There is a section of northeast Monroe County, Georgia known as Cabaniss. It was also known beforehand as Gulletsville, and earlier as New Market. After the Civil War the area was well-known for the prosperity of its citizens. The history of the county includes a planter named R.C. McGough. He was a member of the Georgia General Assembly from Monroe County (1894-95), and was the son of Bob G. and Sandal (Cabaniss) McGough. His maternal grandfather was George Cabaniss (3ʳᵈ generation).

Thomas Banks Cabaniss, soldier, lawyer, state senator, congressman, was born Aug. 31, 1835 in Forsyth, Ga. Thomas was a son of Elbridge Gerry Cabaniss and Sarah Ann Chipman; his older brother was George Augustus Berrien Cabaniss who was William J. Cabaniss Jr.'s great grandfather. Thomas entered the Confederate Army in 1861 and surrendered with General Robert E. Lee at Appomattox Courthouse. He was elected to the House of Representatives of Georgia in 1865, and four times subsequently to the state senate. He was solicitor-general of the Flint Circuit for a term of four years, and had been mayor of his native city. In 1893-95 he was a representative from Georgia to the fifty-third Congress as a Democrat.[5]

E.G. Cabaniss was elected the principal of the Academy of Forsyth and he was admitted to the bar in Thomaston, Georgia in 1827. He served in several legal offices over the years. He was clerk of the Georgia Superior Court in 1840, became Judge of the Court of the Ordinary, and was Judge of the Superior Court for the Flint Circuit. He was elected Collector of Georgia Revenue during the Civil War and after the war became auditor of the State Railway. The latter assignment required him and his family to relocate from Forsyth, Georgia to Atlanta where he died around 1872.[6]

Before the Civil War, Elbridge Gerry Cabaniss was a Whig (pre-Republican) and after the war he became chairman of the Executive Committee of the Georgia Democratic Party.[7] Elbridge's son, George Augustus, said of his father that "he was not an offensive politician, but he was a decided Whig and Union man until the election of [Abraham] Lincoln and the secession of his state."[8] After the Civil War ended Georgia was under the control of Union General George Meade when delegates to the state constitutional convention framed a new constitution for the Reconstruction government.

Once the new constitution was drafted, General Meade ordered a statewide popular vote not only to ratify a new constitution but to elect state officers. The voting occurred for four days beginning on April 20, 1868. In the year prior, conservative groups began to organize across Georgia and on December 5, 1867 a conservative state convention met in Macon. It would be Georgia's first state political convention after the end of the Civil War. Very few northern Georgia counties sent delegates to that convention. In March 1868 Elbridge Gerry Cabaniss, chairman of the Georgia Democratic executive committee, issued an appeal to the voters of the state in the interest of nominating a Judge Reese for governor. In part the appeal read,

"Resolved, That the opinions and feelings of the National Democratic Party of Georgia, and the United States, upon the unconstitutionality and injustice of the Reconstruction Acts of Congress, are too decided and well known to require iteration here, … and to place the destinies of those [southern] states in the hands of adventurers and irresponsible persons, is equally decided and well known; yet warned by the fate of Alabama, and actuated by the instinct of self-preservation, we feel it to be our duty, to the extent of our power, to provide against every contingency; and therefore would urge upon our friends to participate in the election which is to be held on the 20th of April next …"

With that preamble E.G. Cabaniss and the Democratic Executive Committee nominated the Democratic candidate for governor, Augustus Reese. But Reese, an 1835 graduate of Yale Law School, withdrew himself from consideration due to his ineligibility under the Fourteenth Amendment.

Reese had been removed from his judgeship by Union General John Pope, the military commander of the Department of Georgia under General Meade. Apparently, Reese refused to obey orders by Pope directing him to place the names of Negroes in the jury [selection] boxes of the Ocmulgee Judicial Circuit.[9] But it was his Confederate service as a combatant during the Civil War that probably made Reese ineligible for holding public office under Section 3 of the Fourteenth Amendment, the second of the three so-called Reconstruction Amendments. E.G. Cabaniss and the Democratic Executive Committee then nominated David Irwin, another judge, to replace Reese. Then General Meade himself pronounced Irwin ineligible. Before nominating a third candidate Cabaniss and his committee consulted with General Meade and General John B. Gordon was cited as eligible.[10] A practical man, Elbridge Gerry Cabaniss found a way to work with his opposition, or in this case, a Union military overseer, to get his candidate on the ballot.

The Georgia town of Forsyth was incorporated on December 10, 1823 in Monroe County. It was named for John Forsyth, a former Governor of Georgia. As United States Minister to Spain, he negotiated the purchase of Florida from King Ferdinand II. Forsyth was created out of land acquired from the Creek Indians. Names of early settlers were Sharp, Roddy, Thomas, Sanford, Johnson, Harman, and Cabaniss, among many others. The early political leaders were Elbridge G. Cabaniss, the leading Whig and Dr. E.L. Roddy, the Democrat. Both belonged to the local Masonic Order where Cabaniss was the worshipful master of the lodge, and Roddy the high priest. Forsyth became an educational center in Georgia where the first male academy was organized. In the school's charter of 1854 some of the named trustees were Zachary E. Harman, John H. Thomas, Benjamin Watkins, and Elbridge G. Cabaniss. Cabaniss was noted as one of Forsyth's distinguished residents as well as his son, Judge Thomas B. Cabaniss, who was a member of the United States Congress and a judge on the Superior Court of Georgia.[11]

Judge Elbridge Gerry Cabaniss had become a large landowner over his lifetime. Years after his death a law suit was filed in Macon Superior Court in 1904 by a Mrs. M.M. Kelsoe. The suit, filed against the Town of

Oglethorpe, was an attempt at stopping a process to build roads and buildings on land to which she claimed to have absolute title. She denied that the town had any claim to the land. But the town claimed that the land had not only been owned by Judge E.G. Cabaniss but that he had a map drawn, directing the disposition of his land.

The 1849 town map divided Cabaniss's land into squares, streets, and alleys, with the remaining lots designated to be sold with reference to the plan, and dedicated to the municipality for public use. Some of that land had not been used in forty years and was within the geographical boundaries of Mrs. Kelsoe's claim. She argued for relief. In 1877 she had purchased her land from a Mr. W.B. Hill who held title under Judge Cabaniss and his grantees.[12] Irrespective of the results of that particular law suit, the documents in the case clearly showed that Judge E.G. Cabaniss was a civic-minded, public-spirited person by his generosity in providing land to the Town of Oglethorpe. One of the sons of E.G. and Sarah was George Augustus Cabaniss.

Alabama Territory

Alabama would take its place in the new, faster-paced world as its own territory and then as a state. In 1815 John Crowell moved from Halifax, North Carolina, having been appointed as agent to the Government of the Muscogees. He settled in St. Stephens, Alabama in 1817.[13] On March 3, 1817 the Alabama Territory was created when Congress passed the enabling act which allowed the division of the Mississippi Territory and the admission of Mississippi into the union as a state.[14] It was not until December 10, 1817 that Alabama became a Territory at the same time that Mississippi became a state.[15] When the Alabama Territorial Legislature assembled, it created three judicial districts and elected John Crowell as the territory's first delegate to the United States Congress.[16]

Crowell was the brother of Matilda Ann Crowell, the first wife of James Alexander Jelks, an older brother of Joseph William Dorsey Jelks [all yet to be born]. In the November, 1818 session, the territorial legislature petitioned for statehood.[17]

On March 2, 1819 President James Monroe signed the Alabama enabling act and on July 5 a constitutional convention began in

Huntsville that would end on August 2 after adopting a state constitution – the first of many state constitutions for Alabama. In September the new state would hold its first general election making territorial governor William Wyatt Bibb Alabama's first state governor. Between October 25 and December 17, 1819 the newly elected state legislature would meet in Huntsville.

The new capitol in Cahaba was still under construction. During this first state legislative session William Rufus King and John W. Walker were elected as Alabama's first United States senators. On December 13, "Old Hickory, Andrew Jackson, was on hand in person when the naming [of Jackson County, Alabama] occurred. He was visiting in Huntsville when the first state legislature created a county out of Alabama's northeast corner and gave it his name."[18] And on the next day, December 14, 1819, Alabama entered the union as the twenty-second state.[19]

Joseph William Dorsey Jelks

On March 30, 1819, Joseph William Dorsey (J.W.D.) Jelks was born in Halifax County, North Carolina to Robert and Mary Nicholson Jelks. J.W.D. was one of seven full siblings. The Crowell family is related to the Jelks family by marriage only. J.W.D. married Jane Goodrum Frazier and they had three sons and one daughter.[20] William Dorsey Jelks would become Governor of Alabama and Martha Frazier Jelks would marry into the Cabaniss family.

James Monroe began his second term as President of the United States in 1820 and King George IV came to the crown in England. Thomas Bibb became Alabama's second governor and served from 1820 to 1821. Israel Pickens became governor in 1821 and served until 1825.[21] John Quincy Adams began his only term as President of the United States and served from 1825 to 1829. The election process in 1824 was viewed with high suspicion. The Democratic-Republican Party was the only real political party at that time. The Whig Party in Alabama, for example, had its beginnings when statehood was granted. But there was no Federalist Party.

The Democratic-Republican Party split into four factions during the 1824 campaign and rumors circulated that John Quincy Adams of Massachusetts and Henry Clay of Kentucky had stolen the election from

Andrew Jackson.[22] In 1825 John Murphy became governor of Alabama and served until 1829.[23] Andrew Jackson addressed his 1824 loss by being elected President of the United States in 1828 and serving from 1829 to 1837. Gabriel Moore became Alabama governor and served only from 1829 to 1831. Moore resigned in 1831 to take a seat in the United States Senate. Samuel B. Moore, not a relative, was appointed to fill the remainder of Gabriel Moore's term. John Gayle was elected governor and served until 1835.[24]

Differences within the Democratic-Republican Party deepened during the 1830s. President Andrew Jackson vetoed the Bank of the United States, some say because of his dislike for the institution. The bank's lending policies were beneficial to Alabamians who were wary of what they saw as an increase in presidential power. The other party faction were followers of Henry Clay who advocated national economic expansion. The Whig Party had its strongest point of development during the presidency of Andrew Jackson.[25] The Nat Turner rebellion in Southampton County, Virginia occurred in 1831 and Jackson was re-elected to the presidency in 1832.

George Augustus Cabaniss (5ʰ generation)

George Augustus Berrien Cabaniss was born on December 12, 1832 in Forsyth and died on December 14, 1907 in Atlanta, Georgia. [26] George Augustus married Juliette McKay. Educated in high school at Forsyth, George studied law and had a practice beginning in 1861. In a volunteer Confederate army company of the First Georgia Regiment, the Quitman Guards, formed in Forsyth, George Augustus was chosen a lieutenant and sent to the hills of what became the State of West Virginia.[27] It was probably in the Battle of Cheat Summit Fort in mid-September, 1861 when George Augustus was taken prisoner. This was the first battle where Confederate General Robert E. Lee led a command of troops. George Augustus escaped from his captors, but became lost in the dense mountain forest.

There was a garrison of Union troops at the summit of Cheat Mountain and Lee had planned to surround it and then attack it. Because of faulty scouting reports and bungled communications among Confederate Army leaders, the attack never happened.[28] After five days and almost starving to death George Augustus and the other Confederate escapees came upon a guide who led them out of the forest. George and the rest of the men returned home for the remainder of the War. Later in life George was made a trustee of a sanatorium named the Georgia Lunatic Asylum in Milledgeville. One of the buildings on the campus was named after him.[29] George and Juliette had two sons, Dan and Edward Harman.[30]

In 1834 the formerly nascent Whig Party formally organized. Nationally it was an opposition party to President Jackson.[31] In 1835 Clement Comer Clay served as Alabama governor until 1837 when he resigned to take a seat in the United States Senate. He was succeeded by Hugh McVay who served from August to November, 1837, the remainder of Clay's term.

Arthur P. Bagby had already won election as Alabama's next governor. To many Bagby "looked" like a governor, standing more than six feet tall. He had the walk and the talk of a gentleman.[32] 1837 was also the year that Victoria became the British monarch. Her years on the throne would last until 1901, years in which the world would dramatically change. An economic depression spread nationally – it was known as the Panic of 1837. Martin Van Buren assumed the office of the presidency on March 4, 1837 and served until 1841.[33]

By 1840 the population of Alabama was 590,756. Its white population totaled 335,185 and its African American population was 255,571 of which 2,039 were free blacks and 253,532 were slaves. Alabama was a rural state with a ratio of slightly more than 45 to one, rural to urban.[34] During the 1840 election cycle Alabama Whig party leaders focused on the economic depression and the Democrats' failure to resolve it. Whigs believed in economic development encouraged by a government banking system, support for business, and aid for internal improvements such as roads, railroads, and canals. The Whigs made gains against Democrats in Alabama's legislature. Nationally they accused Martin Van Buren of being soft on slavery, causing the depression. Although Van Buren won the presidential election in Alabama, Whigs won 45 percent of the vote.[35]

William Henry Harrison, a Whig, became President of the United States and served from March 4, 1841 to April 4, 1841. John Tyler, vice president when Harrison died, became the tenth president. Tyler, also a Whig, declared himself a No Party on September 13, 1841 and remained so until March 4, 1845. In Alabama, Benjamin Fitzpatrick served as governor from 1841 to 1845. Although he was a Jacksonian Democrat he led a faction of the Democratic Party known as the "Montgomery Regency." The "regency" was more family and personal than ideological. During Fitzpatrick's term, the dominating issue was the state-owned Bank of Alabama which was still suffering due to the Panic of 1837 and was on the verge of bankruptcy.[36]

James K. Polk became the eleventh President of the United States in 1845 and Joshua L. Martin became governor of Alabama. Martin was a descendant of French immigrant Louis Montaigne who came to South Carolina in 1724 and changed his surname to Martin. Governor Martin put an end to the Bank of Alabama.[37]

Up until the election of Reuben Chapman as governor of Alabama (1847-1849), politics were mainly the discussion of internal issues such as state banking and Indian removal. This Jacksonian-style of politics was rapidly transitioning to discussion of national issues, thereby placing local or state issues in the background. The discussion would shift to pro-slavery and pro-secession.[38]

Whig Presidents of the United States

Two Whigs, Zachary Taylor and Millard Fillmore, would serve as President of the United States between 1849 and 1853. When Taylor died in office on July 9, 1850, Fillmore completed his term. Henry W. Collier would serve as Alabama's governor from 1849 to 1853. After America's war with Mexico (1845-48) sectional politics dominated not only in Washington but in Alabama. The Democratic Party in Alabama was split between a states' rights faction and Unionists. Unionist sentiments were strongest in northern Alabama. There was opposition to Democratic Governor Chapman's re-nomination by Unionists because of his appointment of former governor Fitzpatrick to fill an unexpired United States Senate term. Fitzpatrick was a pro-secessionist. Therefore, Collier was a compromise candidate for governor and won election.[39]

By 1850 the population of Alabama had grown from 590,000 to 771,623. The ratio of rural to urban population dropped from 45:1 to 21 to one. The free black population remained relatively constant at 2,265 from 2,039, but Alabama's slave population grew to 342,844 from 253,532 in 1840.[40] Changes were taking place in industry and the state began reporting the number of manufacturing establishments which numbered 1,026 in 1850. Whig Party unity was being fractured by the issue of southern rights related to the expansion of slavery and fears of expanding federal power.[41] In the United States Congress a set of five laws dealing with the issue of slavery was passed in September known as the "Compromise of 1850."

California had requested in 1849 to enter the Union as a free state which would have destroyed the balance between free and slave states in the United States Senate. It was Henry Clay who on January 29, 1850 introduced a series of resolutions seeking a compromise that would ease tensions between North and South. The five parts of the compromise included amending the Fugitive Slave Act and abolishing slave trading in Washington, D.C. California was admitted to the Union as a free state and the Utah Territory was created. Finally, an act was passed which settled a dispute between Texas and New Mexico which included the establishment of a territorial government for New Mexico.[42]

J.W.D. Jelks to Alabama from North Carolina

By the 1850s J.W.D. Jelks, and his father Robert Jelks, had moved from Halifax County, North Carolina to Russell County, Alabama. Robert Jelks, it has been reported, owned and operated a plantation near Uchee, Alabama. The reasons for the Jelks family move from northeastern North Carolina to Alabama can only be speculation.

In 1972 Louise Jelks Sills provided an oral history of her family to East Carolina University in Greenville, North Carolina.[43] According to Miss Sills at her oral history session, "When Louisa [M.P.M.N. Jelks] Sills' father [Robert Jelks, husband of Mary Nicholson] died in 1845 [in Alabama], he left his estate to be divided into ten parts. Dr. Gray [Sills] gave each of his children some land about a half mile from Belford. His youngest son, Thomas Alfred [Sills], who was my father, was given the home place. He and his bride, Pattie Thompson of Mississippi, lived there with his parents and two maiden sisters until their deaths. One of the sisters, the oldest one, outlived my father."[44] Sills was first cousin to

William [Dorsey] Jelks, son of Louisa's brother Joseph William Dorsey Jelks. But William Dorsey Jelks would have been ten years old at the time she places on these events. It is more likely that Robert Jelks moved to Alabama because of the potential fortunes to be made there. Alabama was "opened up" for settlement when it was made a Territory in 1817 and then a State in 1819.

The four children of Joseph William Dorsey Jelks and Jane Goodrum Frazier were born between 1852 and 1856, all in Uchee, Russell County, Alabama. J.W.D. wrote three letters to his sister Louisa in North Carolina. The first of the three was dated October 10, 1851 and a second letter was dated May 11, 1852. The third letter was undated. In the undated letter J.W.D. wrote that "… instead of going up to Macon County, as we had once expected, on the land we bought there, I concluded to buy a dwelling and store in Uchee, so we are now residing there."

Not only the store, but their "dwelling" provided the family some revenue. "Have opened a one-horse hotel. We have nine regular boarders, transient custom is worth about 50 dollars per month, we have from ten to twelve dollars per month for board. We have several horses to board also." The income from all boarding ran between $160.00 to $170.00 per month. J.W.D. and Jane both worked their family business but not without help. J.W.D. wrote that Jane, though "up to her eyes in business, has only two Negro women and one boy to do all the cooking, washings, and ironing."[45]

Further into the undated letter J.W.D. wrote that "Jim Tom and Bob are two of the fattest and finest looking boys in all Hayti – the mothers all through this land give it up so you know it is so, for they are the last to acknowledge that other children are better looking than theirs, are they not?" His reference to Hayti might be a reference to an area or section of Uchee. But by writing about his sons Jim Tom and Bob he gets us closer to the probable dating of this letter. James Thomas was born on May 20, 1852, and Robert was born in 1853. Whether the two boys were toddlers or older cannot be discerned from the letter.

J.W.D. Jelks then returns to the business at hand which provides a broader understanding of the family business and family. He wrote "I believe when I wrote you last I informed you that I expected Mr. Frazier and myself would farm together this year." By using the formal "Mr. Frazier" he could have been referring to his father-in-law. Instead of farming together, J.W.D. wrote that he decided to give the farm management to Mr. Frazier and an over-seer and that he alone would run the mercantile business in Uchee. The over-seer was Mr. Johnson, a clever young man according to J.W.D.. Mr. Johnson must have been highly trusted by J.W.D. and Mr. Frazier because the letter states that Mr. Johnson that night will leave from Columbus, Georgia for New York City with $4,400.00 to purchase between $5,000 and $7,000 worth of stock and goods. "Mr. Johnson having been engaged in the business several years, we thought it best for him to go [to New York], I think I shall go next fall in order to pay you a visit. If I do go, Mary Drake, I reckon, will go with me as far as Nash County [North Carolina]."

Louisa's full name was Louisa Marie Penelope Mann Nicholson [M.P.M.N.] Jelks Sills. She married a shy medical doctor in Nash County, North Carolina named Gray Sills. J.W.D. wrote "Tell Dr. Sills that I have not given up that trip to Texas yet … Perhaps he will get in the notion before many years and to let me know when he gets ready." These sentences provide clues to the dating of this letter, by getting closer to the period of proximity. The State of Texas was admitted to the Union on December 29, 1845 and apparently both J.W.D. and Dr. Sills saw opportunities within the newest and largest state in the Union. Perhaps they were thinking and talking about land acquisition or of setting up a business there. But J.W.D. opined that he would be "content to remain here [in Alabama] if he will move out here." This suggests a strong relationship between J.W.D. and his sister, Mrs. Sills.

In his letter to "Sis Lou" dated October 10, 1851, J.W.D. opens with an apology for "my long silence after promising you so faithfully that I would write you as soon as I got home." J.W.D. wrote that he had been to Macon [County, Alabama] to see sister Martha and Green.[46] He wrote of a good time there and then he scribbled plaintively "If you and all of your family could be here we would have a real jollification." This sounds like another plea for Louisa to move from North Carolina to Alabama.

Joseph William Dorsey Jelks was a family man, and if not homesick for North Carolina, he was homesick for the rest of his family. He went on to write "Do you think you will ever come? You have no idea how glad we would be to see you all out here, but I fear we never shall." These written words evidence J.W.D.'s woes of family separation.

"Can't you break loose from those old red hills?" The "red hills" refers to the area of Nash County, North Carolina where the Belford Plantation existed. The transcription of J.W.D.'s letter had "Bedford" instead of Belford. The area around the plantation though called Belford was probably never incorporated as a town. That area today is known as Castalia. The transcribed letter also located J.W.D. as writing from Allen Dail on Oct. 10, 1851. The closest named area in Alabama is Allendale, a community outside Montgomery. In any event the Alabama counties of Macon, Russell, Bullock, and Barbour are east and south-southeast of Montgomery, in fairly close proximity. Those counties are part of Alabama's eastern Black Belt. The Black Belt is a fertile section of central Alabama that runs between its borders with Mississippi and Georgia. The soil is rich for growing cotton.

The May 11, 1852 letter from J.W.D. to Louisa is more of an update of conditions in Alabama, the plantation, and the "one-horse" hotel business. J.W.D. wrote that "wife Jane and hotel keeping are not a good match. But the mercantile business is prosperous." The transcriber of the letter simply summarizes by saying that the letter "tells of conditions on the plantation in Maton [Macon] County." Near the end of the letter J.W.D. writes that the "way we do masticate the garden peas, lettuce, beets, irish [sic] potatoes, squash, cucumbers etc., is a caution to tavern keepers." That sentence gave evidence of a good harvest but one of subsistence farming and not a cotton plantation.

Plantation cotton farming would have required large numbers of helpers for the harvest. They ground their vegetables so finely that they could be used to make moonshine. Or perhaps the "caution to tavern keepers" meant that they were to keep away from his "stash." The letters provide information about the Jelks family and its Alabama businesses as well as give insight on the state of mind of Joseph William Dorsey Jelks, a man who was quite family-centric and industrious. None of the three letters expressed or implied any political inclination. Certainly nothing was made of Alabama or national politics of the day. On November 7, 1855, the third son of J.W.D. and Jane Jelks was born – William Dorsey

Jelks. Within the next forty-five years the Governor of Alabama would be a Jelks.

Endnotes

Chapter 1 Introduction

[1] Interviews – Kenneth Hillas; William J. Cabaniss, Jr.

[2] "Fahrenheit all day" http://weathersource.com/past-weather/weather-history-reports/free, viewed on March 25, 2003.

[3] "Colin Powell hosted" http://2001-2009.state.gov/secretary/former/powell/remarks/2003/26987.htm, viewed on March 22, 2003

[4] Merriam-Webster definition: French (LA) SAVONNERIE, carpet factory manufacturing Savonnerie carpets established in 1628 on the site of a former soap factory at Chaillot, near the Seine, in Paris, from SAVONNERIE soap factory, from SAVONNIER soap maker (from SAVON soap—from Latin SAPO).

[5] http://history.state.gov/departmenthistory/people/dulles-john-foster, viewed on October 7, 2013

[6] Interviews with William J. Cabaniss, Jr., 09/21/2011 and 05/15/2013.

[7] Jack Bass and Walter De Vries. *The Transformation of Southern Politics: Social Change & Political Consequence Since 1945*. (Athens: The University of Georgia Press, 1995), 58.

[8] Leah R Atkins. *Developed for the Service of Alabama: The Centennial History of the Alabama Power Company 1906-2006*. Birmingham: Alabama Power Company, 2006.

[9] Václav Havel. *The Power of the Powerless (Routledge Revivals): Citizens Against the State in Central-eastern Europe*, 125, 157, 195; http://en.wikipedia.org/wiki/Jan_Pato%C4%8Dka, viewed July 31, 2013.

[10] Václav Havel, *The Art of the Impossible: Politics as Morality in Practice*. (New York: Alfred A. Knopf, 1997), 159.

[11] "The Charter 77 Declaration" reproduced in Havel, *The Power of the Powerless*, 217-221.

[12] Havel, *The Art of the Impossible*, 33.

[13] The genealogy of the greater Cabaniss family documents different modes and conditions of ancestors as they came to colonial America from France, as in the case of the Cabaniss name, and from England and Ireland as in the Jelks family. One family received benefits from the sponsoring English government and receiving colonial government, while the other family migrated as indentured servants, most to the Royal Colony of Virginia, others to New England. The circumstances that led them to seek new lives in the New World are presented in the Appendices.

[14] Rustbelt or Rust Belt refers to the northern tier of the lower 48 states from northeastern part of the United States to the Midwest.

Chapter 2 Growing Up in Alabama – 1951-1960

[1] Samuel L., Webb, and Margaret E. Armbrester, eds. *Alabama Governors: A Political History of the State*. (Tuscaloosa: The University of Alabama Press, 2001), 207-8.

[2] http://en.wikipedia.org/wiki/Victory_at_Sea, viewed on December 24, 2012.

[3] Cabaniss Family Records. Resume of William Jelks Cabaniss [Sr.] dated March 1, 1950.

[4] C. Vann Woodward. *The Battle for Leyte Gulf: The Incredible Story of World War II's Largest Naval Battle*. (Nashville: The Battery Press, 1989), 41-66.

[5] Interview Francis Crockard and Cullom Walker, Feb. 28, 2012.

[6] Interview, William J. Cabaniss, Jr. March 28, 2011.

[7] William C. Havard, ed. *The Changing Politics of the South*. (Baton Rouge: Louisiana State University Press, 1972). 436.

[8] Ivan Volgyes. *Politics in Eastern Europe*. (Chicago: Irwin Professional Publishing, 1986), 89.

[9] Bishop C.C.J. Carpenter was one member of the Birmingham clergy addressed by Dr. Martin Luther King, Jr. in his "Letter from Birmingham Jail" about their statement of King's present activities as "unwise and untimely."

[10] Alabama Department of Archives and History Timeline 1861-1900, see 1896 entry, http://www.archives.alabama.gov/timeline/usa186.html, viewed on February 13, 2014.

[11] *Encyclopedia of Alabama*, "Albert Patterson,"

http://www.encyclopediaofalabama.org/face/Article.jsp?id=h-1250, viewed on February 13, 2014.
[12] Carl Grafton, and Anne Permaloff. *Big Mules & Branchheads: James E. Folsom and Political Power in Alabama*. (Athens: The University of Georgia Press, 1985), xi, 10, 32,68, 107.
[13] *Alabama Governors*, 203.
[14] Interview, Drayton Nabers, Jr., March 8, 2013.
[15] Alabama Department of Archives and History Timeline 1951 to present, see 1954 entry, http://www.archives.alabama.gov/timeline/al1951.html, viewed on February 13, 2014.
[16] Alabama Department of Archives and History Timeline 1951 to present, see 1956 entry, http://www.archives.alabama.gov/timeline/al1951.html, viewed on February 13, 2014.
[17] Helen Shores Lee, Barbara Sylvia Shores, and Denise George. The *Gentle Giant of Dynamite Hill: The Untold Story of Arthur Shores and His Family's Fight for Civil Rights*. Grand Rapids, MI: Zondervan, 2012, 166.
[18] Interview, William J. Cabaniss, Jr., March 28, 2011.
[19] Winton Blount with Richard Blodgett. *Doing It My Way*. (Lyme, Conn: Greenwich Publishing Group, 1996), 34-5.
[20] Interview, John Beau Grenier, May 23, 2012. Mignon Smith died on February 10, 2012. Obituary found in *The Birmingham News* between February 14 and February 17, 2012.
[21] Alabama Department of Archives and History Timeline 1951 to present, see 1956 entry, http://www.archives.alabama.gov/timeline/al1951.html, viewed on February 13, 2014.
[22] *Alabama Governors*, 210-11.
[23] Interview, William J. Cabaniss, Jr., March 28, 2011.
[24] Alabama Department of Archives and History Timeline 1951 to present, see 1960 entry, http://www.archives.alabama.gov/timeline/al1951.html, viewed on February 13, 2014.
[25] *The Changing Politics of the South*, 427-8.
[26] Interview, John Beau Grenier, May 23, 2012.

Chapter 3 Alabama Republican Politics – 1961-1965
[1] Alabama Department of Archives and History Timeline 1951 to present, see 1961 entry, http://www.archives.alabama.gov/timeline/al1951.html, viewed on February 13, 2014.
[2] Westmoreland led United States forces in Vietnam from 1964 to 1968 and then served as Army Chief of Staff from 1968 to 1972. He died in 2005 at the age of 91.
[3] Interview, William J. Cabaniss, Jr. March 28, 2011.
[4] Earl Black and Merle Black. *The Rise of Southern Republicans*. (Cambridge: Belknap Press, 2002), 126.
[5] Ibid, 126-7.; Interview, Bill Harris, October 22, 2013.
[6] Havard. *The Changing Politics of the South*, 439.
[7] Interview, John Beau Grenier, May 23, 2012.
[8] Ibid.
[9] Wayne Greenhaw. *Elephants in the Cottonfields*. (New York: McMillan Publishing Company, 1982), 91.
[10] *Alabama Governors*, 216-20.
[11] Alabama Department of Archives and History, "Governor George C. Wallace's School House Door Speech,"
http://www.archives.alabama.gov/govs_list/schooldoor.html, viewed on February 13, 2014.
[12] Havard. *The Changing Politics of the South*, 438.
[13] Interview, John Beau Grenier, May 23, 2012.
[14] Interview, Bill Harris, Oct. 22. 2012.
[15] Encyclopedia of Alabama, "Bloody Sunday,"
 http://www.encyclopediaofalabama.org/face/Article.jsp?id=h-1876, viewed on February 13, 2014.
[16] Encyclopedia of Alabama, "Voting Rights Act of 1965,"
http://www.encyclopediaofalabama.org/face/Multimedia.jsp?id=m-5825, viewed on February 13, 2014.
[17] Interview, William Armistead, October 18, 2013.
[18] Cabaniss Family Timeline.

Chapter 4 Alabama Republican Politics – 1966-1970

---

[1] *The Birmingham News*, November 3, 1982, 19A.

[2] Havard, *The Changing Politics of the South*, 466.

[3] Ibid.

[4] Gould, *GOP*, 372.

[5] *Alabama Governors*, 230.

[6] *Alabama Governors*, 235-7.

[7] Vlk, Wikipedia article, http://en.wikipedia.org/wiki/Miloslav_Vlk, viewed on February 13, 2014.

[8] Volgyes. *Politics in Eastern Europe*, 91.

[9] Alabama Department of Archives and History Timeline 1951 to present, see 1969 entry, http://www.archives.alabama.gov/timeline/al1951.html, viewed February 13, 2014.

[10] Alabama Department of Archives and History Timeline 1951 to present, see 1970 entry, http://www.archives.alabama.gov/timeline/al1951.html, viewed February 13, 2014.

[11] Interview, William J. Cabaniss, Jr., March 28, 2011.

Chapter 5 Politics and Business in Alabama – 1971-1977

[1] *Alabama Governors*, 239.

[2] Blount. *Doing It My Way*, 119.

[3] Interview, William J. Cabaniss, Jr., March 28, 2011; Letter from William J. Cabaniss, Jr. to "Red" Blount dated December 27, 1971.

[4] Wikipedia article, http://en.wikipedia.org/wiki/Winton_M._Blount; http://en.wikipedia.org/wiki/James_D._Martin, viewed July 31, 2013.

[5] Blount. *Doing It My Way*, 119.

[6] Interview, Walter McCullers, March 19, 2013.

[7] A "C-level" corporate officer would be the Chief Executive Officer (CEO), Chief Operating Officer (COO), or Chief Information Officer (CIO).

[8] Ibid. McCullers.

[9] Interview, William J. Cabaniss, Jr., February 5, 2014.

[10] Interview, Bill Harris, Oct. 22, 2012.

[11] Havard. *The Changing Politics of the South*, 433.

[12] Alabama Department of Archives and History or ADAH.

[13] Blount. *Doing It My Way,* 139.

[14] Sam Hodges. Article in the *Mobile Press Register*, December 11, 1994.

[15] John Hayman with Clara Ruth Hayman. *A Judge in the Senate*. (Montgomery: NewSouth Books, 2001), 188-9.

[16] Interview, Ann Bedsole. January 10, 2012.

[17] Alabama Department of Archives and History Timeline 1950 to present, see entries for 1970 and 1980, http://www.archives.alabama.gov/timeline/al1951.html, viewed on February 13, 2014.

[18] http://en.wikipedia.org/wiki/Robert_E._Lee; www.wiki.answers.com viewed on July 31, 2013

[19] Bass, DeVries. *The Transformation of Southern Politics: Social Change & Political Consequence Since 1945*, 76.

[20] *The Gadsden Times*, Thursday, May 8, 1975, page 32.

[21] Interview, John Beau Grenier, May 23, 2012.

[22] Interview, William J. Cabaniss, August 17, 2012.

[23] Interview, Judy Bewley, May 29, 2012.

[24] Interview, Bill Harris, October 22, 2012.

[25] Ibid.

[26] Interview, William J. Cabaniss, Jr, April 18, 2011.

[27] James A. Baker III with Thomas M. DeFrank. *The Politics of Diplomacy: Revolution, War & Peace, 1989-1992.* (New York: G.P. Putnam's Sons, 1995), 33.

[28] Václav Havel. *The Power of the Powerless (Routledge Revivals): Citizens Against the State in Central-Eastern Europe*, 125, 157, 195; http://en.wikipedia.org/wiki/Jan_Pato%C4%8Dka, viewed July 31, 2013.

Chapter 6 Alabama Retail Politics – 1978-1980

[1] Interview, Peggy Balliet, May 24, 2012.

[2] Interview, Edgar Welden, March 30, 2012.

[3] Interview, William J. Cabaniss, Jr., Aug. 17, 2012.

[4] "Pavarotti fans have big night at Civic Center." Review by Oliver Roosevelt. *The Birmingham News*, Sunday, November 5, 1978.

[5] Interview, Bob Riley, November 5, 2012.

[6] Interview, Gerald Dial, February 14, 2012.

[7] Bert Nettles interview by Jack Bass and Walter De Vries, July 13, 1974. *Interview A-0015. Southern Oral History Program Collection (#4007)*. University of North Carolina-Chapel Hill.

[8] "Alabama's second GOP representative since Reconstruction, Doug Hale, named Republican Pioneer." Paul Huggins, *AL.Com* article, September 16, 2013.

[9] *The Birmingham News*, Wednesday, November 8, 1978, "GOP ends up with four-seat House total; Senate chamber to be exclusively Demo," 2.

[10] *The Birmingham News*, Wednesday, November 5, 1978, paid political advertisement "He Knows How You Feel. You Know Where He Stands," 44-A.

[11] Interview. Edgar Welden, March 20, 2012.

[12] Hayman. *Judge in the Senate*, 213-14.

[13] Leah Rawls Atkins. *Developed for the Service of Alabama: The Centennial History of the Alabama Power Company 1906-2006*. (Birmingham: Alabama Power Company, 2006). 405.

[14] Hayman. *Judge in the Senate*, 205.

[15] Interview, William J. Cabaniss, Jr. April 18, 2011.

[16] Interview, Ann Bedsole, January 10, 2012.

[17] Interview, William J. Cabaniss, Jr. April 18, 2011.

[18] Interview, Ann Bedsole, January 10, 2012.

[19] Interview, William J. Cabaniss, Jr., April 4, 2011.

[20] *Interest Group Politics in the Southern States*, 249. Chapter 11, authored by David L. Martin on Alabama politics wrote "… from 1901, when the Alabama Constitution forbad legislators from accepting free railroad passes, to today, Alabamians have been skeptical of lobbyists and interest groups. … [but] interest groups thrived throughout the 1970s …".

[21] Interview, Cullom Walker, February 28, 2012.

[22] Interview, Larry Dixon, October 10, 2012.

[23] Interview, Gerald Dial, February 14, 2012.

[24] Interview David Bronner, February 14, 2012.

[25] Ibid.

[26] Interview, William J. Cabaniss, Jr., March 28, 2011.

[27] Interview, Judy Bewley, May 29, 2012.

[28] William and Catherine Cabaniss Family Archives: "Letter from William J. Cabaniss, Jr. to John Claypool", November 15, 1979.

[29] William and Catherine Cabaniss Family Archives: "Letter from John Claypool to William J. Cabaniss, Jr.", not dated, handwritten on stationery of Northminster Baptist Church, Jackson, Mississippi.

[30] Václav Havel. *The Art of the Impossible: Politics as Morality in Practice*. (New York: Knopft, 1997), book jacket.

[31] Interview, William J. Cabaniss, Jr., Mar. 28, 2011.

[32] Some Alabama political pundits have written that William Jelks Cabaniss, Jr. and George W. Bush were childhood friends and both sets of parents owned summer estates in Kennebunkport, Maine. Such is not the case and the record should be corrected.

[33] Lewis L. Gould. *Grand Old Party*. (New York: Random House, 2003), 417.

[34] *Southern Republicans*, 127.

[35] "Timeline of the Czech Republic", http://www.datesandevents.org/places-timelines/13-timeline-of-the-czech-republic.htm, viewed on January 10, 2014.

Chapter 7 Civil Strife – 1861-1870
[1] Alabama Department of Archives and History.

[2] "3rd Alabama Infantry Regiment." http://www.civilwarintheeast.com/CSA/AL/3AL.php, viewed on January 10, 2013; "3rd Alabama Infantry in the American Civil War". See link

http://civilwarindex.com/armyal/3rd_al_infantry.html, viewed on January 10, 2013; Colonel Mahone was probably William Mahone who became a United States Senator from Virginia in the 1880s. He was educated at Virginia Military Institute and served in the Virginia General Assembly. He commanded the Norfolk brigade and was eventually promoted to Brigadier General. He fought in the Battle of Seven Pines in 1862. He is better known for his service in the Battle of the Crater during the Union siege of Petersburg in 1864.

[3] *Alabama Governors*, 70.

[4] Notes of James Marion Keener on Battle of Seven Pines. See link viewed on January 11, 2013 http://familytreemaker.genealogy.com/users/k/e/e/Janiece-Keener/GENE1-0002.html

[5] Martha Frazier Jelks married Edward H. Cabaniss. She is the paternal grandmother of William J. Cabaniss, Jr.

[6] Ibid., Keener.

[7] "3rd Alabama Infantry Regiment." See link http://www.civilwarintheeast.com/CSA/AL/3AL.php, viewed on January 10, 2013; "3rd Alabama Infantry in the American Civil War". See link http://civilwarindex.com/armyal/3rd_al_infantry.html, viewed on January 10, 2013; THE HUDSON NORTH STAR and THE PRESCOTT JOURNAL, both of May 14, 1862. Viewed on December 23, 2013 at http://thecivilwarandnorthwestwisconsin.wordpress.com/2012/05/17/1862-may-14-norfolk-evacuated-merrimac-blown-up/.

[8] "3rd Alabama Infantry in the American Civil War" see http://www.civilwarindex.com/armyal_3rd_al_infantry.html, viewed on January 13, 2013; "Battle of Seven Pines-Fair Oaks"; http://www.encyclopediavirginia.org/Seven_Pines_Battle_of#start_entry, viewed on January 13, 2013.
Some documents record the death of J.W.D. Jelks in a hospital in Richmond. The genealogy document created by Barbara Swaim from the *Jelks Family Bible* dates his death as June 2, 1862.

[9] Barbara Swaim's genealogies documents Charles Napoleon Jelks as a son of Robert Jelks and his third wife, Letti Reed.

[10] "Jelks burial sites". http://www.fightingjoewheeler.org/images/CSA_soldiers_J.txt viewed on January 13, 2013.

[11] "Monroe County, Georgia Biographies." http://genealogytrails.com/geo/monroe/bio1.html, viewed on November 12, 2013.

[12] *Alabama Governors*, 73.

[13] "The Battle of Mobile Bay." http://www.encyclopediaofalabama.org/face/Article.jsp?id=h-1257 viewed on February 12, 2014; Alabama Department of Archives and History, http://www.archives.alabama.gov/timeline/1861/diary1.html viewed on February 12, 2014.

[14] Alabama Department of Archives and History 1800-1860 Timeline. http://www.archives.alabama.gov/timeline/al1801.html viewed on February 12, 2014.

[15] Many southern Whigs moved into the American Party around 1856 to avoid having to make a decision between their region and the nation. The other parties demanded a decision, one way or another. When asked about any position they held they would say "I know nothing." Hence the party's nickname, "Know Nothings." Carl N. Degler. *The Other South: Southern Dissenters in the Nineteen Century*. (New York: Harper & Row Publishers, 1974), 115-116.

[16] *Alabama Governors*, 77.

[17] *Alabama Governors*, 80.

[18] Peter Kolchin. *First Freedom: The Responses of Alabama's Blacks to Emancipation and Reconstruction*. (Westport, Connecticut: Greenwood Press, 1972), 152.

[19] Sarah Woolfolk Wiggins. The *Scalawag in Alabama Politics, 1865-1881*. (Tuscaloosa: The University of Alabama Press,1977), 9.

[20] *Alabama Governors*, 83.

[21] Peter Kolchin, *First Freedom*, 151, 154.

[22] Kolchin, *First Freedom*, 157.

[23] Wiggins. *The Scalawag in Alabama Politics, 1865-1881*, 21.

[24] William Warren Rogers: *Black Belt Scalawag: Charles Hayes and the Southern Republicans in the Era of Reconstruction*. (Athens, Georgia: the University of Georgia Press, 1993), 19.

[25] Kolchin, 154.

[26] Wiggins, 21, 22.

[27] Wiggins, 32.

[28] McMillan, *Constitutional Development in Alabama*, 154.

[29] *Alabama Governors*, 87-8.

[30] Wiggins, 39; Alabama Republican Party website. http://algop.org/about-us/history-of-algop/ viewed on February 12, 2014.

[31] McMillan, *Constitutional Development in Alabama*, 101.

[32] Alabama Department of Archives and History Timeline 1861-1900. http://www.archives.alabama.gov/timeline/al1861.html viewed on February 12, 2014.

[33] Wiggins, 40.

[34] Kolchin, *First Freedom*, 186.

[35] *Alabama Governors*, 90-93.

Chapter 8 Post-War Growth – 1871-1880

[1] *Alabama Governors*, 95.

[2] John Temple Graves II; *The Book of Alabama and the South*, 110.

[3] *Alabama Governors*, 96.

[4] University of Virginia, School of Law. http://libguides.law.virginia.edu/content.php?pid=135150&sid=1158363 viewed on February 12, 2014.

[5] Thomas McAdory Owen. *Dictionary of Alabama Biography*, *Vol III*. (Chicago: The S.J. Clarke Publishing Company, 1921), 899-901. Encyclopedia of Alabama, http://www.encyclopediaofalabama.org/face/Article.jsp?id=h-1438 viewed on February 12, 2014.

[6] Kolchin, *First Freedom*, 187.

[7] Greenhaw, *Elephants in the Cottonfields*, 33.

[8] *Alabama Governors*, 118.

[9] Alabama Department of Archives and History Timeline 1861-1900. See 1875 Constitution to replace 1868 Constitution at http://www.archives.alabama.gov/timeline/al1861.html viewed on February 12, 2014.

[10] Arthur M. Hull and Sydney A. Hale, eds. *Coal Men of America: A Biographical and Historical Review of the World's Greatest Industry*. (Chicago: The Retail Coalman, 1918), 26.

[11] Greenhaw. *Elephants in the Cottonfields*, 34.

[12] *Alabama Governors*, 106.

[13] Joel C. DuBose, ed. *Notable Men of Alabama*, (Atlanta: Southern Historical Association, 1904),105.

[14] Owen. *A History of Alabama and Dictionary of Alabama Biography*, 277.

[15] Alabama Department of Archives and History, http://www.archives.alabama.gov/govs_list/g_jelksw.html viewed on February 12, 2014; http://www.encyclopediaofalabama.org/face/Article.jsp?id=h-1438.

[16] Alabama Department of Archives and History Timeline 1861-1900. http://www.archives.alabama.gov/timeline/al1861.html viewed on February 12, 2014.

Chapter 9 Politics and Opportunity – 1881-1890

[1] Booker T. Washington and Tuskegee Institute. http://www.encyclopediaofalabama.org/face/Article.jsp?id=h-1506, viewed on February 12, 2014,

[2] *Alabama Governors*, 109-11.

[3] Thomas McAdory Owen. *History of Alabama and Dictionary of Alabama Biography, Vol III*. (Chicago: The S.J. Clarke Publishing Company, 1921), 277-278.

[4] J.A.B. Besson. *History of Eufaula, Alabama: the Bluff City of the Chattahoochee*. (Atlanta: Franklin Steam Printing House – Jas. P. Harrison & Co. Printers, 1875).

[5] David Alsobrook master's thesis. Online Encyclopedia of Alabama, See link http://www.encyclopediaofalabama.org/face/Article.jsp?id=h-1438, viewed on January 10, 2013

[6] *Alabama Governors*, 113-4.

[7] Ibid. Owen.

[8] *Union Springs Herald and Times*, April 27, 1887; Cindy Holland. "A History of the Firm of Cabaniss, Johnston, Gardner, Dumas & O'Neal." (Birmingham: Cabaniss Johnston unpublished manuscript, 1989), 2-3.

[9] Cindy Holland, 5-6.

---

[10] George M. Cruikshank. *A History of Birmingham and Its Environs: A Narrative Account of Their Historical Progress, Their People, and Their Prinicpal Interests, Vol II*. (Chicago: The Lewis Publishing Company, 1920), 42-44; http://www.archives.alabama.gov/judicial/weakley.html, viewed on July 15, 2012.

[11] Joel C. DuBose, ed. *Notable Men of Alabama: Personal and Genealogical with Portraits, Vol II*. (Atlanta: Southern Historical Association, 1904), 104-5.

[12] Birmingham Bar Association Resolution of December 18, 1936; Cindy Holland, 21-23.

[13] Alabama Department of Archives and History, http://www.alabamamoments.alabama.gov/sec33det.html viewed on February 12, 2014.

[14] *Alabama Governors*, 115.

[15] *Alabama Governors*, 116-119.

[16] Alabama Department of Archives and History Time Line 1861-1900 http://www.archives.alabama.gov/timeline/al1861.html; http://www.census.gov/population/www/documentation/twps0056/tabs15-65.pdf, viewed on February 12, 2014.

[17] Richard E. Welch, Jr. "The Federal Elections Bill of 1890: Post-scripts and Prelude." *Journal of American History* 52 (1965): 511–526; http://www.answers.com/topic/compromise-of-1890, viewed on November 3, 2013.

[18] "History of Prague through the Centuries: 9th Century to 2002", http://www.myczechrepublic.com/prague/history/prague_history.html, viewed on July 9, 2013.

Chapter 10 Alabama Politics and Business – 1891-1900

[1] *Alabama Governors*, 199-120.

[2] Alabama Department of Archives and History Time Line 1861-1900, see 1893 entry, http://www.archives.alabama.gov/timeline/al1861.html viewed on February 12, 2014

[3] Ibid.

[4] *Alabama Governors*, 124-5.

[5] *Alabama Governors*, 127.

[6] Alabama Department of Archives and History Time Line 1861-1900, see 1896 entry, http://www.archives.alabama.gov/timeline/al1861.html viewed on February 12, 2014.

[7] http://www.bhamwiki.com/w/Truman_Aldrich, viewed on February 12, 2014; http://algop.org/about-us/history-of-algop/.

[8] Owen. *Alabama Official Statistical Register 1903*, 6; http://www.archives.alabama.gov/govs_list/g_jelksw.html, viewed on January 10, 2013; David Alsobrook. Online Encyclopedia of Alabama; Thomas McAdory Owen. *History of Alabama and Dictionary of Alabama Biography, Vol III*. (Chicago: The S.J. Clarke Publishing Company, 1921), 899-901.
See link http://www.encyclopediaofalabama.org/face/Article.jsp?id=h-1438, viewed on January 10, 2013.

[9] *The Sixth Decennial Catalogue of the Chi Psi Fraternity, 1902*. (Auburn, New York: 58th Annual Convention, 1902), 565.

[10] *Alabama Governors*, 135.

[11] *Alabama Governors*, 137-8.

[12] David Alsobrook master's thesis; Online Encyclopedia of Alabama, See link http://www.encyclopediaofalabama.org/face/Article.jsp?id=h-1438, viewed on January 10, 2013; http://www.archives.alabama.gov/govs_list/g_jelksw.html, viewed on January 10, 2013.

[13] Alabama Department of Archives and History Timeline 1861-1900, see 1900 entry, http://www.archives.alabama.gov/timeline/al1861.html viewed on February 12, 2014.

Chapter 11 Alabama Politics and Business – 1901-1910

[1] Alabama Department of Archives and History; http://www.archives.alabama.gov/findaids/v6462.pdf, viewed on February 13, 2014; http://www.encyclopediaofalabama.org/face/Article.jsp?id=h-1495, viewed on February 14, 2014.

[2] Some Alabama historians ssuggest that the Progressive Era began with Governor Braxton Bragg Comer (1907-1911). His progressive successes were in education, railroad regulation, tax funding and education. A successful industrialist himself, his progressive measures were biased toward the

emerging industrial and urban segments of the state while at the same time careful not to disturb the remnants of the old plantation system. See
http://www.encyclopediaofalabama.org/face/Article.jsp?id=h-1529, viewed on February 13, 2014;

Maureen A. Flanagan. *America Reformed: Progressives and Progressivisms 1890s – 1920s*. (New York: Oxford University Press, 2007), 285. Flanagan concludes that "America was reformed in this time period [between the 1890s and 1920s]. Federal government was strengthened and the presidency began to accumulate more power to determine the country's political and economic course. ... Most Americans accepted that it was the government's job to help regulate the economy and to provide at least a modicum of protections for all people."

[3] "History of the Alabama Department of Archives and History."
http://www.archives.alabama.gov/intro/adah.html, viewed on February 13, 2014;
Samuel L. Webb and Margaret E. Ambrester, eds. *Alabama Governors: A Political History of the State*. (Tuscaloosa: The University of Alabama Press, 2001), 140.
[4] Jelks was the last of the "Bourbon" governors of Alabama denoting a change in the structure of politics in the state.
[5] Thomas McAdory Owen. *Alabama Official and Statistical Record, 1903*. (Montgomery: The State Department of Archives and History, 1908), 5-6.
[6] David E. Alsobrook. "William Dorsey Jelks: Alabama Editor and Legislator." (West Virginia University: Masters Thesis., 1971), 20, 21. Alsobrook is a (probably the first) Jelks biographer. See also the only *Encyclopedia of Alabama*.
[7] Cindy Holland. "A History of the firm Cabaniss, Johnston, Gardner, Dumas & O'Neal." Unpublished internal manuscript. (Birmingham: Cabaniss, Johnston, 1989), 13. Attorney Forney Johnston, the son of former Alabama Governor and United States Senator Joseph Forney Johnston, partnered with Edward H. Cabaniss in 1920 to form the firm of Cabaniss, Johnston, Cocke and Cabaniss.
[8] Owen. *History of Alabama and Dictionary of Alabama Biography,* 899-901.
[9] Alsobrook, 15; Owen, *Dictionary*, 900.
[10] Alsobrook, 23; Jelks Official Papers, Alabama Department of Archives and History
[11] Alsobrook, 46.
[12] Alsobrook, 50 citing an interview on March 18, 1972 with Jelks former chauffeur, Mr. Lee Moore.
[13] Alsobrook, 50. Owens. *Dictionary of Alabama Biography, III.*, 899.
[14] Ibid. 139, 140.
[15] A "beat" is a small geographic area. In this case a "beat meeting" would include persons in an area smaller than a political party precinct; a county could be divided into precincts, and precincts could be divided into beats.
[16] Owens. 146, 147.
[17] Ibid. 150, 151.
[18] Ibid.
[19] Ibid.
[20] *The Sixth Decennial Catalogue of the Chi Psi Fraternity, 1902*. (Auburn, New York: 58th Annual Convention, 1902), 565.
[21] Andrew Robert Warner, ed. *The Purple and Gold, Vol XX*. (Auburn, New York: Published by the [Chi Psi] Fraternity, 1903), 65.
[22] http://www.encyclopediaofalabama.org/face/Article.jsp?id=h-1438, viewed on January 10, 2013.
[23] *American Manufacturer and Iron World* magazine, Vol. 73, No. Pittsburg[h], PA. July 2, 1903, 84.
[24] The office of Lt. Gov. was re-instated by the 1901 Constitution.
http://www.encyclopediaofalabama.org/face/Article.jsp?id=h-1438, viewed on January 10, 2013.
[25] *Alabama Governors*, 147.
[26] Alabama Department of Archives and History,
http://www.alabamamoments.alabama.gov/sec42qs.html, viewed on February 13, 2014.
[27] Alabama Department of Archives and History Timeline 1901-1950, see 1904 entry
http://www.archives.alabama.gov/timeline/al1901.html, viewed on February 13, 2014.
[28] "Alabama Republicans and the Populists (1890-1916) as found in
http://en.wikipedia.org/wiki/Alabama_Republican_Party, viewed on January 10, 2014.

[29] http://www.bizapedia.com/al/CAHABA-SOUTHERN-COAL-MINING-COMPANY.html, viewed on January 10, 2014.

[30] Charles Carroll Brown, ed. *Directory of American Cement Industries*. (Indianapolis: Municipal Engineering Company, 1906), 84.

[31] http://www.archives.alabama.gov/judicial/weakley.html, viewed on July 15, 2012.

[32] Alabama Department of Archives and History, "Iron and Steel in Alabama: The Technical Story," http://www.alabamamoments.alabama.gov/sec30det.html, viewed on February 13, 2014.

[33] *Alabama Governors,* 150-1.

[34] Alabama Department of Archives and History, http://www.archives.alabama.gov/govs_list/g_jelksw.html, viewed on July 15, 2012.

[35] "Gus Cabaniss Goes to Beyond" from the *Atlanta Constitution*, December 15, 1907, page 5 as found on http://www.findagrave.com/cgi-bin/fg.cgi?page=gr&GRid=52180461, viewed on June 13, 2013.

[36] John Temple Graves, ed. *The Book of Alabama and the South: Commemorating the Silver Anniversary of the Protective Life Insurance Company*. (Birmingham: Protective Life, 1934), 179.

[37] Alabama Department of Archives and History Timeline 1901-1950, see 1910 entry, http://www.archives.alabama.gov/timeline/al1901.html, viewed on February 13, 2014; Federal Census 1910, http://www.census.gov/population/www/documentation/twps0056/tabs15-65.pdf, viewed on February 13, 2014.

[38] "Alabama Republicans and the Populists – 1890-1916." Alabama Republican Party website. http://algop.org/about-us/history-of-algop/ viewed on May 25, 2014.

[39] Alabama Republican Party office documents, Hoover, Alabama.

Chapter 12 Alabama, World War I, New World Order – 1911-1920

[1] *Alabama Governors,* 157.

[2] Alabama Department of Archives and History, http://www.archives.alabama.gov/govs_list/g_jelksw.html, viewed on July 15, 2012.

[3] Thomas McAdory Owen. *History of Alabama and Dictionary of Alabama Biography, Vol III*. (Chicago: The S.J. Clarke Publishing Company, 1921), 899-901.

[4] Ibid. 51.

[5] "Direct Elections to the United States Senate 1914-98." http://psephos.adam-carr.net/countries/u/usa/congress/senate1.txt, viewed on January 10, 2014. Also, Ratification was completed on April 8, 1913. The amendment was subsequently ratified by Louisiana, on June 11, 1914; Alabama, April 16, 2002. The amendment was rejected by Utah, February 26, 1913; Delaware, March 18, 1913. Florida, Georgia, Rhode Island, and South Carolina did not complete action. Source: U.S. Government Printing Office document found at http://www.gpo.gov/fdsys/pkg/HMAN-112/pdf/HMAN-112-pg106.pdf viewed on September 17, 2014.

[6] "Timeline of the Czech Republic" as found on http://www.datesandevents.org/places-timelines/13-timeline-of-the-czech-republic.htm, viewed on January 10, 2014.

[7] *Alabama Governors,* 163-4.

[8] House of Windsor, http://en.wikipedia.org/wiki/House_of_Windsor, viewed on January 10, 2014

[9] Richard Holbrook in the Foreword to Margaret MacMillan. *Paris 1919: Six Months that Changed the World*. (New York: Random House, 2001/2002), viii.

[10] Margaret MacMillan, *Paris 1919*. (New York: Random House, 2001), 229.

[11] United States Department of State "Czech Republic Profile 2006".

[12] "History of Prague through the Centuries: 9th Century to 2002"; See http://www.myczechrepublic.com/prague/history/prague_history.html, viewed on July 9, 2013

[13] "Timeline of the Czech Republic".

[14] *Alabama Governors,* 166-7.

[15] Alabama Department of Archives and History Timeline 1901-1950, see entry for 1920, http://www.archives.alabama.gov/timeline/al1901.html, viewed on February 13, 2014; http://www.census.gov/population/www/documentation/twps0056/tabs15-65.pdf, viewed on February 13, 2014.

[16] Arthur M. Hull and Sydney A. Hale, eds. Coal Men of America. (Chicago: The Retail Coalman, 1918), 26.

[17] *The Insurance Year Book 1920-1921: Life, Casualty and Miscellaneous*. (New York: The Spectator Company, 1920), 262.

¹⁸ *Birmingham and Its Environs*, 43 (Vol II, 1920), 42-3.

Chapter 13 Home and Abroad – 1921-1930
¹ *The Encyclopedia Britannica* online, http://www.britannica.com/EBchecked/topic/367110/Bohuslav-Martinu, viewed on January 10, 2014.
² *Alabama Governors*, 170-1.
³ Garland S. Tucker, III. *The High Tide of American Conservatism: Davis, Coolidge, and the 1924 Election.* (Austin: Emerald Book Company, 2010), 13-27.
⁴ Alabama Department of Archives and History Timeline 1901-1950, see 1926 entry, http://www.archives.alabama.gov/timeline/al1901.html, viewed on February 13, 2014.
⁵ Graves also served from 1935 to 1939; *Alabama Governors*, 173.
⁶ *Alabama Governors*, 171.
⁷ Various images of The Class of 1906 in the *Lucky Bag*, the Naval Academy newsletter, pages 28 and 29. Sources include a letter from Fred "B" Mitchell, curator of the Navy Museum in Pensacola, Florida to William J. Cabaniss, Jr. dated October 16, 1998; A letter dated January 12, 1998 from Alice S. Creighton, Head of Special Collections and Archives of the Department of the Navy to Joe Cabaniss of San Antonio, Texas. The letter, in part, reads "Enclosed in reply to your 6 December e-mail query are copies of the 1906 *Lucky Bag* [U.S. Naval Academy yearbook] entry for Robert Wright Cabaniss …"; an Associated Press article "Cabaniss Field sees little aviation use, except for the occasional errant jet airline" dated May 11, 1997 on Internet at http://homepage.mac.com/cabaniss/genealogy/cabaniss_field_landing.html, viewed on May 6, 2011. Cabaniss Field was named after Robert Wright Cabaniss. On May 11, 1997 a commercial jet plane landed there by mistake.
⁸ William Jelks Cabaniss [Sr.] Resume dated March 1, 1950. Resume shows an undergraduate degree earned in 1928 from the University of Alabama as well as three months at Harvard Law School in 1928, and a business course from Massie Business College in Birmingham. His board memberships included Children's Hospital, Phenix Natural Gas Company, and Protective Life Insurance. He was also a former member of the Mountain Brook City Council and a past president of the Jefferson County Alumni Association of the University of Alabama.
⁹ Alabama Department of Archives and History Timeline 1901-1950, see 1928 entry, http://www.archives.alabama.gov/timeline/al1901.html, viewed on February 13, 2014.
¹⁰ *Alabama Governors*, 181. Democratic National Candidate for President, Al Smith, was a Roman Catholic. Alabama U.S. Senator Thomas Heflin, a Democrat, led a "bolting" of the Democratic Party and voted for Republican Herbert Hoover.
¹¹ *Alabama Governors*, 181
¹²Ibid. Cabaniss [Sr.] Resume
¹³ Alabama Department of Archives and History Timeline 1901-1950, see 1930 entry, http://www.archives.alabama.gov/timeline/al1901.html, viewed on February 13, 2014; http://www.census.gov/population/www/documentation/twps0056/tabs15-65.pdf, viewed on February 13, 2014.

Chapter 14 Rural Alabama, TVA, Big Mules – 1931-1940
¹ *Alabama Governors*, 180-1.
² Encyclopedia of Alabama, http://www.encyclopediaofalabama.org/face/Article.jsp?id=h-1438, viewed on February 13, 2014.
³ Encyclopedia of Alabama "Scottsboro Trials", http://www.encyclopediaofalabama.org/face/Article.jsp?id=h-1456, viewed on February 13, 2014.
⁴ Birmingham Public Library "Alabama Episcopal Church Register" http://bpldb.bplonline.org/db/formProc/episcopal?parish=14&atnum=810.
⁵ Tennessee Valley Authority website, http://www.tva.com/abouttva/history.htm, viewed on February 13, 2014; Alabama Department of Archives and History, see 1933 entry, http://www.archives.alabama.gov/timeline/usa191.html, viewed on February 13, 2014.
⁶ Alabama Department of Archives and History, see 1934 entry, http://www.archives.alabama.gov/timeline/usa191.html, viewed on February 13, 2014; Walter J.

Heacock. "William B. Bankhead and the New Deal." *Journal of Southern History* 21 (August 1955): 347–359.
[7] *Alabama Governors,* 176-8.
[8] Alabama Department of Archives and History Timeline 1901-1950, see 1936 entry, http://www.archives.alabama.gov/timeline/al1901.html, viewed on February 13, 2014.
[9] Ibid. Birmingham Public Library.
[10] Barbara Swaim. "Descendents of Richard Jelks" genealogy from *Jelks Family Bible*
[11] Alabama Department of Archives and History Timeline 1901-1950, see 1936 entry for William B. Bankhead, http://www.archives.alabama.gov/timeline/al1901.html, viewed on February 13, 2014.
[12] Alabama Department of Archives and History Timeline 1901-1950, see 1937 entry, http://www.archives.alabama.gov/timeline/al1901.html, viewed on February 13, 2014.
[13] Ibid.
[14] "Timeline of the Czech Republic" as found on http://www.datesandevents.org/places-timelines/13-timeline-of-the-czech-republic.htm, viewed on January 10, 2014.
[15] Henry Kissinger. *Diplomacy.* (New York: Simon & Schuster, 1994), 311.
[16] Josef Korbel, *The Communist Subversion of Czechoslovakia 1938-1948: The Failure of Coexistence.* (Princeton: Princeton University Press, 1959), 33.
[17] *Alabama Governors,* 186.
[18] Alabama Department of Archives and History Timeline 1901-1950, see 1940 entry, http://www.archives.alabama.gov/timeline/al1901.html, viewed on February 13, 2014.

Chapter 15 Industrial Alabama, World War II, Change - 1941-1950
[1] Birmingham Public Library. "Alabama Episcopal Church Register." http://bpldb.bplonline.org/db/formProc/episcopal?parish=14&atnum=, viewed on February 13, 2014
[2] Alabama Department of Archives and History, "Alabama and World War II," http://www.alabamamoments.alabama.gov/sec50det.html, viewed on February 13, 2014.
[3] Alabama Department of Archives and History, "The Tuskegee Airmen," http://www.alabamamoments.alabama.gov/sec52qs.html, viewed on February 13, 2014.
[4] Birmingham Public Library. "Alabama Episcopal Church Register."
[5] Marilyn Davis Barefield. *A History of Mountain Brook, Alabama and Incidentally of Shades Valley.* (Birmingham: Southern University Press, 1989), 107-8.
[6] Barefield, 71.
[7] Barefield, 70, 71, 73, 75, 78.
[8] Barefield, 86.
[9] *Alabama Governors*, 190-1.
[10] http://en.wikipedia.org/wiki/USS_Birmingham (CL-62), viewed on December 24, 2012; Department of the Navy – Naval History and Heritage Command at http://www.history.navy.mil/danfs/b6/birmingham-ii.htm, viewed on January 10, 2014.
[11] Alabama Department of Archives and History, http://www.archives.alabama.gov/map/23.html, viewed on February 13, 2014.
[12] Interview, William J. Cabaniss, Jr. March 28, 2011.
[13] Interview, William J. Cabaniss, Jr. July 17, 2012.
[14] "Timeline of the Czech Republic" http://www.datesandevents.org/places-timelines/13-timeline-of-the-czech-republic.htm, viewed on January 10, 2014.
[15] Interview, William J. Cabaniss, Jr March 28, 2011.
[16] Alabama Department of Archives and History Timeline 1901-1950, see 1945 entry, http://www.archives.alabama.gov/timeline/al1901.html, viewed on February 13, 2014.
[17] "Timeline of the Czech Republic" as found on http://www.datesandevents.org/places-timelines/13-timeline-of-the-czech-republic.htm, viewed on January 10, 2014.
[18] *Alabama Governors,* 195.
[19] *Alabama Governors,* 197.
[20] Alabama Department of Archives and History, "Hank Williams," http://www.archives.alabama.gov/famous/music/hank.html, viewed on February 13, 2014.
[21] Patrick Buchanan. *Churchill, Hitler, and the Unnecessary War: How Britain Lost Its Empire and the West Lost the World.* (New York: Three Rivers Press, 2008), 418.

[22] Paul Johnson. *Modern Times: The World from the Twenties to the Nineties*. (New York: Harper Perennial, 1991), 440.

[23] Kissinger, *Diplomacy*, 457.

[24] http://en.wikipedia.org/wiki/Jan_Masaryk, viewed on January 10, 2014.

[25] "History of Prague through the Centuries: 9th Century to 2002";
See http://www.myczechrepublic.com/prague/history/prague_history.html, viewed on July 9, 2013

[26] Alabama Department of Archives and History, "Dixiecrats – The States' Rights Party, 1948," http://www.alabamamoments.alabama.gov/sec54.html, viewed on February 13, 2014.

[27] The term "Post Office Republicans" refers to federal patronage positions with a state. In the case of the state of Alabama, between the end of Reconstruction and the 1970s Republicans were not elected to statewide or even county-wide offices. The northern counties of Alabama were, for the most part, anti-slavery and pro-Union counties during before, during and after the Civil War. Winston County reliably, however, elected Republicans to the county-wide offices. Other counties with Republican leanings had to rely on federal patronage appointments such as the local postmaster. Hence, Post Office Republicans.

[28] Gould. *Grand Old Party*, 306.

[29] Alabama Department of Archives and History Timeline 1901-1950, see 1950 entry, http://www.archives.alabama.gov/timeline/al1901.html, viewed on February 13, 2014.

[30] Cathedral Church of the Advent-Birmingham Archives - Birmingham Public Library. "Alabama Episcopal Church Register".
http://bpldb.bplonline.org/db/formProc/episcopal?parish=14&atnum=

[31] Interview, Cullom Walker, February 28, 2012.

[32] Interview, Francis Crockard, February 28, 2012.

[33] Black and Black. *The Rise of Southern Republicans*, 2.

Chapter 16 Alabama House of Representatives – 1981-1982

[1] Alabama Department of Archives and History Timeline 1951 to present, see 1981 entry, http://www.archives.alabama.gov/timeline/al1951.html, viewed on February 14, 2014.

[2] Interview, Bill Harris, October 22.2012.

[3] Interview, David Bronner, February 14, 2012.

[4] Interview, William J. Cabaniss, Jr. August 17, 2012

[5] "GOP candidates generally take in on the chin", *The Birmingham News*, November 3, 1982.

[6] "GOP says GOP candidates need to plan to get black support" syndicated article by Fred Barnes in *The Birmingham News*, November 7, 1982.

[7] "Did voters tell politicians to cooperate?" an analysis of the mid-term election of 1982 by AP correspondent Walter R. Mears, appearing in *The Birmingham News*, Nov. 3, 1982.

[8] Alabama Department of Archives and History Timeline 1951 to present, see 1982 entry, http://www.archives.alabama.gov/timeline/al1951.html, viewed on February 14, 2014

[9] *The Birmingham News*, Nov. 1, 1982 also endorsed senate candidates Bill Cabaniss (R), John Amari (D), and Spencer Bachus (R). George Seibels (R) for re-election to the House and statewide Emory Folmar (R) for Governor, Bill Baxley (D) for Lt. Governor, and Don Siegelman (D) for Secretary of State.

[10] *The Birmingham News*, November 3, 1982.

[11] Interview, William J. Cabaniss, Jr., April 18, 2011.

[12] *The Birmingham News*, "Reapportionment Again", editorial, January 6, 1983.

[13] "The Alabama Legislature Reapportionment History" as viewed on March 30, 2012 on the Alabama Legislature's website. See www.legislature.state.al.us/reapportionment/history.html. The legislative acts involved between 1980 and 1983 were *Act No. 81-1049 (S.1)* dated October 26, 1981; Attorney General objection cited section SS5 of the Voting Rights Act; *Act No. 82-629 (H.19)* dated June 1, 1982. The suit was Burton v. Hobbie, 543 F. Supp. 235 (M.D. Ala. 1982). *Act No. 83-154 (H.1)* on February 23, 1983, the final re-districting plan received federal approval on April 11, 1983.

[14] In the State of Alabama there are 35 Senate districts, each with three House districts. Therefore there are 105 members in the House of Representatives, the total Legislature having 140 members.

[15] Interview, Ann Bedsole, January 10, 2012.

Chapter 17 Alabama Senate and Republican Successes – 1983-1984
[1] Interview, Ann Bedsole, January 10, 2012.
[2] *The Birmingham News,* January 3, 1983.
[3] *The Birmingham News,* January 9, 1983.
[4] *The Birmingham News,* January 11, 1983.
[5] Alabama Department of Archives and History Timeline 1951 to present, see 1983 entry, http://www.archives.alabama.gov/timeline/al1951.html, viewed on February 14, 2014.
[6] Blount. *Doing It My Way,* 193-5.
[7] Interview, Frank Ellis, February 23, 2012.
[8] Interview, Larry Dixon, October 10, 2012.
[9] Interview, William J. Cabaniss, Jr., September 13, 2012.
[10] Interview, Larry Dixon, October 10, 2012.
[11] "Ambassador in lace-up shoes" by Alan Levy. *The Prague Post,* February 12, 2004.
[12] "Pro: New Legislature is said to be coming in tune with people", *The Birmingham News,* Sunday, November 6, 1983, days before the special election.
[13] "Con: Business leaders: Special interests may hurt us badly", *The Birmingham News,* Sunday, November 6, 1983, days before the special election.
[14] Ibid.
[15] "Coalition Definitions", *The Birmingham News,* November 6, 1983.
[16] Interview, William J. Cabaniss, Jr., September 21, 2011; "Friends of Baxley, coalition win key Senators", an analysis by staff writer Michele MacDonald in *The Birmingham News,* November 6, 1983.
[17] "Friends of Baxley, coalition win key Senators", *The Birmingham News,* November 6, 1983.
[18] "Independents and GOPers profit from backlash", *The Birmingham News,* November 9, 1983.
[19] "GOP, independents expect to be heard", *The Birmingham News,* November 10, 1983.
[20] Interview, Larry Dixon, October 10, 2012.
[21] Interview, Frank Ellis, February 23, 2012.
[22] "County voters make changes in delegation"; "Independents and GOPers profit from backlash", *The Birmingham News,* November 9, 1983.
[23] "Wallace election in '82 cited healthy sign for South's Demos", *The Birmingham News,* November 6, 1983. University of Mississippi professor Alexander Lamis, speaking in Birmingham at a meeting of the Southern Political Science Association speculated that Wallace's victory in 1982 might have boosted an Democratic election revival "from the shock of the civil rights movement."
[24] *The Birmingham News,* November 2, 1982, South Edition. "Historian Woodward takes new look at state, says he's puzzled." In an after-speech question and answer session C. Vann Woodward was asked about Governor George Wallace's political comeback with black support. Woodward said "I better leave that to the people of Alabama."
[25] Interview, Perry Hand, January 11, 2012.
[26] Interview, Ann Bedsole, January 10, 2012.
[27] Ibid.
[28] Interview, Frank "Butch" Ellis, February 23, 2012.
[29] "State now has most black legislator", *The Birmingham News,* November 12, 1983.
[30] "Effects on Delegation", *The Birmingham News,* November 11, 1983.
[31] Interview, Edgar Welden, March 30, 2012.
[32] Interview, David Bronner, February 14, 2012.
[33] Interview, Bill Harris, October 22, 2012.

Chapter 18 Republican Challenges, Democrats Implode – 1985-1989
[1] History of the Tenn-Tom Waterway, http://history.tenntom.org/, viewed on February 13, 2014.
[2] Interview, Larry Dixon, October 10, 2012.
[3] Legislators in Alabama, both House Representatives and Senators, have assigned offices in a white building named the Alabama State House.
[4] Ibid.
[5] "Buy American filibuster ends", *The Birmingham Post-Herald,* Friday, February 28, 1986.
[6] Interview, William J. Cabaniss, Jr., August 17, 2012; Interview, Walter McCullers, March 19, 2013.
[7] Ibid. "Buy American".
[8] Ibid.

[9] Interview, John Beau Grenier, May 23, 2012.

[10] Interview, Luther Strange, February 15, 2012.

[11] *The Birmingham News*, July 20, 1986.

[12] Black and Black. *The Rise of Southern Republicans*, 128.

[13] Interview, Ann Bedsole, January 10, 2012.

[14] Interview, William J. Cabaniss, Jr., April 18, 2011; "Sage Lyons remembered as trustworthy insider", *The Tuscaloosa News*, March 6, 1999.

[15] David L. Martin "Alabama: Personalities and Factionalism" *Interest Group Politics in the Southern States*, eds. Ronald Hrebenar and Clive S. Thomas. (Tuscaloosa: The University of Alabama Press, 1992), 264-7.

[16] Phil Gailey. "Hearings on Disputed Primary Open in Alabama" in *The New York Times*, Tuesday, July 15, 1986.

[17] *The Birmingham News*, June 29, 1986.

[18] Martin, 266-7.

[19] *The Birmingham Post-Herald*, December, 1985. "Cabaniss pre-files stronger ethics bill" article by reporter Ted Bryant.

[20] Ibid.

[21] *The Tuscaloosa Times*, January 1, 1986. "Ethics bill would provide proper tools."

[22] Interview, William J. Cabaniss, Jr., April 18, 2011.

[23] "The Unfinished Business of Tort Reform." Birmingham: The Alabama Policy Institute, 2006.

[24] Interview, David Bronner, February 14, 2012.

[25] Hrebenar and Martin. *Interest Group Politics*, 255.

[26] Interview, William J. Cabaniss, Jr. 09-13-2012.

[27] Online un-credited article "1988: Thank you, New Hampshire." *The New Hampshire Union Leader*, May 3, 2011 at http://www.newhampshire.com, viewed on August 10, 2013.

[28] Interview, William J. Cabaniss, Jr., March 28, 2011; "Bill Cabaniss for United States Senate" speech, May 17-18, 1989.

[29] Interview, Larry Dixon, October 10, 2012.

[30] "Campaign '88/Bush/Competency Issue", CBS Evening News, September 22, 1988, Vanderbilt University Television News Archive, viewed on February 25, 2012 at http://tvnews.vanderbilt.edu/diglib-fulldisplay.pl?SID=20130810913970947&code=tvn&RC=323337&Row=373

[31] Ibid *The New Hampshire Leader*.

[32] Interview, Frank "Butch" Ellis, February 23, 2012.

[33] Ibid.

[34] Interview, Larry Dixon, October 10, 2012.

[35] Hayman. *A Judge in the Senate*, 364.

[36] "Bill Cabaniss for United States Senate." Announcement speech for May 17-18, 1989.

[37] "Cabaniss Launches Eight City Announcement Tour for U.S. Senate" press release May 16, 1989. Marty Connors, Executive Director of the Alabama Republican Party and Lee Styslinger, Jr., campaign finance chairman.

[38] *The Tuscaloosa News*, May 17, 1989. "Cabaniss begins campaign for Heflin's seat."

[39] Johnson. *Modern Times*, 761; also http://www.pragueexperience.com/information/history.asp viewed on July 9, 2013.

Chapter 19 Challenge for Change – 1990

[1] Alabama Department of Archives and History Timeline 1951 to present, see 1990 entry, http://www.archives.alabama.gov/timeline/al1951.html, viewed on February 13, 2014.

[2] "Ethics Bill for Alabama." *The Times Daily* March 5, 1990.

[3] Interview, Cabaniss, March 28, 2011.

[4] "Speech to A Joint Session of the U.S. Congress." Václav Havel. February 21, 1990.

[5] Baker, *The Politics of Diplomacy*, 200.

[6] Ibid. Baker, 63.

[7] Madeleine Albright with Bill Woodward. *Madam Secretary: A Memoir*. (New York: Miramax Books, 2003), 149.

[8] Interview, Peggy Balliet, May 24, 2012. Ironically, when Heflin decided to run for the U.S. Senate in 1978 against Governor George Wallace, Heflin claimed that business leaders and other supporters were concerned about Wallace and the possible negative image he would bring to Alabama. *A Judge in the Senate*, 203-4.

[9] Interview, Judy Bewley, May 29, 2012.

[10] Interview, Frank "Butch" Ellis, February 23, 2012.

[11] Interview, Bill Harris, October 22, 2012.

[12] Interview, Lee Styslinger, Jr., December 21, 2011.

[13] Interview, Peggy Balliet, May 24, 2012.

[14] Interview, David Bronner, February 14, 2012.

[15] Hayman. *A Judge in the Senate*, 205.

[16] Interview, Cabaniss, September 13, 2012.

[17] Interview, Lee Styslinger, Jr., December 21, 2011.

[18] Kim Fridkin Kahn and Patrick J. Kenney. *The Spectacle of U.S. Senate Campaigns*. (Princeton: Princeton University Press, 1999), 16-18.

[19] Interview, Luther Strange, February 15, 2012.

[20] Interview, Peggy Balliet, May 24, 2012.

[21] Interview, Peggy Balliet, May 24, 2012.

[22] *Gadsden Times*, July 20, 1990. Article "Cabaniss plans two-month tour of waterways."

[23] Interview, Peggy Balliet, May 24, 2012.

[24] Interview, Judy Bewley, May 29, 2012.

[25] George H.W. Bush: "Remarks at a Fundraising Luncheon for Senatorial Candidate Bill Cabaniss in Birmingham, Alabama," April 20, 1990. Online by Gerhard Peters and John T. Woolley, *The American Presidency Project*.
See http://www.presidency.ucsb.edu/ws/?pid=18382.

[26] Ibid.

[27] "Cabaniss plans two-month tour of state's waterways." *The Gadsden Times*, July 20, 1990.

[28] "Heflin criticizes Bush; Cabaniss blasts Heflin." *The Gadsden Times*, July 21, 1990.

[29] Interview, William J. Cabaniss, Jr., August 17, 2012.

[30] Ibid.

[31] Ibid; www.leadershipal.org/about-us, viewed on February 13, 2014.

[32] "Bill Cabaniss for Senate" Friday, September 28, 1990 Campaign Agenda.

[33] "Heflin's hasty exit." *The Tuscaloosa News*, November 1, 1990.

[34] Hayman, 160-1.

[35] *The Birmingham News*, Wednesday, November 7, 1990. Article "HEFLIN: I won because state's voters like me"

[36] Interview, William J. Cabaniss, Jr., November 8, 2011.

[37] Interview, Peggy Balliet, May 24, 2012.

[38] *The Birmingham News*, Nov 7, 1990.

[39] Interview, Ann Bedsole, January 10, 2012.

[40] Interview, Marty Connors, March 14, 2012.

[41] Interview, Gerald Dial, February 14, 2012.

[42] Interview, Perry Hand, January 11, 2012.

[43] Interview, Bob Riley, November 5, 2012.

[44] Interview, Luther Strange, February 15, 2012.

[45] "Damage Control for Democrats." *The Cook Political Report*, February, 2010; http://cookpolitical.com/node/579, viewed on February 25, 2012. The *Cook Report*, though 20 years after the Cabaniss U.S. Senate race in Alabama, emphasized the irony of Senator Howell Heflin's characterization of Cabaniss as "one of them silk stockings boys" from wealthy town of Mountain Brook while the Democratic Party that considered itself an elite group of leaders or privileged people (noblesse oblige) qualified to act and govern with generosity and nobility for those less privileged.

Chapter 20 Exit from Elective Politics – 1991-2000

[1] *Alabama Governors*, 251.

[2] *The Birmingham News*, Wednesday, November 7, 1990, page 2B.

[3] Interview, Peggy Balliet, May 24, 2012.

[4] Interview, Mike Thompson, December 21, 2012.

[5] Black and Black, *The Rise of Southern Republicans*, 296.
[6] BBC News, http://news.bbc.co.uk/2/hi/europe/country_profiles/1844391.stm   viewed July 9, 2013.
[7] *Alabama Governors*, 254; Alabama Department of Archives and History.
[8] Alabama Department of Archives and History timeline.
[9] Ted vonCannon, interview, February 1, 2013.
[10] Mike Thompson, interview, December 21, 2012.
[11] Ibid. vonCannon.
[12] *Alabama Governors*, 246; Interview, Cabaniss, September 21, 2011.
[13] http://www.theatlantic.com/magazine/archive/2004/11/karl-rove-in-a-corner/303537/ Viewed December 29, 2012.
[14] Mike Thompson, interview, December 21, 2012.
[15] *South Union Steet*. December 3, 2012. "Karl Rove talks about his time in Alabama, about 2012 election."
[16] *The Decatur Daily*, October 29, 2005. "Rove built reputation in Alabama court races."
[17] Interview, William J. Cabaniss, Jr., April 18, 2011.
[18] *The Rise of Southern Republicans*, 304.
[19] Wayne Flynt. *Alabama in the Twentieth Century*, 102-3.
[20] Black and Black. *The Rise of Southern Republicans*, 314.
[21] Black and Black. *The Rise of Southern Republicans*, 128.
[22] Flynt, 103.
[23] http://en.wikipedia.org/wiki/Perry_O._Hooper,_Sr., viewed January 16, 2014; http://www.archives.state.al.us/judicial/hooper.html, viewed January 16, 2014.
[24] Interview, Bob Riley, November 5, 2012.
[25] *Alabama Governors*, 247.
[26] U.S. Government Accountability Office (GAO) document NSIAD-95-53dated April 5, 1995 about Radio Free Europe.
[27] Timeline of the Czech Republic 1993-2011.
[28] Interview, William J. Cabaniss, Jr. September 8, 2011.
[29] Timeline of the Czech Republic 1993-2011 http://news.bbc.co.uk/2/hi/europe/country_profiles/1844391.stm, viewed July 9, 2013.
[30] Ann Bedsole Academy of Honor; http://www.archives.alabama.gov/famous/academy/a_bedsol.html, viewed on January 15, 2014.
[31] *The Rise of Southern Republicans*, 308.
[32] Timeline of the Czech Republic 1993-2011
[33] http://www.archives.alabama.gov/famous/academy/l_styls.html, viewed on January 15, 2014
[34] http://www.archives.alabama.gov/famous/academy/ahome.html, viewed on January 16, 2014
[35] Steve Windom; http://www.stevewindom.com/; http://en.wikipedia.org/wiki/Steve_Windom, viewed on January 15, 2014.
[36] Timeline of the Czech Republic 1993-2011.
[37] Interview, Cabaniss, March 28, 2011.
[38] Timeline of the Czech Republic 1993-2011.
[39] "St. Luke's throws fond 'family' farewell for the Claypools" by Susan Strictland. *The Birmingham News*, December 21, 2000.
[40] Bill Cabaniss's farewell speech handwritten on twelve 4x6 index cards.

Chapter 21 New Openings on International Stage – 2001-2003
[1] "Timeline of the Czech Republic 1993-2011", http://news.bbc.co.uk/2/hi/europe/country_profiles/1844391.stm, viewed on January 16, 2014
[2] Alabama Department of Archives and History [ADAH]; Alabama Timeline, November, 2001 "Honda Manufacturing of Alabama in Lincoln begins production"; http://www.archives.alabama.gov/timeline/al1951.html viewed on January 17, 2014.
[3] "Timeline of the Czech Republic 1993-2011".
[4] Letter from William J. Cabaniss, Jr. to President George W. Bush dated October 24, 2002, on official stationery of Precision Grinding, Inc.
[5] http://www.encyclopediaofalabama.org/face/Article.jsp?id=h-1507, viewed on January 17, 2014.

[6] Interview, Bob Riley, November 5, 2012.

[7] Interview, William J. Cabaniss, Jr., September 21, 2011.

[8] The gubernatorial election in 2002 was controversial because it had the narrowest winning margin in Alabama history; Riley won by just 3,000 votes. Riley challenged incumbent Don Siegelman and the early voting returns showed Siegelman winning by 2,000 votes.

[9] The Birmingham Post-Herald, November 26, 2002, article "Resumes inundate Riley's staffers"

[10] Interview, Bob Riley, November 5, 2012; Mike Hubbard with David Azbell. *Storming the State House: The Campaign that Liberated Alabama from 136 Years of Democrat Rule*. (Montgomery: NewSouth Books, 2012), 70.

[11] Interview, William J. Cabaniss, Jr., September 21, 2011.

[12] Interview, Bob Riley, November 5, 2012.

[13] Interview, Marty Connors, March 14, 2012.

[14] Interview, Bob Riley, November 5, 2012.

[15] Interview, Mike Thompson, December 21, 2012.

[16] Ambassadorial Appointment, American Friends of the Czech Republic; http://www.afocr.org/leadership/bill-cabaniss, viewed on January 17, 2014.

[17] Interview, William J. Cabaniss, Jr., March 28, 2011.

[18] Ibid.

[19] "Timeline of the Czech Republic 1993-2011".

[20] Interview, William J. Cabaniss, Jr., September 21, 2011;Interview, Bob Riley, November 5, 2012; Interview, Marty Connors, March 14, 2012; Interview, Gerald Dial, February 14, 2012.

[21] Interview, Marty Connors, March 14, 2012.

[22] Mike Hubbard. *Storming the State House*, 75-85.

[23] Interview, Wayne Flynt, November 26, 2013.

[24] http://www.archives.alabama.gov/judic.html viewed on January 17, 2014.

[25] "A Pioneer Comes Home." White House for Sale Blog, September 25, 2003. http://www.sourcewatch.org/index.php?title=Craig_Roberts_Stapleton

[26] Paul Zahl. "Cabaniss Nominated for Ambassadorial Post." Dean's Bulletin Board, Cathedral Church of the Advent, Birmingham, Alabama http://www.adventbirmingham.com/advent/articles.asp?ID=1404 viewed on January 4, 2012.

[27] "Confirmation Hearing Statement, William Jelks Cabaniss, Jr. Ambassador-designate to the Czech Republic Before the Senate Committee on Foreign Relations, September 30, 2003."

[28] Interview, Wayne Flynt, November 26, 2013.

[29] Interview, William J. Cabaniss, Jr., September 21, 2011; U.S. Department of State Archives, Secretary of State Colin Powell; http://2001-2009.state.gov/secretary/former/powell/remarks/2003/26987.htm, viewed on January 17, 2014; U.S. Department of State - The Benjamin Franklin Room; https://diplomaticrooms.state.gov/Pages/rooms.aspx?rm=8, viewed on January 17, 2014.

Chapter 22 U.S. Ambassador to the Czech Republic – 2004-2007

[1] Statement before the United States Senate Committee on Foreign Relations, September 30, 2003.

[2] New York University-Prague website. http://www.nyu.edu/global/global-academic-centers/prague.html?utm_source=Google&utm_medium=cpc&utm_content=CopyC&utm_campaign=Prague_FallC&gclid=COubpfi8q7wCFQPl7AodJkcA2g, viewed on February 1, 2014.

[3] Speech to students at NYU-Prague, June 24, 2004.

[4] IMDb website http://www.imdb.com/name/nm0001232/, viewed on February 11, 2014; http://www.estatestheatre.cz/et_history.html, viewed on March 14, 2014.

[5] J.M. Lau. *Prague Then & Now*. (San Diego: Thunder Bay Press, 2007), 5.

[6] American Friends of the Czech Republic (AFofCR) website http://www.afocr.org/us-embassy-prague-0, viewed on February 11, 2014.

[7] http://prague.usembassy.gov/ambassadors_residence.html, viewed on March 14, 2014.

[8] Ibid.

[9] Interview, William J. Cabaniss, Jr., March 5, 2014.

[10] U.S. Embassy in Prague website, http://prague.usembassy.gov/ambassadors_residence.html viewed on February 11, 2014.

---

[11] Interview, Kenneth Hillas, April 13, 2013.

[12] Ibid. Hillas.

[13] American Friends of the Czech Republic website.
http://www.afocr.org/leadership/bill-cabaniss, viewed on February 4, 2014.

[14] Cabaniss interviews 4/18/2011, 4/18/2011, 09/08/2011/

[15] Ian Willoughby, "One on One – William Cabaniss – the new United States ambassador to Prague." *Czech Radio 7, Radio Prague*. February 3, 2004.

[16] Ibid: Willoughby press interview with Cabaniss; Hillas interview.

[17] Alan Levy. "Ambassador in lace-up shoes." *The Prague Post*. February 12, 2004.

[18] Ibid. Levy.

[19] Speech. "AmCham Luncheon." March 17, 2004.

[20] Interview, William J. Cabaniss, Jr., September 8, 2011.

[21] Speech. "European Banking and Financial Forum." March 23, 2004.

[22] Letter from Bill Cabaniss to friends. April 28, 2004.

[23] Dorothy "Dodie" Day died on January 6, 2012. She was survived by husband Horace Corbin Day, a Birmingham investment banker.

[24] Interview, William J. Cabaniss, Jr., March 28, 2011.

[25] Ibid. Letter from Bill Cabaniss to friends.

[26] Interview, Kenneth Hillas, April 13, 2013.

[27] Interview, William J. Cabaniss, Jr., September 8, 2011.

[28] Ibid.

[29] Alison Siskin. "Visa Waiver Program." (Washington: Congressional Research Service, Jan. 15, 2013), fn63, 11-12.

[30] Interview, William J. Cabaniss, Jr., September 8, 2011.

[31] "Prague History 5500 BC to 2008".
http://www.pragueexperience.com/information/history.asp, viewed on February 4, 2014.

[32] Václav Klaus speech at U.S. Embassy in Prague, July 2, 2004.

[33] Ibid.

[34] "Ambassador's [Cabaniss] July 4 Remarks 2004".

[35] "Ambassador Weekly Itinerary July 26 – August 1, 2004."

[36] "Elections in Iraq Will Be Successful – Interview with U.S. Ambassador to the Czech Republic William Cabaniss." December 22, 2004.

[37] The Alabama Academy of Honor, Class of 2005
http://www.archives.alabama.gov/famous/academy/year04.html, viewed on February 3, 2014.

[38] Interview, William J. Cabaniss, Jr. September 8, 2011. The Ambassador became quite emotional during this segment of the interview.

[39] Originally an arms manufacturer in 1859, Škoda became an automobile manufacturer and has a long-term history in parallel with Tatra, Peugeot, Daimler, and Opel.

[40] Patton Museum website. http://www.patton-memorial.cz/en/museum/ viewed on May 25, 2014.

[41] Interview, Kenneth Hillas, April 13, 2013.

[42] Interview, William J. Cabaniss, Jr. September 8, 2011.

[43] Interview, Kenneth Hillas, April 13, 2013.

[44] American Friends of the Czech Republic website.
http://www.afocr.org/leadership/bill-cabaniss, viewed on February 4, 2014.

[45] Space One Eleven. http://spaceoneeleven.org/about-soe/ viewed on February 4, 2014.

Appendix A Historical Matters – 1500-1700

[1] Barbara Swaim *Jelks Family Bible* and genealogy resources.

[2] Edmund S. Morgan. *American Slavery, American Freedom*. (New York: W.W. Norton, 1975), 250.

[3] Ibid. Barbara Swaim.

[4] http://www.surnamedb.com/Surname/Jelks#ixzz1sVyrst8X;
http://www.surnamedb.com/Surname/Jelks, viewed April 19, 2012.

[5] Barbara Swaim's *Jelks Family Bible* and genealogy charts.

[6] Ambassador Cabaniss's maternal family history has always been thought to be connected to Abraham Pierson, even though a documented lineage is yet to be completed.

[7] Lizzie B. Pierson's record of the Piersons in America. Original documents located in The Library of Brigham Young University, Provo, Utah. The Internet source viewed on December 17, 2013 and found at http://archive.org/stream/piersongenealogi00pier/piersongenealogi00pier_djvu.txt. According to this document Abraham Pierson was "Episcopally ordained" before leaving England. This could have only meant ordination in the Church of England.

[8] Charles Washington Baird. *History of the Huguenot Emigration to America.* Vol I (New York: Dodd, Mead & Company, 1884), 24-66.

[9] Huguenot Society of America. http://huguenotsocietyofamerica.org/?page=Huguenot-History, viewed on December 26, 2012.

[10] Francis Fukuyama. *The Origins of Political Order: From Prehuman Times to the French Revolution.* (New York: Farrar, Straus, and Giroux, 2011), 338.

[11] http://www.britannica.com/EBchecked/topic/261684/Henry-IV, *viewed on November 29, 2013*

[12] Huguenot Noteworthy Dates.   http://www.huguenot.netnation.com/general/dates.htm viewed on September 11, 2013.

[13] Also known as the *Declaration of Liberty of Conscience*, two proclamations were issued by James II, one for Scotland followed by one for England; these declarations amounted to the beginnings of the establishment of the freedom of religion in Britain.

[14] The significance of the *Act of Toleration* is not simply the Act's content but that the Act was passed by Parliament and not a proclamation of a monarch. The relationship between the English monarchy and Parliament began to change after the Glorious Revolution of 1688.

[15] Morgan. *American Slavery, American Freedom*, 346.

[16] Niall Ferguson. *Civilization: The West and the Rest.* (New York: The Penguin Press, 2011), 39, 41, 76.

[17] John Plath Green. *Henry Cabaniss and His Descendents.* (Dallas: unpublished manuscript, 1956); Allen Cabaniss. *Cabaniss Through Four Generations: Some Descendents of Matthew and George.* (Oxford: University of Mississippi, 1971); Alloa Caviness Anderson. Henry Cavinis: *The Immigrant Infant and Some of His Descendents.* (Leland, MI., 1971).

[18] Historical records have several spellings for the French name Cabaniss. For example, Cabinis; Cabanet; Cavinis; Caviness; Cavinder. These multiple spellings are resolved in this project as Cabaniss.

[19] John Plath Green. Henry Cabaniss and His Descendents. (Dallas: self published, 1956), 1,2.

[20] Ibid; Joe Cabaniss genealogy documents, commentary of first generation of Cabanisses in America.

Appendix B Family Matters – 1701-1800
[1] Queen Anne, http://en.wikipedia.org/wiki/Anne,_Queen_of_Great_Britain/, viewed on January 20, 2014.

[2] John Plath Green. *Henry Cabaniss and His Descendents.* (Dallas: unpublished manuscript, 1956); Allen Cabaniss. *Cabaniss Through Four Generations: Some Descendents of Matthew and George.* (Oxford: University of Mississippi, 1971); Alloa Caviness Anderson. Henry Cavinis: *The Immigrant Infant and Some of His Descendents.* (Leland, MI., 1971).

[3] Thomas McAdory Owen. *History of Alabama and Dictionary of Alabama Biography*, Vol III. (Chicago: The S.J. Clarke Publishing Company, 1921), 277-8; entry is about Edward H. Cabaniss but mentions the "body of land" that ancestor Henri Cabaniss received in Henrico County, Virginia;

[4] Henrico County, Virginia Orders, 1707-1709, p.35, as found in document by Allen Cabaniss, "Cabaniss Through Four Generations: Some Descendants of Matthew and George," The University of Mississippi, 1969, 1970, 1971.

[5] John Plath Green, compiler. "Henry Cabaniss and His Descendants," Dallas, TX, 1956 as modified and updated by Joe Cabaniss of San Antonio, TX.

[6] Ibid. John Plath Green.

[7] Grady Garrett. "Cabaniss", *The Huguenot,* Volume XI, 1941-1943. 84-87.; Prince George County, Virginia, Will of Henri Cabanis, recorded in Deeds, etc., 1713-28 (part 2), 414.

[8] Allen Cabaniss. *Cabaniss Through Four Generations: Some Descendents of Matthew and George.* (Oxford: University of Mississippi, 1971), 24.

[9] These are speculations about Henri Cabaniss's history based on the events of his day and his Will. Between his arrival in Manakintown in 1700 and his death in 1720, little to no documentation of his life is extant. What is known is that Henri Cabaniss is the patriarch of a vast American family.

[10] Huguenot Noteworthy Dates.

[11] Paul Johnson. *The Birth of the Modern: World Society 1815-1830.* (New York: HarperCollins Publishers, 1991), xvii.

[12] "Second Generation of the Cabaniss Family in America." Joe Cabaniss, Allen Cabaniss, John Plath Green compilers. 1954, 7.

[13] Rhys Isaacs. *The Transformation of Virginia 1740-1790.* (Chapel Hill: The University of North Carolina Press, 1982), 133.

[14] Grady Garrett. "Cabaniss", *The Huguenot*, Volume XI, 84-87.; Nottoway County, Virginia, Will Book, 1790.

[15] "Second Generation of the Cabaniss Family in America." Joe Cabaniss, Allen Cabaniss, John Plath Green compilers. 1954, 7.

[16] An Internet record of the obituary of George Cabaniss (son of Matthew). The Internet record cites a DAR listing reading "13 Dec. 1815 Greene Co. Vincent Haralson has applied for letter of adm'r on esate of Griffin Cabaniss, late of Jones Co.. signed E.Torrence, Clerk Jones County All persons having demands against the estate of.... George Cabaniss Sr. deceased.. signed Palitier Cabaniss adm'rx. Harrison and Henry B. Cabaniss..Robert McGough adm'rs...." It also states both father and son were soldiers in the American Revolutionary War. See link http://www.findagrave.com/cgi-bin/fg.cgi?page=gr&GRid=38494116, viewed on November 12, 2013.

[17] *Alabama Governors*, 7.

[18] George M. Cruikshank. *A History of Birmingham and its Environs: A Narrative Account of their Historical Progress, their People, and their Principle Interests, Volume II.* (Chicago: The Lewis Publishing Company, 1920), 42-3.

[19] This date comes from a genealogy by Lana Sawey, a descendant of George Cabaniss. The posting for this record in found on the Internet at http://archiver.rootsweb.ancestry.com/th/read/GAJONES/2003-12/1070603665, viewed on November 12, 2013; another record fixes the marriage in 1781 as found on the Internet at http://www.findagrave.com/cgi-bin/fg.cgi?page=gr&GRid=38494116, viewed on November 12, 2013.

[20] "Third Generation of the Cabaniss Family in America." Joe Cabaniss, Allen Cabaniss, John Plath Green compilers. 1954, 12.

[21] Barbara Swaim document "Descendants of Thomas Mann and William Nicholson."

[22] There appears to be no family linkage between William Nicholson II or his father with Colonial Virginia Governor Francis Nicholson.

[23] Ibid.

[24] "1790 Heads of Family, Edgecombe County, North Carolina." Internet link http://genealogytrails.com/ncar/edgecombe/cen_1790_headsoffamilies.html, viewed on March 14, 2013.

[25] Barbara Swaim document "Descendents of Richard Jelks."

Appendix C Family Matters – 1801-1860

[1] Alabama Department of Archives and History http://www.archives.alabama.gov/teacher/creekwar/creek.html, viewed on January 20, 2014

[2] Source: http://en.wikipedia.org/wiki/Elbridge_Gerry, viewed on February 23, 2013.

[3] David McCollough. *John Adams.* (New York: Simon & Schuster Paperbacks, 2001), 73-75, 585; Wikipedia link http://en.wikipedia.org/wiki/Elbridge_Gerry, viewed on February 23, 2013.

[4] The current day Cabaniss family pronounces "Gerry" with a hard "g" as in the name "Gary."

[5] "Monroe County, Georgia Biographies" http://genealogytrails.com/geo/monroe/bio1.html, viewed on November 12, 2013.

[6] Grady Garrett. "Cabaniss", The Huguenot, Vol XI, pages 84-87.

[7] According to family genealogist Joe Cabaniss of San Antonio, Texas, Elbridge Gerry Cabaniss was the subject of an extensive paper by George C. Smith entitled a "Genealogical Sketch of Judge E.G. Cabaniss," prepared in 1904. Much of Joe Cabaniss's work and University of Mississippi professor Allen Cabaniss in his book "Cabaniss Through Four Generations" provide much of the documentation of the Cabaniss lineage from 1700 in Hampton, Virginia to present day. It is interesting to understand the business and political life of this great-great grandfather of William Jelks Cabaniss, Jr.

[8] Nathaniel Cheairs Hughes, Jr. *Yale's Confederates: A Biographical Dictionary*. (Knoxville: The University of Tennessee Press, 2008), 35-6.

[9] Hughes, *Yale's Confederates*, 172.

[10] C. Mildred Thompson. *Reconstruction in Georgia: Economic, Social, Political 1865-1872*. (New York: The Columbia University Press, 1915), 199-201.

[11] Lucian Lamar Knight. *Georgia's Landmarks, Memorials and Legends, Volume II*. (Atlanta: The Byrd Printing Company, 1914), 878-880.

[12] Supreme Court of the State of Georgia. "Reports of Cases Decided in the March Term, 1904, Volume 120." (Atlanta: The State Library, 1904), 951-953.

[13] http://bioguide.congress.gov/scripts/biodisplay.pl?index=C000942, viewed January 10, 2013.

[14] *Alabama Governors*, 11; Website http://www.netstate.com/states/government/al_government.htm viewed on February 12, 2014.

[15] Website http://www.netstate.com/states/government/al_government.htm viewed on February 12, 2014..

[16] Malcolm Cook McMillan. *Constitutional Development in Alabama 1798-1901*. (Chapel Hill: University of North Carolina Press, 1955), 25, 28.

[17] McMillan, *Constitutional Development*, 24-28.

[18] John Temple Graves II, ed. *The Book of Alabama and the South: Commemorating the Silver Anniversary of the Protective Life Insurance Company.*, 2nd edition. (Birmingham: The Company, 1934), 105.

[19] *Encyclopedia of Alabama* http://www.encyclopediaofalabama.org/face/Article.jsp?id=h-1548, viewed on January 20, 2014.

[20] Barbara Swaim, "Descendants of Richard Jelks"; David Alsobrook. "William Dorsey Jelks: Alabama Editor and Legislator." Master's thesis, West Virginia University, 1972.

[21] *Alabama Governors*, 13, 17.

[22] *Encyclopedia of Alabama*, http://www.encyclopediaofalabama.org/face/Article.jsp?id=h-1500, viewed on January 20, 2014.

[23] *Alabama Governors*, 21.

[24] *Alabama Governors*, 24, 28, 31.

[25] *Encyclopedia of Alabama*, http://www.encyclopediaofalabama.org/face/Article.jsp?id=h-1500, viewed on January 20, 2014.

[26] http://familytreemaker.genealogy.com/users/h/o/b/Hardy-M-Hobbs/WEBSITE-0001/UHP-1079.html, viewed on May 13, 2013.

[27] West Virginia was admitted to the Union on June 20, 1863. These former western counties of Virginia separated from Virginia while the American Civil War was an ongoing battle.

[28] Jack Zinn. *R.E. Lee's Cheat Mountain Campaign*. Parsons, West Virginia: McClain Publishing Company, 1974.

[29] "Henry Cabaniss and His Descendents," 27.

[30] "Gus Cabaniss Goes To Beyond." *The Atlanta Constitution*, December 15, 1907, 5.

[31] *Encyclopedia of Alabama*, http://www.encyclopediaofalabama.org/face/Article.jsp?id=h-1500, viewed on January 20, 2014.

[32] *Alabama Governors*, 38-41.

[33] http://www.encyclopediaofalabama.org/face/Multimedia.jsp?id=m-6629; http://en.wikipedia.org/wiki/Panic_of_1837, viewed on January 20, 2014

[34] Alabama Department of Archives and History: Alabama History Timeline http://www.archives.alabama.gov/timeline/al1801.html, viewed on January 20, 2014

[35] Martin Van Buren, http://www.encyclopediaofalabama.org/face/Multimedia.jsp?id=m-2682, viewed on January 20, 2014.

[36] *Alabama Governors*, 45.

[37] *Alabama Governors*, 49.

[38] *Alabama Governors*, 53.

[39] *Alabama Governors*, 57.

[40] ADAH   Alabama History Timeline http://www.archives.alabama.gov/timeline/al1801.html, viewed on January 20, 2014.

[41] "Whig Party." http://www.encyclopediaofalabama.org/face/Article.jsp?id=h-1173, viewed on January 20, 2014.

[42] http://en.wikipedia.org/wiki/Fugitive_Slave_Act_of_1850, viewed on January 20, 2014

<hr>

[43] Sills Family Papers, 1792-1969 (Manuscript Collection #201). Special Collections, Joyner Library, East Carolina University, Greenville, North Carolina. In addition to the oral history, 110 items were made available to the University for copies, June 27, 1972 by Miss Louis [Jelks] Sills, Nashville, N.C. Other papers were donated on November 11, 1982 and March 21, 2000 by Mrs. Charlotte Perry and Mr. Bill Dameron, respectively. Internet source found at http://digital.lib.ecu.edu/10919#details.
[44] Louise Jelks Sills "Oral History," 1972, 17.
[45] Barbara Swaim. The three letters written by Joseph William Dorsey Jelks were transcribed by Swaim and other family members over the years. The transcribed letters were not word-for-word. In some cases the transcriber commented on or summarized a paragraph.
[46] Martha E.A. Jelks married Green W. Drake and their daughter was Mary Drake. Green Drake died in 1938 [at age 32] so they could not have spent the day with J.W.D. if this letter was written in 1851. Or, Green could have been William Green Drake a son of Martha and Green born in 1935. Martha had to have married William Threadgill either in or before 1845.

Books, Journals, Magazines

Abernethy, Thomas Perkins. *The Formative Period in Alabama – 1815-1828*. Publication of the Alabama State Department of Archives and History Historical and Patriotic Series No. 6. Montgomery: The Brown Printing Company, 1922.

Albright, Madeleine. *Madam Secretary: A Memoir*. New York: Miramax Books, 2003.

Alsobrook, David Ernest. "William Dorsey Jelks: Alabama Editor and Legislator." Master's thesis, West Virginia University, 1972.

Anderson, Lisa, ed. *Transitions to Democracy*. New York: Columbia University Press, 1999.

Arent, Hannah. *The Origins of Totalitarianism*. Introduction by Samantha Power. New York: Schocken Books, 2004.

Atkins, Leah Rawls. *Developed for the Service of Alabama: The Centennial History of the Alabama Power Company 1906-2006*. Birmingham: Alabama Power Company, 2006.

----------------------- *John M. Harbert III: Marching to the Beat of a Different Drummer*. Birmingham: Tarva House, 1999.

----------------------- *The Building of Brasfield & Gorrie*. Birmingham: Brasfield & Gorrie, LLC., 2002.

Baird, Charles Washington. *History of the Huguenot Emigration to America, Volume I*. New York: Dodd, Meade & Company Publishers, 1884.

--------------------------------. *History of the Huguenot Emigration to America, Volume II*. New York: Dodd, Meade & Company Publishers, 1885.

Baker, James A. III. *The Politics of Diplomacy: Revolution, War and Peace 1989-1992*. New York: G.P. Putnam's Sons, 1995.

Barefield, Marilyn Davis, *A History of Mountain Brook, Alabama & Incidentally of Shades Valley*. Birmingham: Southern University Press as the Press of Birmingham Publishing Company, 1989.

Bass, Jack and Walter De Vries. *The Transformation of Southern Politics: Social Change & Political Consequence Since 1945*. Athens: The University of Georgia Press, 1995.

Battle, Cullen Andrews. *The Civil War Memoir*. Edited by Brandon Beck. Tuscaloosa: University of Alabama Press, 2000.

Berg. A. Scott. *Wilson*. New York: G.P. Putnam's Sons, 2013.

Besson, J.A.B. *History of Eufaula, Alabama: the Bluff City of the Chattahoochee*. Atlanta: Franklin Steam Printing House – Jas. P. Harrison & Co. Printers, 1875.

Betts, Edward Chambers. *Early History of Huntsville, Alabama 1804 to 1870*. Montgomery: The Brown Printing Company, 1909, revised 1916.

Bickley, Jr. R. Bruce. *Joel Chandler Harris*. Athens: Brown Thrasher Books - The University of Georgia Press, 1978, 1987.

Black, Earl and Merle Black. *The Rise of Southern Republicans*. Cambridge, MA: The Belknap Press of Harvard University Press, 2002.

Blackmon, Douglas A. *Slavery by Another Name: The Re-Enslavement of Black Americans from the Civil War to World War II*. New York: Anchor Books, 2008.

Blount, Winton M. "Red" with Richard Blodgett. *Doing It My Way*. Lyme, Conn: Greenwich Publishing Group, 1996.

Boddie, John Bennett. *Historical Southern Families, Vol. 5*. Baltimore: Genealogical Publishing Company, 1967.

Bonhoeffer, Dietrich. *Ethics*. New York: A Touchstone Book-Simon & Schuster, 1995.

Brock, R.A., editor and compiler. *Documents Chiefly Unpublished as Related to the Huguenot Immigration to Virginia and to the Settlement at Manakin-Town*. Richmond: Virginia Historical Society, 1886.

Brokaw, Tom. *The Greatest Generation*. New York: Random House, 1998 & 2004.

Brown, Charles Carroll, ed. *Directory of American Cement Industries, Fourth Edition.* Indianapolis: Municipal Engineering Company, 1906.

Bryson, W. Hamilton, ed. *Virginia Law Books: Essays and Bibliographies*, Volume 239. Philadelphia: American Philosophical Society, 2000.

Buchanan, Patrick J. *Churchill, Hitler, and the Unnecessary War: How Britain Lost Its Empire and the West Lost the World*. New York: Random House, 2008.

Bugg, Jr., James L. "The French Huguenot Frontier Settlement of Manakin Town." *Virginia Magazine of History and Biography* 61, no. 4 (October, 1953): 359-92.

Cabaniss, James Allen. *Cabaniss Through Four Generations: Some Descendants of Matthew and George*. Oxford, MS: University of Mississippi, 1971.

Caldwell, H.M. *History of the Elyton Land Company and Birmingham, Alabama*. Birmingham: Caldwell-Garber Company, 1892, reprinted 1926.

Carmer, Carl. *Stars Fell on Alabama*. Introduction by J. Wayne Flynt. Tuscaloosa: The University of Alabama Press, 1985. Published originally by Farrar and Rinehart, 1934.

---------------. *Stars Fell on Alabama*. Introduction by Howell Raines. Tuscaloosa: The University of Alabama Press, 2000. Published originally by Farrar and Rinehart, 1934.

Carpenter, Douglas, M. A *Powerful Blessing: The Life of Charles Colcock Jones Carpenter, Sr. 1899-1969, Sixth Episcopal Bishop of Alabama 1938-1968*. Birmingham: TransAmerica Printing, 2012.

Carrick, John Charles. *Wycliffe and the Lollards*. New York: Charles Scribner's Sons, 1908.

Clark, Cal and Don-Terry Veal. *Public Opinion in Alabama: Looking Beyond the Stereotypes*, Lanham, MD: Lexington Books, a division of Rowman & Littlefield Publishers, Inc., 2010.

Conway, Alan. *The Reconstruction of Georgia*. St. Paul, MN: North Central Publishing Company, 1966.

Cooper, John Milton, Jr. *Woodrow Wilson: A Biography*. New York: Alfred A. Knopf, a division of Random House, 2009.

Cooper, William J., Jr. and Thomas E. Terrill. *The American South: a History*. 2nd ed. New York: McGraw-Hill Companies, Inc., 1995.

Cottrell, Robert C. *The Czech Republic: The Velvet Revolution*. Philadelphia: Chelsea House Publishers, 2005.

Cross, F.L., ed. *The Oxford Dictionary of the Christian Church*. Oxford: Oxford University Press, 1983.

Cruikshank, George M. *A History of Birmingham and its Environs: A Narrative Account of their Historical Progress, their People, and their Principle Interests, Volume I*. Chicago: The Lewis Publishing Company, 1920.

---------------------------. *A History of Birmingham and its Environs: A Narrative Account of their Historical Progress, their People, and their Principle Interests, Volume II*. Chicago: The Lewis Publishing Company, 1920.

Curran, Eddie. *The Governor of Goat Hill*. Bloomington, IN: iUniverse, 2009.

Degler, Carl N. *The Other South: Southern Dissenters in the Nineteenth Century*. New York: Harper and Row, 1974.

------------------. *Place Over Time: The Continuity of Southern Distinctiveness*. Baton Rouge: The Louisiana State University Press, 1977.

DuBose, Joel C. *Notable Men of Alabama: Personal and Genealogical with Portraits, Vol II*. Atlanta: Southern Historical Association, 1904.

DuBose, John Witherspoon. *Jefferson County and Birmingham, Alabama: Historical and Biographica*l. Birmingham: Teeple & Smith Publishers; Caldwell Printing Works, 1887.

Eskew, Glenn T. *But for Birmingham: The Local and National Movements in the Civil Rights Struggle*. Chapel Hill: The University of North Carolina Press, 1997.

Evans, M. Stanton. *The Future of Conservatism*. New York: Holt, Rinehart and Winston, 1968.

Fallin, Wilson Jr. *The African American Church in Birmingham, Alabama, 1815-1963: A Shelter in the Storm (Studies in African American History and Culture)*. Edited by Graham Russell Hodges. New York: Routledge, 1997.

Feldman, Lynne B. *A Sense of Place: Birmingham's Black Middle-Class Community, 1890-1930*. Tuscaloosa: The University of Alabama Press, 1999.

Ferguson, Niall. *Empire: The Rise and Demise of the British World Order and the Lessons for Global Power*. New York: Basic Books, 2002.

------------------. *Civilization: The West and the Rest*. New York: Penguin Press, 2011.

Flanagan, Maureen A. *America Reformed: Progressives and Progressivisms, 1890s-1920s*. New York: Oxford University Press, USA, 2007.

Fleming, Walter L. *Civil War and Reconstruction in Alabama*. Spartanburg, South Carolina: The Reprint Company, Publishers, 1978, from Birmingham: Tutwiler Collection of Southern History and Literature, Birmingham Public Library, 1905 edition.

Flynt, Wayne. *Alabama in the Twentieth Century*. Tuscaloosa: The University of Alabama Press, 2004.

---------------. *Keeping the Faith: Ordinary People, Extraordinary Lives.* Tuscaloosa: The University of Alabama Press, 2011.

---------------. *Alabama Baptists: Southern Baptists in the Heart of Dixie.* Tuscaloosa: The University of Alabama Press, 1998.

Foner, Eric. *Reconstruction: America's Unfinished Revolution – 1863-1877.* New York: HarperCollins, 1988.

Frederick, Jeffrey. *Stand Up for Alabama: Governor George Wallace.* Tuscaloosa: University of Alabama Press, 2007.

Gantt, Mary & Butch Gantt; compiled by Edgar Welden. *Wetumpka: The Golden Years.* Birmingham: Will Publishing, LLC, 2011.

Georgia, State of. *Reports of Cases Decided in the Supreme Court of Georgia at the March Term 1904, Volume 120.* Atlanta: The State Library, 1904.

Gould, Lewis L. *Grand Old Party: A History of the Republicans.* New York: Random House, 2003.

Grafton, Carl and Anne Permaloff. *Big Mules & Branchheads: James E. Folsom and Political Power in Alabama.* Athens: The University of Georgia Press, 1985.

Graves II, John Temple, ed. *The Book of Alabama and the South: Commemorating the Silver Anniversary of the Protective Life Insurance Company. Birmingham, 2nd edition:* The Company, 1934.

Greenhaw, Wayne. *Alabama On My Mind: Politics, People, History, and Ghost Stories,* Montgomery: Sycamore Press, 1987.

--------------------- *Elephants in the Cottonfields: Ronald Reagan and the New Republican South,* New York: McMillan Publishing Co., 1982.

Gregg, Robert. *Origin and Development of the Tennessee Coal, Iron and Railroad Company.* New York: Newcomen Society, 1948.

Griffith, Lucille. *Alabama: A Documentary History to 1900.* Tuscaloosa: The University of Alabama Press, 1972.

Hackney, Sheldon. *Populism to Progressivism in Alabama.* Princeton: Princeton University Press, 1969.

Hamilton, Virginia Van der Veer. *Alabama: A History.* New York: W.W. Norton and Co., 1977.

Havard, William C., ed. *The Changing Politics of the South.* Baton Rouge: Louisiana State University Press, 1972.

Havel, Václav. *The Power of the Powerless (Routledge Revivals): Citizens Against the State in Central-eastern Europe*. Edited by John Keane. Armonk (NY): M.E. Sharpe, Inc., 1985.

------------------ *Open Letters: Selected Writings, 1965-1990*. Edited by Paul Wilson. New York: Vintage, 1992.

------------------ *The Art of the Impossible: Politics as Morality in Practice*. Translated by Paul Wilson and others. New York: Alfred A. Knoft, 1997.

Hayman, John with Clara Ruth Hayman. *A Judge in the Senate: Howell Heflin's Career of Politics and Principle*. Montgomery: New South Books, 2001.

Hayman, Ronald. *K: A Biography of Kafka*. Phoenix Press: a division of Orion Publishing Group Ltd., 2005.

Hayward, Steven F. *The Age of Reagan: The Conservative Counterrevolution 1980-1989*. New York: Crown Forum, 2009.

Hobson, Charles F. "St. George Tucker, Spencer Roane, and the Virginia Court of Appeals, 1804-11." *Virginia Magazine of History and Biography* 121, no. 1 (2013): 1-43.

Holmes, David L. *The Faith of the Postwar Presidents: From Truman to Obama*. Athens: University of Georgia Press, 2012.

Hrebenar, Ronald J. and Clive S. Thomas, eds. *Interest Group Politics in the Southern States*. Tuscaloosa: University of Alabama Press, 1992.

Hubbard, Mike and David Azbell. *Storming the State House: The Campaign that Liberated Alabama from 136 Years of Democratic Rule*. Montgomery: NewSouth Books, 2012.

Hughes, Jr., Nathaniel Cheairs. *Yale's Confederates: A Biographical Dictionary*. Knoxville: The University of Tennessee Press, 2008.

Hull, Arthur M. and Sydney A. Hales, eds. *Coal Men of America: A Biographical and Historical Review of the World's Greatest Industry*. Chicago: The Retail Coalman, 1918.

Isaac, Rhys. *The Transformation of Virginia 1740-1790*. Chapel Hill: The University of North Carolina Press, 1982.

Jackson III, Harvey H. *Inside Alabama: A Personal History of My State*. Tuscaloosa: The University of Alabama Press, 2004.

Johnson, Paul. *The Birth of the Modern: World Society 1815-1830*. New York: HarperCollins, 1991.

----------------. *Modern Times: The World From the Twenties to the Nineties*. New York: HarperPerennial, 1992.

Kahn, Kim Fridkin and Patrick J. Kenney. *The Spectacle of U.S. Senate Campaigns*. Princeton: Princeton University Press, 1999.

Kemp, Jack. *An American Renaissance: A Strategy for the 1980s*. New York: Harper & Row, Publishers, 1979.

Key, V.O., Jr. *Southern Politics in State and Nation*. Knoxville: The University of Tennessee Press, 1984.

Kissinger, Henry. *Diplomacy*. New York: Simon & Schuster, 1994.

Klein, Maury. *Rainbow's End: The Crash of 1929*. New York: Oxford University Press, 2001.

Knight, Lucian Lamar. *Georgia Landmarks, Memorials, and Legends, Volume 2*. Gretna, Louisiana: Pelican Press, 1914, 2006.

Kolchin, Peter. *First Freedom: The Responses of Alabama's Blacks to Emancipation and Reconstruction*. Westport, Conn.: Greenwood Press, Inc., 1972.

Korbel, Josef. *The Communist Subversion of Czechoslovakia, 1938-1948: The Failure of Coexistence*. Princeton: Princeton University Press, 1965.

Lambert, David E. *The Protestant International and the Huguenot Migration to Virginia*. New York: Peter Lang, 2010.

Lamberth, Minnie with Jennifer Korneygay. Forward by William J. Canary. *Alabama: Moving Forward*. Montgomery: Beers & Associates LLC, 2012.

Lau, J.M. (Jenni Meili). *Prague Then & Now*. San Diego: Thunder Bay Press, 2007.

Lee, Helen Shores, Barbara Sylvia Shores, and Denise George. *The Gentle Giant of Dynamite Hill: The Untold Story of Arthur Shores and His Family's Fight for Civil Rights*. Grand Rapids, MI: Zondervan, 2012.

Lichtman, Allan J. *White Protestant Nation: The Rise of the American Conservative Movement*. New York: The Atlantic Monthly Press, 2008.

Luker, Ralph E. *The Social Gospel in Black and White: American Racial Reform, 1885-1912*. Chapel Hill: The University of North Carolina Press, 1991.

MacMillan, Margaret. *Paris 1919: Six Months that Changed the World.* New York: Random House, 2001.

Mapp, Jr., Alf J. *Thomas Jefferson: A Strange Case of Mistaken Identity.* Lanham, MD: Madison Books, 1987.

Marks, Henry, compiler. *Who Was Who in Alabama.* Huntsville: The Strode Publishers, 1972.

McCullough, David. *John Adams.* New York: Simon & Schuster Paperbacks, 2001.

McGrath, Alister. *Christianity's Dangerous Idea: The Protestant Revolution – A History from the Sixteenth Century to the Twenty-First.* New York: HarperOne of Harper Collins, 2007.

McKiven, Jr. *Iron and Steel: Class, Race, and Community in Birmingham, Alabama, 1875-1920.* Chapel Hill: The University of North Carolina Press, 1995.

McMillan, Malcolm Cook. *Constitutional Development in Alabama, 1798-1901: A Study in Politics, the Negro, and Sectionalism.* Chapel Hill: University of North Carolina Press, 1955 – reprint 1978.

McWhorter, Diane. *Carry Me Home: Birmingham, Alabama: The Climactic Battle of the Civil Rights Revolution.* 2nd ed. New York: Simon & Schuster, 2002.

Meacham, Jon. *Thomas Jefferson: The Art of Power.* New York: Random House, 2012.

Morgan, Edmund S. *American Slavery, American Freedom.* New York: W.W. Norton, 1975.

Nabers, Drayton. *The Case for Character: Looking at Character from a Biblical Perspective.* Tulsa: Christian Publishing Services, 2006.

--------------------. *The Hidden Keys to Happiness.* Birmingham: Cornerstone Books, 2010.

Nelson, Linda J. and Marjorie L. White. *Mountain Brook Village Then & Now.* Birmingham: Birmingham Historical Society, 2009.

Noles, James L., Jr. *Hearts of Dixie: Fifty Alabamians and the State They Called Home.* Birmingham: Will Publishing, LLC., 2004.

Norrell, Robert J. *Up From History: The Life of Booker T. Washington.* Cambridge, MA: Harvard Univesity Press, 2009.

--------------------- *Reaping the Whirlwind: The Civil Rights Movement in Tuskegee.* Chapel Hill: The University of North Carolina Press, 1998.

--------------------- *The Making of Modern Alabama.* Tuscaloosa: Yellowhammer Press, 1993.

Owen, Thomas McAdory. *Alabama Official and Statistical Register 1903 (The State of Alabama Department of Archives and History)*. Montgomery: Brown Printing Company, 1908.

---------------------------- *History of Alabama and Dictionary of Alabama Biography, Vol. III*. Chicago: The S.J. Clarke Publishing Company, 1921.

Phillips, Kevin. *Wealth and Democracy: A Political History of the American Rich*. New York: Broadway Books of Random House, 2002.

Price, John. *When the White House Calls: From Immigrant Entrepreneur to U.S. Ambassador*. Salt Lake City: The University of Utah Press, 2011.

Raper, Dennis L. and Constance M. Jones. *A Goodly Heritage: The Episcopal Diocese of Southern Virginia 1892-1992*. Norfolk: Pictorial Heritage Publishing Company, 1992.

Rogers, William Warren; Robert David Ward; Leah Rawls Atkins; and Wayne Flynt. *Alabama: The History of a Deep South State*. Tuscaloosa: The University of Alabama Press, 1994.

Rogers, William Warren. *Black Belt Scalawag: Charles Hays and the Southern Republicans in the Era of Reconstruction*. Athens: The University of Georgia Press, 1993.

Rove, Karl. *Courage and Consequence: My Life as a Conservative in the Fight*. New York: Threshold Editions, A Division of Simon and Schuster, 2010.

Rushton, William J. III. *A Sense of Quality, A Sense of Growth: The Story of Protective Life*. Princeton: Princeton University Press for The Newcomen Society in North America, 1977.

Sager, Ryan. *The Elephant in the Room: Evangelicals, Libertarians, and the Battle to Control the Republican Party*. Hoboken: John Wiley & Sons, 2006.

Scarborough, Joe. *The Right Path: From Ike to Reagan, How Republicans Once Mastered Politics – and Can Again*. New York: Random House, 2013.

Sellers, James Benson. *Slavery in Alabama*. Tuscaloosa: The University of Alabama Press, 1950.

Shlaes, Amity. *The Forgotten Man: A New History of the Great Depression*. New York: HarperCollins, 2007.

------------------. *Collidge.*. New York: HarperPerennial, 2013.

Sobel, Robert. *Panic on Wall Street: A History of America's Financial Disasters*. London: The MacMillan Company, 1968.

Stanton, Elvin. *Faith and works: The business, politics, and philanthropy of Alabama's Jimmy Faulkner*. Montgomery: NewSouth Books, 2002.

Stewart, John Craig. *The Governors of Alabama*. Gretna, LA: Pelican Publishing Co., 1975.

Suitts, Steve. *Hugo Black of Alabama : How His Roots and Early Career Shaped the Great Champion of the Constitution*. Montgomery: NewSouth Books, 2005.

Taylor, Sandra Baxley. *Governor Fob James: His 1994 Victory, His Incredible Story*. Mobile: Greenberry Publishing Company, 1995.

Thomas, James D. and William H. Stewart. *Alabama Government and Politics*. Lincoln: University of Nebraska Press, 1988.

Thompson, Clara Mildred. *Reconstruction in Georgia: Economic, Social, Political, 1965-1872*. New York: Columbia University Press, 1915.

Thompson, Wesley, S. *Tories of the Hills*. Vernon, AL: The Pareil Press, 1960.

Thornton, J. Mills. *Politics and Power in a Slave Society – Alabama, 1800-1860*. Baton Rouge: Louisiana State University Press, 1978.

Tocqueville, Alexis de. *Democracy in America*. New York: Alfred E. Knopf, 1979.

Trest, Warren. *Nobody but the People: the Life and Times of Alabama's Youngest Governor*. Montgomery: NewSouth Books, 2008.

Tucker, Garland S. III. *The High Tide of American Conservatism: Davis, Coolidge, and the 1924 Election*. Austin: Emerald Book Company, 2010.

Volgyes, Ivan. *Politics in Eastern Europe*. Chicago: Irwin Professional Publishing, 1986.

Walton, Jr., Hanes, *Black Republicans: The Politics of the Black and Tans*, Metuchen, NJ: The Scarecrow Press, Inc., 1975.

Ward, Robert D. and William Warren Rogers. *Labor Revolt in Alabama: The Great Strike of 1894*. Tuscaloosa: The University of Alabama Press, 1965.

Webb, Samuel L., and Margaret E. Armbrester, eds. *Alabama Governors: A Political History of the State*. Tuscaloosa: The University of Alabama Press, 2001.

Webb, Samuel L. *Two-Party Politics in the One-Party South: Alabama's Hill Country, 1874-1920*. Tuscaloosa: The University of Alabama Press, 1997.

Welden, Edgar and Keith Dunnavant, *Time Out: A Sports Fan Dream Year*, Birmingham: Will Publishing, 1999.

Whitaker, Walter C. *History of the Protestant Episcopal Church in Alabama 1763-1891*. Birmingham: Roberts & Son, 1897.

Weiner, Jonathan M. *Social Origins of the New South – Alabama, 1860-1885*. Baton Rouge: Louisiana State University Press, 1978.

Wiggins, Sarah Woolfolk. *The Scalawag in Alabama Politics, 1865-1881*, Tuscaloosa: The University of Alabama Press, 1977.

------------------------------. *From Civil War to Civil Rights: Alabama 1860-1960*. Tuscaloosa: University of Alabama Press, 1987.

Wills, Matthew B. *The Lindbergh Report: The Untold Story of Lindbergh's Report of September 22, 1938*. Central Milton Keynes, Buckinghamshire: AuthorHouse, U.K., 2008.

Wilmer, Richard Hooker, *The Recent Past From a Southern Standpoint: Reminiscences of a Grandfather*. New York: Thomas Whitaker, 1887.

Woodlief, Ann Matthews, *In River Time: The Way of the James*. Chapel Hill: Algonquin Books, 1985.

Woodward, C. Vann. *The Battle for Leyte Gulf: The Incredible Story of World War II's Largest Naval Battle*. Nashville: The Battery Press, 1989, 2007.

------------------------. *The Burden of Southern History*. Baton Rouge: Louisiana State University Press, 1960.

------------------------. *Origins of the New South 1877 – 1913*. Baton Rouge: Louisiana State University Press, 1971 (1999 printing).

Yeager, Alice. *Guy Hunt: Governor Who Leveled the Field*. Birmingham: Seacoast Publishing, 2010.

Newpapers (referenced in endnotes)
The Birmingham News
The Birmingham Post-Herald
The Mobile Press-Register
The Montgomery Advertiser

Magazines and Journals
Alabama Heritage
Alabama Review
American Manufacturer and Iron World
Business Alabama
Inside Alabama Politics
The Prague Post

Alabama Department of Archives and History (ADAH)
House Legislative Journals 1978-1982
Senate Legislative Journals 1983-1990
Jefferson County (Alabama) Library System
Archives of the Episcopal Church in the Diocese of Alabama
Chi Psi Fraternity
The Sixth Decennial Catalogue of the Chi Psi Fraternity, 1902. Auburn,
New York: The Fifty-Eighth Annual Convention, 1902.
Warner, Andrew Robert, ed. *The Purple and Gold, Volume XX*. Auburn,
New York: Published by the Chi Psi Fraternity, 1903.
Cabaniss, Johnston, Gardner, Dumas & O'Neal LLP
Birmingham, Alabama
Jelks Family Bible
Barbara Hudgens Swaim and Helen Dean Jelks Hicks
England, Arkansas

Permissions
(public domain; explicit; implied)
Alabama Republican Party
American Friends of the Czech Republic
Cabaniss Family Albums/Archives
Encyclopedia of Alabama (Internet-based)
Persons interviewed by author
Ms. Lillis Werder, photojournalist
United States Department of State

Cabaniss Genealogy Authorities/Sources

Brock, R.A. *Documents, Chiefly Unpublished, Relating to the Huguenot Emigration to Virginia and to the Settlement at Manakin-Town.*

Cabaniss, Allen. *Cabaniss Through Four Generations: Some Descendents of Matthew and George*. Oxford, MS, 1971.

DAR Patriot Index, Centennial Edition, Part I. Washington: Daughters of the American Revolution Centennial Administration, 1990.

Daughters of the American Revolution, National Society of. *Directory 1904*. Washington, D.C.: Compiled by the Order of the Thirteenth Continental Congress, 1904.

Garrett, Grady. "Cabaniss," *The Huguenot*, Volume XI, 1941-1943, 84-87.

Green, John Platt. "Henry Cabaniss and His Descendents" internet-based family tree Dallas, 1958. Reproduced in 1998 by Joe Cabaniss, San Antonio, TX.

Prince George County, Virginia. Will of Henry Cabanis, recorded in Deeds, etc., 1713-28 (Part 2), 414.

Virginia Historical Society, *Miscellaneous Papers*

Virginia Magazine of History and Biography

Virkus, Abridged Compendium of American Genealogy, Volume I, 40

Acknowledgements

This is a story about the man, William Jelks Cabaniss, Jr. I approached him in late 2010 and asked him if he intended to write his memoirs. Bill Cabaniss was in his early seventies and very much an active person in multiple local, statewide, national, and international endeavors. He is one of those persons whose very physical presence commands a high level of attention. Slightly leaning forward as he stands and walks, he carries himself with a confident gait and his face expresses an honest authority and personal stability. In other words, he looks important. And he is. That is why I asked him about his future memoirs. He was not interested in memoirs. But he listened to me.

Before asking Mr. Cabaniss about writing his memoirs I conducted research on him. Even though I had met him a couple of years earlier than that day of questioning, I had no idea of his history. I just knew that he had to be important not only by the way he presents himself but how he interacts with everyone he meets. He knows no stranger and makes a person feel important. He remembers names and events and is very good at recalling previous conversations. Given all that, it was one event that caused me to find out who he really is. It was at a funeral service.

My wife Patricia and I were standing on a sidewalk outside St. Luke's Episcopal Church in Mountain Brook, Alabama, a suburb of Birmingham. Standing with us were John Richardson and Glandion Carney, the rector and assistant rector, respectively, of St. Peter's Anglican Church, and Bill and Catherine Cabaniss. A funeral service having just ended minutes earlier, we were waiting on the sidewalk next to the road for the cortege of the family of William Ireland to pass by the crowd on their way to the cemetery for the interment. Patricia, noticing a crossed-flags lapel pin on Bill Cabaniss's suit jacket asked "What's the other flag?" The recognizable flag was the American "stars and stripes." The other flag was that of the Czech Republic. "Are you native Czech," she asked? "No, I just worked there for a few years." That was all he said, but that reply was not sufficient for me. Thus began my research which led to my question to him about his memoirs. Even though Bill

Cabaniss had no interest in writing his memoirs he expressed an interest in my inquiry and he agreed to meet with me at a later time provided that I write him a letter of my intent. So I wrote a proposal offering to write his memoirs for him.

In March, 2011 I met with Bill and Catherine Cabaniss in his small, narrow nook of an office in Mountain Brook's Office Park off U.S. Highway 280. For one hour we discussed my proposal. In the end we agreed that an objective biography would be better than a memoir. And with that I went to work developing an agreement between Mr. Cabaniss and me and expanded my research which included a series of interviews not only with the subject of my book but with his many friends, business associates and former political colleagues. The doors were opened for me to peer into the circumstances that made William Jelks Cabaniss, Jr. one of the most respected and honored citizens of Alabama and the United States. To be sure, many people have never heard of this Alabama Gentleman and American Statesman. But they will now. A biography such as this could not have been written without the cooperation of many people.

In the political sphere I wish to thank former Alabama State Senators Ann Bedsole; Perry Hand; Frank "Butch" Ellis; Larry Dixon; current Alabama Attorney General Luther Strange; former Alabama Governor Bob Riley; State Senator Gerald Dial; Edgar Welden; Marty Connors; Bill Armistead, and Bill Harris. Friends of Bill Cabaniss who helped him in his campaigns, namely Peggy Balliet; Judy Bewley; and Lee Styslinger, Jr. Several business associates: Walter McCullers; Miles Cunningham; Andrew Cunningham; Drayton Nabers; Mike Thompson; and Ted vonCannon. There were others who provided valuable insight about Bill Cabaniss and political activity within Alabama: John Beau Grenier, chairman of the Birmingham law firm of Bradley Arant Boult Cummings LLP, provided a historical perspective of the development of the Alabama Republican Party from the time his father John Grenier became head of the Alabama GOP in the early 1960s; Dr. David Bronner, the chief executive officer of The Retirement Systems of Alabama gave valuable insight on Mr. Cabaniss's legislative acuity; William J. Canary contributed to the understanding of the development of the Business Council of Alabama as successor to the former state Chamber of Commerce. Close friends of Bill Cabaniss, Cullom Walker and Francis

Crockard, spoke of his character from childhood days until now. Steve Still, a Birmingham attorney and chair of the Governmental & Regulatory Affairs Section of the firm where he practices, explained the political environments of the times when Bill Cabaniss served in government. Richard Randolph III situated the town of Mountain Brook from its unincorporated status to a city composed of many of Alabama's wealthiest citizens. Some have referred to Mountain Brook as Birmingham's equivalent of the Highland Park and University Park suburbs of Dallas, Texas. The mere existence of Mountain Brook and its politicized mischaracterization play a role in any statewide election when a political candidate is a resident of that town.

I am grateful for receiving assistance from the *American Friends of the Czech Republic* and their official photographer Lillis Werder.

Bill Cabaniss comes from several lines of significant Americans. I am grateful for the work of genealogists who have either conducted research for me or have provided me with their own original efforts at documenting the Cabaniss family. Joe Cabaniss of San Antonio, Texas is the source for many of the notes included in the book about Bill Cabaniss's heritage. Joe Cabaniss's work is an extension of research conducted by former University of Mississippi professor Allen Cabaniss. Joe Cabaniss also amplified the work of John Platt Green's "Henry Cabaniss and His Descendents" produced in 1958 and re-worked by Joe Cabaniss with the permission of Mr. Green's wife.

I am indebted to Barbara Swaim who over the years has produced large volumes of genealogies of the Jelks, Nicholson, and Mann family lines.

David Alsobrook, Executive Director of the Museum of Mobile, wrote his master's thesis in the 1970s on Alabama Governor William Dorsey Jelks. I am grateful to Dr. Alsobrook for mailing to me a copy of his insightful and valuable thesis about Alabama's most frugal governor.

At the annual meeting of the Alabama Historical Association in 2012 in Huntsville, I had brief conversations about Ambassador Cabaniss with Dr. Edwin Bridges, then Executive Director and now Executive Director Emeritus of the Alabama Department or Archives and History (ADAH), and Dr. Wayne Flynt, Distinguished Professor Emeritus at Auburn University. Bridges told me that Mr. Cabaniss was one of a few state legislators who came to ADAH requesting research on aspects of bills pending before the Alabama House and Senate. Dr. Flynt described Mr. Cabaniss as an honest and faithful servant of the people of Alabama. A year later I visited Dr. Flynt at Auburn University and interviewed him.

It is an honor to have had this book reviewed and commented upon in its manuscript and proof stages. Appreciation goes to former United States President George Herbert Walker Bush; Margaret Tutwiler, former Ambassador to Morocco; Bob Riley, former Governor of Alabama; Bill Harris, former Chairman of the Alabama Republican Party; Dr. Wayne Flynt, Distinguished Professor Emeritus at Auburn University and Alabama historian; and Stephen W. Still, attorney and writer of this book's *Foreword*.

Denise George and Carolyn Tomlin, founders of *Boot Camp for Christian Writers* at Beeson Divinity School in Birmingham, taught me not only how to develop and submit book proposals, but how to format biographies, histories, memoirs, and fiction.

Writing is a spiritual endeavor and there were times when I approached the edges of the depths of futility. My dear friend, Donna Read, could always discern these ups and downs during my time writing this book. I thank her for her on-the-spot prayers and words of encouragement.

I thank my three adult children who have been supportive of this project from its inception: Michael Norman and Cynthia Norman Williams. The Rev. Curtis Kemper Norman, having an interest in genealogy and a clear understanding of the intricacies of navigating through genealogical websites, has been a great help in researching Ambassador Cabaniss's family history for me.

I wish to thank William J. and Catherine Cabaniss for their efforts at fact checking then many iterations of the manuscript. There had been times when I simply got dates, name spellings, and events wrong. Although not requested, they also advised me about misplaced or missing commas, semi-colons, and colons. Unbelievable, I know.

Mike Edwards, my friend and former consulting partner, kept calling me from Texas every now and then to ask "When will the book be finished?" I thank him for his assertive nature.

Finally, I thank my wife Patricia Ann Padrick Norman for her work as the primary editor of the manuscript.

I take full responsibility for any errors in this book.

Index

A

Czech business leaders, 211
Czech Foreign Minister, 3
Czech Ministry of Justice, 214
Czech Mobile Military Hospital, 229
Czech Radio 7, 211
Czech Republic, 3,5,189,181-193,200-205,239
Czech Republic Constitution, 184
Czech Social Democratic Party, 190,191
Czech-Americans, 226,227
Czechoslovakia, 12,20,38,39,49,63,65,105,112,
    113,118.119,161,164,184,209,222,231,234

D

Dallas County, Alabama, 80
Dallas, Texas, 146
Davidson, Julius W., 101
Davis, John W., 107
Day, Corbin, 60,183,219
Day, Dodie, 60,219
de la Muce, Marquess, 265,272
de Sailly, Charles, 265,266
Decatur, Alabama, 154,173
Declaration of Independence, 277,278
Declaration of Indulgence, 262
Deep South, 33,140
deGraffenreid, Mrs. Ryan, 191
delve into details, 60
Democrat Bourbon Redeemers, 80
Democratic Coalition, 138,139,140,141,142
Democratic Executive Committee, 141
Democratic Legislative Maneuvering, 147
Democratic National Convention 1912, 103
Democratic National Union Party, 72
Democratic Party, 285
Democratic-Republican Party, 277,282,283
Denton, Bobby, 150
Denton, Elizabeth, 274
Denton, Jeremiah, 65,151
Department of Homeland Security, 222,223
Deputy Chief of Mission, 210
Detroit, Michigan, 65
Devon, 260
Dial, Gerald, 52,59,137,138,142,145,150,176,246
    "the bulldog", 150
Dickinson, Bill, 34,135
Dillon, J.L., 99
Dine, Thomas A., 239,240
Directory of American Cement Industries, 99
Discharge Rule, 53
Dixie Eagles Rifle Company, 69,70
Dixiecrats, 33,119
Dixon, Larry, 59,113,135-137,142,143,145,
    147,148,150,158,159,173,191,246
    "office fate", 148
Dole, Bob, 157,158,160,167
Don Marwell Show, 173
doo-rag, 195
Dothan, Alabama, 151,161
Doubek, Robert, 239

Doyle, Dane and Bernback, 60
Drake, Mary, 288
Drake, Tom, 132,138
Drebitko, Iva, 218
Drennen, Laurie, 191
Dubček, Alexander, 38
Dukakis, Michael, 159
DuPont, Pete, 158
Duskova, Lenka, 218
Dutch Republic, 262
Dvořák, Antonin, 99,101

E

East Anglia, 260
East Berlin, 20
East Carolina University, 286
East Orange, New Jersey, 81,98,106
Eastern Europe, 20,161,234
Economic Panic of 1837, 284
Edgecombe County, North Carolina, 274
Edict of Nantes, 262,265,266
Edwards, Jack, 34,135
Edwards, Mike, 330
Eisenhower, Dwight D., 4,18,18,24,119
    "Citizens for Eisenhower", 18
Ellis, Frank "Butch", 136,142-145,159,165,246
    "...would follow [Bill] Cabaniss off the
    side of a cliff", 144
    "mass conversion event", 159
Ellis, Handy, 159
Ellison, "Slick", 32
Elyton Land Company, 77
Emancipation Proclamation, 71
Embassy Residence in Prague, 209,217,219,220
Embassy Row, 224
Emperor Joseph II, 271
Energen, Inc., 204,230
England, 15,260,262,264,282
Ensley, Alabama, 99
Epes, Francis, 270
Episcopal Church of the Advent-Birmingham,
    111,113
Episcopal Diocese of Alabama, 20
Erderich, Beverly, 219
Estates Theatre, 208
Estonia, 223
Etheridge, Danielle, 5
Etheridge, David, 5,62
Etheridge, Jessica, 5
Etheridge, Nikki, 5
Etheridge, Sandy, 62
Etheridge, Will, 62
ethics, 53,154,187
Etowah County, Alabama, 30,51
Eufaula, Alabama, 69,84,94,97,98,111
    "The Bluff City", 84
Eufaula Indians, 84
Eufaula Investment and Security Company, 98
Eufaula Times, 81,89
Europe, 164

H

About the Author

Worth Earlwood "Woody" Norman, Jr. served in the United States Marine Corps between 1962 and 1966. His assignments included the Second Marine Aircraft Wing, Cherry Point, North Carolina; the Third Marine Division, Okinawa; and Marine Corps Schools, Quantico, Virginia.

He retired from Electronic Data Systems Corporation and later served as a consultant in the information technology outsource advisory sector with The Everest Group and Technology Partners International.

Mr. Norman is a member of the Alabama Historical Association, the Virginia Historical Society, and the Historical Society of the Episcopal Church. He is a graduate of Norview High School (Norfolk, Virginia) and Old Dominion University (B.A.); Lindenwood University (M.B.A.); the Anglican School of Theology-Dallas (L.Min); and the School of Theology at Sewanee: The University of the South (S.T.M.).

He is a deacon in the Anglican Diocese of the South, within the Anglican Church in North America. He is assigned to Saint Peter's Anglican Church in Mountain Brook, Alabama.

Other books authored by Worth E. Norman, Jr. are *James Solomon Russell: Former Slave, Pioneering Educator and Episcopal Evangelist; Alabama Timelines: Those Republicans;* and *Alabama Timelines: African American Entrepreneurs.* He is a contributing writer to *The Living Church* magazine; *The Anglican Digest; the Historiographer;* and the online *Encyclopedia of Alabama* and *Encyclopedia Virginia.*

A native of Norfolk, Virginia, Mr. Norman is the father of three and grandfather of six. He and his wife Patricia Ann Padrick Norman live in Hoover, Alabama.

Made in the USA
Lexington, KY
27 January 2015